Bears in the Caviar

BEARS IN THE CAVIAR

CHARLES W. THAYER

Introduction by Avis Bohlen

Russian Life
BOOKS

Cover: Original Illustration by Taisiya Kulygina

ISBN 978-1-880100-36-3

Library of Congress Control Number: 2015937764

Russian Information Services, Inc.
PO Box 567
Montpelier, VT 05601-0567
www.russianlife.com
orders@russianlife.com
phone 802-223-4955

CONTENTS

Charles W. Thayer as a boy, dressed in a Cossack costume
purchased by his father on a 1914 business trip to Russia.

INTRODUCTION

None of the young men who were part of the first American embassy to the Soviet Union in the winter of 1933-34 ever forgot the experience. It was a uniquely exciting and challenging period, a privileged moment of their careers. "Words would fail me, " George Kennan wrote some thirty years later, "if I were to try to convey... the excitement, the enjoyment, the fascination and the frustrations of this initial service in Moscow," remembered as "...the high point of life.... at least, in comradeship, in gaiety, in intensity of experience."[1] It is fortunate for the rest of the world that the experience was so memorably captured by Charles W. Thayer in his classic memoir, *Bears in the Caviar*, first published in 1950 and now republished by Russian Life Books.

---

1. George F. Kennan, *Memoirs, 1925-1950* (Boston, 1967), 60; Charles W. Thayer, *Bears in the Caviar* (Philadelphia, 1951). For other memoirs of the period, see also Charles E. Bohlen, *Witness to History* (New York, 1973) 14-36; *A Question of Trust: the Origins of US-Soviet Diplomatic Relations: memoirs of Loy W. Henderson*, ed. George W. Baer (Stanford, 1986). For an interesting interpretation of the impact of this period on the later views of Kennan and the others, see Frank Costigliola, "Unceasing Pressure for Penetration: Gender, Pathology, and Emotion in George Kennan's Formation of the Cold War," *The Journal of American History* (March 1997), 1309-39.

The United States, the last of the Western powers to recognize the Bolshevik regime, established diplomatic relations with the Soviet Union in December 1933. As his first Ambassador to Moscow, Franklin Roosevelt appointed William Bullitt, a brilliant, ebullient, if mercurial figure who had served on Woodrow Wilson's delegation at Versailles and had undertaken a peace mission to Lenin at the height of the Russian Civil War in 1920. Bullitt entertained high hopes for the success of his mission; he made it his first task to recruit the best and the brightest to serve in his Embassy.[2]

They were a distinguished group, career diplomats for the most part. George Kennan and Charles Bohlen (Thayer's future brother-in-law) had spent several years studying Russian in anticipation of this moment. These two men would rise to fame as Soviet experts and Ambassadors to the Soviet Union. There were other future ambassadors as well: Loy Henderson, Elbridge Durbrow, John Wiley, to name only a few. And then there was Charlie Thayer, who had arrived in Moscow before any of them.

Born to a patrician background on the Philadelphia Main Line, Charles W. Thayer, as he recounts in *Bears*, decided soon after graduating from West Point that a military career was not for him and set out to become a diplomat. He was advised that, as there was a State Department hiring freeze on, his only hope of being admitted to the Foreign Service was to learn Russian. Accordingly, he set out for Moscow in the fall of 1933 with his possessions in a trunk – "hoping," as he put it, "that there'd one day be an embassy and that it would hire me."[3] It was an astonishingly bold decision. (Charlie, as one colleague observed, was an adventurer by nature[4]). But not surprisingly, during the next few months, he confessed later, "I often got very cold feet and told myself that I'd been a darn fool to have had

---

2. On Bullitt, see *For the President, Personal and Secret; Correspondence between Franklin D. Roosevelt and William C. Bullitt*, ed. Orville H. Bullitt (Boston, 1972); Will Brownell and Richard N. Billings, *So Close to Greatness: a Biography* (New York, 1987); William C. Bullitt papers, Sterling Library Manuscripts and Archives, Yale University.
3. Thayer to Jacob Beam, May 21, 1953. Thayer papers.
4. Henderson. *Question of Trust*, 310.

such a silly idea."[5] Moscow in late 1933 was freer and more tolerant of foreigners than at any moment thereafter – but even so life was difficult, the authorities ever suspicious and watchful. Amazingly, however, Thayer was able to rent a room with a Russian family. For the next few months he found occasional employment with American journalists posted to Moscow – virtually the only Americans in Russia at the time. More importantly, he found himself a Russian teacher and quickly made friends with a group of young Russians, many of them in the theater world. He travelled to other parts of the Soviet Union. By the time Bullitt arrived to present his credentials in December 1933, Thayer had, after six months of residence in Moscow, knowledge of the language and a direct experience of Soviet life that would prove invaluable to the new American embassy. As the Ambassador later said, "the Americans had arrived in Moscow to find absolutely nothing for them except one young man who knew Russia thoroughly."[6]

And so, during Bullitt's brief stay in Moscow in December, 1933, a snub-faced young man came to call on him at the National Hotel, on the strength of a family acquaintance, in order to offer his services in setting up the new Embassy. George Kennan, who had accompanied the Ambassador to Moscow, was to be left behind to get the Embassy up and running. After interviewing Thayer, he told Bullitt, "He's a nice kid," and recommended hiring him.[7] Thus began the adventures Thayer so vividly described in his book – for several months just with a team of himself, Kennan and one other State Department official, then, after Bullitt returned in March 1934, with the full Embassy.

What followed was a time of unparalleled confusion, a zany, hilarious experience later described by Chip Bohlen as "the hoopla

---

5. Thayer to George Kennan, May 28, 1953, Thayer papers.
6. Thayer Diary, February, 1936, Thayer papers. For Thayer's experiences during his first six months in Moscow, see his letters to his mother and other family members as well as his Diaries for the period. Charles W. Thayer papers, Harry S. Truman Library, Independence, MO.
7. George Kennan to William Bullitt, December 27, 1933, Bullitt papers.

period when the Embassy resembled a circus."[8] The Embassy was
brimful with talent; a conspicuous omission, Kennan recalled, was
anyone "available, qualified and inclined to assume administrative
responsibility."[9] The sheer challenge of setting up a new Embassy in
a city where everything from nails to razor blades had to be imported,
coupled with the daily frustrations of battling Soviet bureaucracy, were
a formula for chaos – further complicated by Bullitt's determination
to throw out the rule book and do everything differently. For months
the Embassy hardly functioned; official business was intermittent
to say the least. As John Wiley wrote, "the struggle for existence
occupied nearly all [our] energy."[10] But these young men brushed
off the frustrations, laughed at the absurdities of Soviet bureaucracy
and got on with the job, whether moving furniture or tearing around
on motorcycles in search of coat hangers. "I am delighted with every
man on the staff," Bullitt wrote to President Roosevelt.[11] They were
young, there were lots of laughs and it was all great fun.

Not least of all, these young Americans shared a common
fascination with the Soviet Union that they were now observing at
first hand, a moment for which so many of them had prepared and
trained. What, more than anything, made this period special was the
freedom they had to mingle with Russians. It was a time midway
between the horrors of Stalin's collectivization and the resulting
famine on the one hand, and the mindless bloodbath of his purges on
the other. The mood was optimistic: many Russians believed that the
worst was behind them, that a brighter future was ahead, when they
could look forward to "increasing freedom and personal security."[12]

---

8. Charles Bohlen to Avis Thayer, November 13, 1934, in Charles E. Bohlen papers,
Library of Congress; "...delighted with every man..." William Bullitt to FDR, April
13, 1934, *For the President*, 83.
9. Kennan, *Memoirs*, 63. For Bullitt's propensity to throw away the rule book see
Bohlen's letters to his mother April 20, 1934 and a subsequent undated letter, Bohlen
papers.
10. John Wiley to Robert Kelley September 27, 1934, John C. Wiley papers, Franklin
Delano Roosevelt Library.
11. Ibid.
12. See Bohlen, *Witness to History*, 29; Kennan, *Memoirs*, George F. Kennan, "Flash-

The idealism of the Revolution had not yet died out. Thayer and his colleagues were able to consort with Russians of all kinds – ballerinas, theater people, musicians, even political figures and military men. Bullitt encouraged his diplomats to get out and meet Russians; he himself cast a wide net with his invitations to Spaso House, where one might meet such legendary figures of the Bolshevik revolution as Nikolai Bukharin, Karl Radek, or Marshal Budyonny, a Civil War hero, a "lovely soul with a pair of moustaches at least a foot long."[13] In those days, Muscovites were not afraid to come to the American ambassador's residence.

Embassy life was continually enlivened and energized by Bullitt's taste for the unconventional, his "determination to make things fun," as Kennan put it, his resolute refusal "to permit the life around him to degenerate into dullness and dreariness." He was ever on the lookout for ingenious new ways and activities to form close relations with the Russians, from baseball to polo; his entertainments too had to be out of the ordinary and for those he turned to his aide Charlie Thayer, whom he had placed in charge of running Spaso House and most importantly of social events.[14]

Thayer was always at the center of the high jinks. Known as "the naughty boy of the embassy," he was remembered by his colleagues with enormous affection. At twenty-three he was younger than most of them – a blue eyed, round-faced young man, whose slightly angelic looks belied an "outrageous sense of humor," and 'fondness for ingenious pranks." Brash, "unabashed by authority," according to his future brother-in-law Chip Bohlen, "…he kept us in good humor with his marvelous sense of the ridiculous." Another colleague, Loy Henderson, wrote, "his "ready wit [and] youthful exuberance pranks promoted gaiety in any social gathering where [he] happened to be." But the mischievous appearance was deceptive; he was also, as his

backs," *New Yorker*, February 25, 1985; Thayer's letters to mother and other family members throughout this period, Thayer papers.
13. Bohlen to his mother, April 15, 1934, Bohlen papers.
14. Kennan on Bullitt: *Memoirs*, 79; Thayer to mother, September 27, 1934.

German colleague and later good friend Jonny Herwarth perceptively noted, "a formidable observer" of the Russian scene, a "far deeper man than many people realized." Thanks to Thayer's creative ingenuity and imagination, *carte blanche* from the Ambassador and the help of Irena Wiley, the artistic wife of the counselor of the Embassy, the Embassy hosted a number of spectacular events ("I am really becoming the most expert social entertainer in the world right now," he boasted to his mother). The most spectacular of these was the ball described in chapter XI of *Bears*; no one who attended it ever forgot it. Among Muscovites it passed into legend and was immortalized in Mikhail Bulgakov's masterpiece, *The Master and Margarita*.[15]

Among other noteworthy events of this period, Charlie's sister, Avis, paid him a visit in the spring of 1934, in the course of which she met his friend and colleague Chip Bohlen, who became her future husband. Avis and her sister Betsy (sent, according to one family legend, by their mother to check up on Charlie) spent several weeks in the Russian capital, and became regular participants in the baseball games, parties and general frolics. Avis achieved brief notoriety when she was arrested for photographing a bridge and detained for three hours in a Soviet police station. There was a great deal of late night dancing at the Metropole Hotel and, by the time she left, her romance with Chip was well advanced. After a desultory correspondence over the winter, the courtship resumed when Chip returned to the U.S. in the late spring of 1935. He and Avis became engaged in and were married in August 1935.[16]

But sadly, by the time the famed Spaso House ball took place in April 1935, this heady, carefree period was already coming to

15. Diary of Avis Thayer, in Avis Bohlen collection, Schlesinger Library, Cambridge, Massachusetts.

16. Irena Wiley, *Around the Globe in Twenty Years* (New York, 1962) 30, Thayer Diaries, in September -February 1935. Thayer papers. For Bullitt's dissatisfaction with Bohlen and Thayer, see Bullitt to Walton Moore, April 25, 1935, May 11, 1935, June 8, 1935, July15, 1935 and August 30, 1935; Walton Moore to Bullitt, June 8, 1935, Box 58, Bullitt papers, Yale University; Thayer diaries for fall and early winter 1935-1936, Thayer papers.

an end. It was, it turned out, no more than a short-lived respite in the brutal history of Stalin's reign. With the benefit of hindsight, we can see how fragile it all was, how misplaced the optimism of ordinary Russians. As we now know, Stalin was already plotting the physical elimination of the rivals whom he had earlier dethroned. The assassination of Sergei Kirov, Leningrad first party secretary, in December 1934, marked the beginning: Irena Wiley, hosting a cocktail party, saw the room empty in minutes as the news spread among her Soviet guests. Although the worst of the purges was still several years off, and contacts between the Americans and Russians continued quite freely for a time, it was the beginning of the end. Within the embassy, too, the happy atmosphere of 1934 dissipated, as Bullitt soured on his Soviet experience. Disappointed in his hopes for a special relationship with Moscow, he became increasingly and vocally anti-Soviet. Malicious gossip and tale bearers within the Embassy turned him against all the bright young men he had praised so highly a year earlier, including for a time Charlie Thayer. Chip Bohlen was reassigned to Washington. Charlie Thayer was demoted to the role of receptionist in the consular section, but by keeping his head down managed to work his way back up into Bullitt's good graces. Bullitt himself left Moscow in mid-1936, having long outlived his welcome with his Soviet hosts.[17]

AFTER PASSING THE Foreign Service exam in 1936, Thayer remained in Moscow until September 1937. It was an increasingly grim experience. Russian friends from the earlier period were arrested and sent to camps or shot. Foreigners led an increasingly isolated existence. The dacha became ever more a refuge for the Americans. After Moscow came assignments in Berlin and Hamburg, each with its own adventures, as Thayer recounts in *Bears*. In 1940, he returned, somewhat reluctantly, to Moscow for a second tour and in 1941 was evacuated with the Soviet government and the American

---

17. Charles W. Thayer, *Hands Across the Caviar* (Philadelphia-New York, 1952).

Embassy to Kuibyshev when the capital appeared on the point of falling to the Germans. In 1942, he was posted to Kabul in order to open a U.S. embassy. A brief stint in London followed, after which he was seconded first to the U.S. Army in 1944, then to the OSS, in which capacity he joined the newly created American Mission to Tito in Yugoslavia. His encounters and adventures with Tito's partisans and the advancing Red Army are described in *Hands Across the Caviar*, the sequel to *Bears*. Thayer ended the war working for the OSS in Vienna and finally as a member of the Joint United States-Soviet Commission on Korea in Seoul. In all these assignments, his Russian experience and knowledge of the Russian language stood him in good stead.

After rejoining the Foreign Service in 1946, Thayer was chosen to head the newly created Voice of America from 1947-1949. He then served a tour as political liaison officer in the Embassy in Bonn. Finally, in 1952 he was appointed to the important post of Consul General in Munich. At 43, he could take some pride in a successful career and a reputation as a well-regarded Soviet expert.

But in March 1953, Thayer's life in diplomacy came to a tragic end. Like many of his State Department colleagues, he fell victim to the witch-hunts of the McCarthy era and the vindictiveness of J. Edgar Hoover. The onset of the Cold War in the late 1940's produced a growing hysteria about Communist subversion, with attacks on the State Department in particular, for allegedly harboring Communists and homosexuals. (Real Communists being scarce, charges of homosexuality became a favored weapon of the witch hunters.) Beginning in 1949, Thayer would be repeatedly investigated on the basis of anonymous denunciations charging him with communist sympathies and homosexuality, some dating back to his years in Moscow. (It is hard today to credit the flimsiness of the evidence – based on lurid accusations, unsubstantiated rumors, spiteful gossip – that was used to destroy people's careers.) In 1951 he was ordered home from Bonn to testify before a security board. He failed one polygraph test; a second was inconclusive. "Distraught, 'in a state of anguish, revulsion and emotion' at the accusations against him and the damage to his career, he checked himself into a clinic in Switzerland.[18] A psychological examination, like the earlier investigations, found no basis for the charge of homosexuality. In short, none of the charges was ever proven and he was repeatedly cleared: by the Civil Service Commission, the Department of Justice and, twice, by State Department loyalty boards.

But the investigations continued; the diplomat was kept under surveillance and the accusations would not go away. Thayer had lost none of his brashness with age and, as Director of Voice of America, he had run afoul of J. Edgar Hoover with his public accusation in 1948 that the FBI investigations were "hamstringing his efforts" to recruit East Europeans and Russians. Thereafter, Hoover ensured that the charges against Thayer were never allowed to die, and he made sure they were known to McCarthy and his allies on the Hill. The one solid fact that emerged from the investigations was that Thayer had fathered a child by Olga Philipoff, a Russian émigré who had worked as his assistant at VOA. The brief affair was followed by a quick marriage and almost immediate divorce. A son, Charles, was born in March 1949. This "morals charge" was added to the dossier as further proof of Thayer's moral turpitude.[19]

After the Republicans returned to power in 1953, the witch-hunts intensified; within the State Department they now had the blessing of John Foster Dulles. Revived yet again, Thayer's case became embroiled in the nomination by Dwight Eisenhower of Chip Bohlen, Thayer's brother-in-law, to be U.S. ambassador to the Soviet Union. It was a controversial appointment in its own right. As Roosevelt's interpreter at Yalta, Bohlen was tainted in Republican eyes. He too faced vague charges of homosexuality dating in part from his early service in Moscow and, as in Thayer's case, based on guilt by

---

18. See Thayer Diaries, Thayer papers. Robert D. Dean, " The Sexual Inquisition and the Brotherhood," in *Imperial Brotherhood: Gender and the Making of Cold War Policy* (Amherst, Mass. 2001), 111, 97-112.

19. Dean, *Imperial Brotherhood*, 101. "Keep on top of this," Hoover instructed his staff on discovering the Olga Philipoff affair.

association. McCarthy and his allies took up the cudgels against him and soon his confirmation was the center of a full-blown debate.[20]

Despite opposition from his own party and from Hoover himself, Eisenhower stood by the appointment. However, it became clear that the price for Bohlen's confirmation would be the resignation of Thayer. Dulles extracted a promise from the ambassador-designate that "no matter what happened" and "regardless of the testimony" he would not embarrass the President by withdrawing from the nomination "for any reason 'whatsoever.' " But, unbeknownst to Bohlen, Thayer with Dulles' assent had been targeted for dismissal as a "homosexual security risk." On the day after Bohlen's conversation with Dulles, Thayer telephoned his brother-in-law from Munich to say his resignation had been requested "to avoid preferment of charges involving his suitability for federal service." Bohlen went to Dulles and asked if the "whatsoever," had meant Thayer's case, "to which Dulles replied blandly, 'yes.' "[21] The promise by which Bohlen felt bound had been extracted from him in order to preclude his resigning over Thayer's firing.

The last sordid act in this tragedy played out in Bohlen's office in the State Department on March 23, 1953, even as a heated Senate debate on his nomination was taking place at the other end of town.[22] Thayer returned unannounced to Washington. Unable to reach Bohlen at first, he "made himself scarce" for several hours at National Airport, hiding behind a copy of the *Washington Post*. Once contact was made, Bohlen, appalled, told him he had been "unwise" to come to the U.S. and instructed him to come to the State Department at once "as inconspicuously as possible" in order to avoid detection and a possible subpoena by McCarthy. It was now clear to Thayer that the State Department's protection had been withdrawn. Fighting the charges would be futile, Bohlen told his brother-in-law, since the

---

20. For the security investigations under Dulles and Bohlen's confirmation fight, see Bohlen, *Witness to History*, 309-336; Dean, *Imperial Brotherhood* 112-132.
21. March 23, 1953, Thayer Diary; Dean, *Imperial Brotherhood*, 122.
22. See March 23, 1953, Thayer Diary, Thayer papers; Dean, *Imperial Brotherhood*, 132-135.

President and Dulles were bent on " 'getting along' with McCarthy." A fight would merely make public all the sordid, if unproven, charges in his file, which would be highly upsetting to his wife and mother. The issue was how to put the best face on his ouster.

A letter of resignation was then negotiated with Under Secretary for Administration Donald Lourie, a political appointee. Thayer requested that the Department make clear that the reason for his resignation was the "girl charge" (i.e. the affair with Olga Philipoff) rather than something less savory. Incredibly, Lourie demurred, agreeing only when Bohlen "got mad, his hands and face twitching with anger," and said if the Department "let [Thayer] down" he'd consider himself released from his promise to the President to go through with the nomination. The scene was surreal: while the teletype continued to clatter out reports of the Senate debate on the Bohlen nomination, Thayer's sister Avis called to ask her husband if he knew where Charlie was; Bohlen, sure his phone was bugged, told her he did not know. When everything was over, Thayer flew back to New York in great secrecy, and "like a fugitive criminal" sat in a corner of Idlewild Airport until it was time for his plane to leave. His visit to the U.S. had lasted all of seven hours. "I really had the feeling I was in a cross between a madhouse and a gangsters' hideout," he wrote later.[23] "Everyone was looking over his shoulder, whispering, sighing and groaning as though the devil was about to get them." Back in Munich, he stayed up until 3 a.m. drinking with John Paton Davies, the State Department's foremost China hand, who predicted, correctly, that he would soon be next on the McCarthy hitlist.[24] News of Thayer's resignation was greeted with stunned disbelief by Americans and Germans alike.[25]

---

23. Thayer to Elbridge Durbrow, April 2, 1953.
24. March 24, 1953, Thayer Diary.
25. Thayer's prolonged and ultimately unsuccessful efforts to change the public characterization of the reason for his resignation: extensive correspondence with Glen Wolff, Sol Rosenblatt and various divisions of the State Department throughout 1953, Thayer papers.

Charles W. Thayer in New York, 1960s.

Thus – not with a bang but a whimper – ended Thayer's diplomatic career. It was a personal tragedy: the Foreign Service had been his life and nothing else he did ever proved as satisfying or as successful. As when he arrived in Moscow twenty years earlier, he was assailed by doubts whether he had done the right thing in resigning rather than facing the charges.[26] Predictably, the State Department did not keep its promise: in the face of attacks from Senator McCarthy, it was given out on background that Thayer had "resigned to avoid preferment of charges involving allegations on his suitability for Federal Employment."[27]

After leaving the Foreign Service, Thayer initially moved with his wife Cynthia and family to Mallorca, a destination both inexpensive and beyond the reach of McCarthy's subpoenas, which he still had reason to fear.[28] (Under Stalin, Thayer joked, you went to Siberia, under Hitler to Dachau, but under McCarthy to Mallorca, which he reckoned was progress.[29]) An added attraction for Thayer was that it offered "the possibility of bringing up the young... more or less as I was brought up with... a wonderful outdoor existence that you couldn't buy in the U.S. without a lot of money."[30]

The former diplomat proposed to support himself by writing, for which he had already demonstrated a real talent. Published before he left the Foreign Service, *Bears in the Caviar* had been a huge success. Over the next fourteen years, he would write many good books and dozens of articles; among other things, he was a frequent contributor to *Sports Illustrated*. Several of his books won critical acclaim, but none enjoyed the success of *Bears* and his career as a writer never really took off. He had many moments of deep discouragement. Money was a perennial problem. Pursued to the end of his life by the ghosts

---

26. Thayer to Kay Bunnell March 30, 1953; Thayer to Durbrow, April 9, 1953.

27. Thayer diary, correspondence.

28. Dean, *Imperial Brotherhood*, 143.

29. Thayer to Avis Bohlen, June 4, 1953.

30. Thayer to George Kennan, July 27, 1953, Thayer papers; Thayer's letters and especially his diary reflect his many moments of discouragement after his retirement. A copy of *An Officer and A Gentleman* in is the Thayer papers.

Laubau, August, 1956. Charles W. Thayer with family. Left to right is Diana Cochrane, daughter of Cynthia Thayer; Thayer's wife Cynthia, and son James (Jimmy) seated in Thayer's lap. Laubau was the family home located in Bavaria.

of the McCarthy era, he found himself blackballed by the FBI when he applied for other jobs: as late as the mid-1960's he was passed over for a professorship at the University of Virginia. He wrote a novel based on his own experiences, entitled *Officers and Gentlemen*, but was strongly dissuaded by friends from publishing it.[31]

After two years in Mallorca, Thayer with his wife and their two children moved back to Munich, where they remained for ten years. They also acquired a chalet near Ruhpolding in the Bavarian Alps, an area "amid the great tall pines and beeches and the green moss and streams underneath," that became a beloved refuge.[32] Later, they began spending part of the year in the United States – first in Washington, then on the Philadelphia Main Line – so that son Jimmy could attend an American school. Summers, however, continued to be spent in the calm and beauty of Ruhpolding, and it was there that Thayer died of a heart attack on August 27, 1969.

An avid outdoorsman all his life, Thayer had hunted game all over the globe, from gazelles in Azerbaijan to ibex in Afghanistan. In later years, he was never happier than when hunting or fishing in his beloved Bavarian Alps. He took enormous pride and pleasure in his son Jimmy – who shared his love of the outdoors – and his stepdaughter Diana. In his final years, he reestablished a somewhat uneasy relationship with his son by Olga Philipoff, also named Charles. (Young Charlie eventually made contact with his father's family, and became friends with several of his cousins, the Bohlens among them.) To the end of his life, Thayer had many devoted friends to whom he wrote wonderful letters. He was adored by his twenty-odd nieces and nephews. It would be hard to exaggerate the charm of his company – he was an amusing, gifted raconteur and always fun to be with. As Loy Henderson had written so many years ago, his presence promoted gaiety wherever he went.[33]

---

31. Frank G. Wisner "Notes and Reflections Upon Thayer's Novel," April 1956, Evan Thomas to Thayer, Thayer papers.

32. April 1953, Thayer Diary, Thayer papers.

33. Henderson *Question of Trust*, 307. Thayer's love of hunting and the outdoors is abundantly documented in his books and diaries.

Thayer certainly deserved better of life than the hand that was dealt him. But it would have given him great pleasure to know the enduring reputation of *Bears in the Caviar*, how many generations of Foreign Service officers and journalists had prepared for life in Moscow by reading the adventures and high jinks of that band of young men so long ago. He would be delighted, as will *Bears'* many fans, to know that some sixty years after its first appearance it was thought worthy of republication.

Avis Bohlen, Winter 2015

Avis Bohlen is the niece of Charles W. Thayer, daughter of Chip and Avis Bohlen. A professional Foreign Service Officer, she served, among other assignments, as Ambassador to Bulgaria and Assistant Secretary for Arms Control. She is currently working on a biography of Charles E. Bohlen and has done extensive research on the Charles W. Thayer papers.

BIBLIOGRAPHICAL NOTE

The papers of Charles W. Thayer are in the Harry S. Truman Library in Independence Missouri. This extensive collection includes his correspondence and the diaries he kept all his life. Other relevant collections include Charles E. Bohlen papers, Library of Congress; John C. Wiley papers, Franklin Delano Roosevelt Library; William C. Bullitt papers, Sterling Library Manuscripts and Archives, Yale University; Avis Bohlen collection, Schlesinger Library, Cambridge, Mass.

The most complete account of the multiple investigations of Thayer and his eventual resignation is to be found in Robert D. Dean, "The Sexual Inquisition and the Brotherhood," in *Imperial Brotherhood: Gender and the Making of Cold War Policy* (Amherst, Mass. 2001), 98-145. See also by Dean, "Charles W. Thayer: Purged from the State Department," in *The Human Tradition in America since 1945*, ed. David L. Anderson (Wilmington, Delaware, 2003), 227-245. I am grateful to Professor Dean for his comments on the Introduction.

PREFACE

To avoid any misunderstanding let it be clear from the start that this is not a diplomatic history of the dreary decade leading up to World War II. There are enough such histories already. It is not even one of those intimate accounts of the diplomatic maneuvering of the period. There are far too many of them, written by everyone from the Ambassadors and Ministers themselves to their daughters and chauffeurs.

It is purely and simply an account of some of the episodes any diplomatic officer is likely to run into during his off hours. Any historical events described in this account are purely coincidental. The writer has never been able to keep a diary for more than a month or two, after which he has, probably fortunately, lost it. Consequently, it has been necessary to rely exclusively on a faulty memory to recall episodes of twenty or more years ago. Names, dates, and places have been recorded mildly accurately but, in some unimportant cases where memory has failed, pseudonyms and approximations have been used.

Bonn, Germany
2 June 1950

Charles Thayer in his cadet's uniform.
He graduated from West Point in 1933.

1

GETTING MILITARY

In its light-hearted way, the U.S. Government took over my formal education on a hot summer morning in 1929 when I entered the sallyport at West Point. Just what happened during the next few hours and weeks has never been very clear in my mind. I have a hazy recollection of a pack of Yearlings, or sophomores, barking, snarling and yelling at me, but I still don't know exactly what they wanted. Some seemed to want me to pick up my suitcase. Others wanted me to drop it. Some preferred that I run, others that I walk and still others that I stand rigid with my chin on my Adam's apple and my shoulder blades touching behind me. But we Plebes were told it was discipline and very good for us and after only 360 days the Yearlings shook our hands and said we were "recognized" and didn't have to say "sir" to them any more. So we were all very happy and waited eagerly to pounce on the next class of Plebes to come in the sallyport.

Just fifteen years later Uncle Sam urged me down the home stretch of my formal education. It led through the floor of a converted bomber into a very black and uninviting night somewhere over the north of England. I landed with a thud on a hard cow pasture, slightly dazed but very pleased with myself and my parachute. They gave me a certificate saying I was a "Third Class Parachutist," and sent me off to General Bill Donovan as an educated agent. Ever since I've been trying in vain to find someone with a "Fourth-Class Parachutist" certificate. Apparently they're only issued posthumously.

But to get back to the beginning. People have a way of asking why anyone should go to West Point when he wanted to join the Foreign Service – or vice versa. Some ex-cadets will tell you they went to West Point because they wanted to be soldiers; others will say they wanted the education; still others will admit candidly they wanted to play on the Army football team. I'm afraid none of these answers is entirely exact in my case. From the age of eight I'd always meant to go into some form of Government service. At first it was the police or fire departments. Then it was the Navy, then the Army and finally the Foreign Service. So I figured I'd better let the Government educate me if it would. But to be perfectly honest, there was another just as compelling reason, namely football. Not that I wanted to play it. I didn't.

Over several decades, my father, uncles, and brother had all gone to the University of Pennsylvania where they had captained the football team, starred on various hypothetical All-American teams and generally enjoyed the roles of football heroes. At school my coaches and I had made a discovery which, while not widely publicized, was nevertheless important to me: I was not a football player. For three years I was on the third intramural club team, and the fourth year they even made me captain, not because of my prowess but because of my overwhelming seniority. It wasn't the coaches' fault either. They'd remembered my brother and uncles and father, and they had done what they could to bring out that football talent they were convinced was lying dormant within me. But after four years of struggling, they shook their heads and admitted mournfully that I wasn't developing according to plan.

So when it came to going to college, there was one thing I was absolutely determined about: I was *not* going to play football or try to play football or be experimented upon by the Penn coaching staff at the expense of my health and temper until they discovered what I had long since so painfully learned – that I couldn't play football.

Hence, I planned to break quietly with the Penn football tradition and sneak unobtrusively to West Point. But I hadn't reckoned with the Army football staff. We'd hardly been in "Beast Barracks" a week before the whole Plebe class was trotted out onto the football field to show what they could do. I explained to the Officer in Charge as politely as I could that I thought they were wasting their time on me. But I was told as impolitely as possible that the coaches would decide who was good at football and who wasn't. It takes only a few hours of Beast Barracks to teach you not to argue with your superiors, so I mentally shrugged my shoulders and ran down under a punt to tackle some bruiser from the Trans-Appalachian Steppes. He caught me on the ear with his knee. The trainer managed to bring me to again in a few minutes. Then someone told New Cadet Thayer to run for a pass. I ran as hard as I could, but the pass caught up with me and landed neatly and painfully in my face. While I was recovering, some optimistic instructor said, "Maybe he's a runner." So they passed me a ball and eleven loyal classmates on the opposing team fell on me before I'd even started to run. Eventually the evidence became overwhelming and the Officer in Charge told me I could "try out" for lacrosse the next day.

For a week or two I went the rounds of the athletic fields while the athletic instructors looked for my niche. Naturally they didn't ask me. That would have been too simple. Lacrosse, soccer, baseball, basketball, hockey, boxing, wrestling – I "tried out" at them all.

Then one day at the mess hall the Adjutant read out among the orders for the day: "New Cadet Thayer will report to the football squad this afternoon." Gloomily I drew a football uniform in the gym and marched out to the field. By this time the football squad had been weeded out considerably and its average weight and vigor had correspondingly increased.

One of the minor coaches growled at me, "Are you any relation to last year's All-American end?" I admitted I was, but started to explain that my brother had cornered the family football talent.

The coach stopped me short. "Get in there at end and see what you can do."

I went in and for a couple of plays all I had to do was to get knocked down by some very energetic interference runner. Then someone on the other team did the wrong thing and I found myself face to face with the ball carrier. I lunged at him as well as I could, but somehow or other he got his hand on my head and pushed it violently against his upcoming knee and went on around my end for a nice gain. They dragged me off the field, doused me with water and told me to rest for a few minutes. "Hard luck," said the coach consolingly. Evidently he still thought he'd made a discovery and wasn't going to let anything stand in the way of my football career.

I've met that type several times since. There was a professor in Iran who said that if I could only learn to read in the right direction – that is from right to left – he could teach me Persian. (He never did.) And there was the Italian ski instructor at Cortina who, after watching me hurtle down the beginners' run at great speed, concluded that I was a promising skier. Somehow he overlooked the fact that I was going so fast only because I couldn't stop. So he took me up a mountain ski run high in the Dolomites with his prize class of pupils. When the snow and blood cleared away several hours later, I was at the bottom of the mountain. After a certain amount of first aid, I was even able to sit up and take nourishment in the form of a stiff glass of brandy. But the ski instructor was a good sport and gallantly pinned a medal on my chest. It proclaimed me a "Third-Class Skier." It was apparently awarded on the same basis as the parachutist certificate: if I'd been any worse, I'd have been dead. The junior football coach at West Point didn't give me any brandy. Instead he had me running down under kicks, charging dummies – artificial and otherwise – bouncing passes off various parts of my anatomy, chiefly my solar plexus, until nightfall. As I hobbled off toward the locker room, he seemed to soften for a moment and I was genuinely touched when he shouted after me, "That'll be all the football for you. You can go back to the gym squad tomorrow."

Several more weeks went by and I began to think I'd finally thrown off my misguided fans. Then again one day at lunch the Adjutant shouted the same fatal formula: "New Cadet Thayer will report for football practice today." I was sure it was a mistake and considered whether just to ignore the order or to check on it. Ignoring orders is a rather dangerous form of sport at West Point, so after lunch I diffidently approached the Adjutant: "Sir, isn't that order for me a mistake? You told me that three weeks ago and I think..."

"Mr. Dumbjohn! Haven't you learned yet that Plebes don't ask questions? What's more, don't you know what happens when Plebes think?"

It was a standard question and I dutifully murmured the set reply: "Yes, sir! They foul it all up, sir."

So for the third time I found myself back with the football squad. This time the head coach himself came over to me and slapped me genially on the back.

"I was going over the Plebe rolls last night," he said, "and ran across your name. Aren't you the brother of the All-American end?"

I admitted I was.

"To think we've missed you all this time! Now get in there at right end and show us what you Thayers can do. We'll have you on the varsity squad in no time. You're a little light but you'll fill out quickly enough."

By this time I'd learned better than to protest and I went in at end. The football squad was now thoroughly purged of all neophytes and was made up exclusively of two hundred pound gorillas whose only ambition, it seemed to me, was to make their colleagues as uncomfortable as possible. I was rapidly beginning to dislike them. My performance on this occasion was shorter but definitely more intensive than on my previous appearances. For several plays I managed to come through with nothing worse than a set of cleats on my face, a bruised shin bone and a wrenched shoulder. I was beginning to feel I was leading a charmed life. Then two of my larger colleagues, going in opposite directions, collided with my left leg. My ankle, being the only thing that could give way, gave.

The squad doctor took one look at it and turned to the head coach: "No more football for him this season."

The head coach murmured something about "too bad." But from the way he said it, I gathered he wasn't as disappointed as he might have been earlier in the day. Perhaps he'd begun to realize that football is an acquired and not an hereditary trait.

Eventually, I was tried out at polo. I'd ridden since I was a small child and the polo coach thought he saw some possibilities in me. At any rate, when the polo squad list came out, my name was hanging to the end of it. For the rest of my four years, polo was my only athletic activity. Not that I could hit a ball, but I could ride and spent most of my time training ponies. Eventually, again from simple seniority, I made my letter, which rehabilitated me in the eyes of my family at least. But it was a "minor" letter – not a "major" letter. It corresponded roughly to a "Third-Class Parachutist" or a "Third-Class Skier" certificate.

Although football and polo were my chief worries in those early days, Beast Barracks kept us busy at a number of other more or less unpleasant duties. They tried to teach us to march, to do squads right, to make our beds, to do the manual of arms. And the whole time they harassed us with a noisy form of discipline which I dare say produced quick results but also was apt to raise doubts about the sanity of our instructors. It consisted chiefly of very loud barking on the part of the instructor and bewildered confusion on the part of the Plebe. If the Plebe's confusion was too great, the Plebe was "backward." If it wasn't great enough, the Plebe was "forward" – a far greater crime. But eventually we learned to keep in the happy middle ground and by the time the academic year started in the fall, we were largely immune to the noisy rantings of our superiors-though the last thing we could do was show it.

I wouldn't say West Point's curriculum is exactly adapted to preparing you for diplomacy. After all, the diplomat is supposed to flourish, while the soldier vegetates – and sometimes vice versa. The chief ingredient of the course was mathematics and its various applications to physics, ballistics and engineering. Its application to diplomacy was a long time in making itself clear, but eventually the calculus and the slide rule proved their indispensability even in the rarefied atmosphere of an Embassy Chancery.

A good ten years after I had last looked at a logarithm, I was in Afghanistan setting up our new Embassy. We were provided with a fine stone house to put the future Ambassador in but there were no decent offices. The war was on and many of the foreign engineers and architects who had been employed by the Afghan Government had gone home. Consequently, the remaining engineers were all occupied in much more vital matters than helping the Americans with their housing problems. So it was not long before my West Point drawing board was dragged from a trunk and, with T-square and ruler, I designed myself what I daresay is the only chancery in the U.S. Foreign Service architected by a Third Secretary. (Incidentally, the Third Secretary's office is the largest, most comfortable and has the finest view of all in the Kabul Chancery.)

But then another problem arose. The Ambassador's house had a large main dining room. Directly above it, on the second floor, was a bedroom of the same size. However, as a bedroom it was a little large even for the most ambassadorial taste. So we decided to divide it in two. Local masons were called in and in no time a good solid brick wall was built across the room. The only trouble was that we had not reckoned with the weight of the bricks or the strength of the wooden beams supporting the dining room ceiling. Very soon the ceiling began to develop a slightly tired, sagging look. Before long, large cracks appeared. It was generally agreed that if something weren't done, the handsome new partition upstairs would soon land in the dining room below. But with no engineers or architects available, the contractor-landlord and I had to cope with the problem alone. (Incidentally, the landlord also doubled in brass as Minister of War.

Today, His Royal Highness Shah Mahmud Khan is Afghanistan's Prime Minister.)[1] I suggested we get a steel beam.

"A steel beam in Kabul?" asked His Royal Highness. "How will we ever find one?"

His majordomo, a bright-eyed fellow called Ahmed Jan whose resourcefulness was bigger than his book learning, broke in:

"I'll get you a beam easily. Wait a few minutes."

Ahmed Jan disappeared in His Royal Highness' carriage and in about half an hour returned dragging behind him what certainly looked like a beam. On closer examination, it turned out to be one of the old streetcar tracks from Afghanistan's ex-railroad. (Among its many other unique qualities, Afghanistan is, so far as I know, the only country in the world that *had* a railroad. A few countries don't have railroads. Most have railroads. But Afghanistan had one and tore it up. It was only a short road – about three miles – but the tribesmen and the Mullahs decided it was a step in the wrong direction. So they tore it up and threw out the King, Amanullah, who'd built it, and elected another King. Anyone who thinks Afghanistan isn't democratic, just ask Amanullah. He lives in Switzerland.)

When I saw the track, I pointed out that it was hardly heavy enough for our purposes. Shah Mahmud threw up his arms in despair and drove off in his carriage. The majordomo was a little crestfallen and more than a little annoyed at my criticism. He started taunting me by asking how I knew the beam was too light.

"I'm an engineer by training," I replied haughtily.

"Do trained engineers tell the strength of beams just by looking at them? I always thought they had to measure them and do some arithmetic before they were sure. But perhaps American engineers are different," he concluded sarcastically.

---

1. Shah Mahmud Khan (1890-1953) was the uncle of Zahir Shah, who ruled as King of Afghanistan from 1933 to 1972, and also the uncle of President Daud Khan, who ruled from 1973 to 1978, when he was assassinated in the Communist coup that eventually led to the Soviet invasion of the country in 1979.

I went home offended, angry and thoroughly frustrated. But that evening it occurred to me that my old engineering manuals were stored with all the other useless books I'd been dragging around the globe at Government expense for ten years. So I set out to calculate the safeload for a streetcar track from ex-King Amanullah's abandoned railroad. It took me nearly a week to brush up my calculus. Another week I spent trying to find the right formulas for steel beams. I'm not quite certain that I ever did get the right one, but I made the rough assumption that a streetcar track is equivalent to an I-beam. Each day the dining room ceiling dropped more despairingly. It was a race with time and the masonry work on the second floor. There was no time to be lost in quibbling over formulas.

At last I finished my calculations and to my consternation arrived at the conclusion that the car track would be quite safe, provided no more than one elephant was kept in each bedroom. As there was only one elephant in Kabul at that time and as she rarely came into the house (she was used to pull the roller on the Palace driveway), it was obvious that Ahmed Jan was right. I checked my figures once more and sent for him. I showed him my calculations which covered about three notebooks while he stared politely. His own knowledge of arithmetic was limited to simple addition, but when I got to the point about the two elephants, he beamed with delight, shook me warmly by the hand and announced that American engineers might be slow but they always came to the right conclusions.

It is entirely possible that the calculations were wrong, but according to the latest reports, the dining room ceiling in the Kabul Embassy is still holding up very nicely. I hope calculus has proved as useful to my fellow graduates.

I suppose that military training at West Point does play a role of some importance, although I did my best to ignore it at the time. It was in this field, I'm afraid, that I fell down most completely. In the first place, upperclassmen were almost unanimous in the view that I couldn't keep step in parades. I eventually convinced them that this wasn't strictly accurate, but then they decided there was something else wrong with my gait. After repeated efforts to cure the string-halt in my hindlegs, they relegated me to the rear rank, where I remained for four years. I was a little offended at first but I soon got used to it. In fact, I found marching behind my colleagues something of an advantage. Inspecting Generals were less apt to discover you'd forgotten to tie your shoes and when you wrinkled your nose during a parade to scare off a mosquito, the Officer of the Day was less likely to detect the "unauthorized movement." Besides it relieved you of the necessity of any undue thinking during drill. An uncle of mine who tried vainly to get commissioned in World War I used to say that only a moron could really be good at close order drill. Anyone with the slightest inclination toward thought invariably got off on to some interesting mental speculation just as the platoon commander said, "Left front into line" or "Squads left into line," and the poor thinker was left clueless. My uncle had something.

Then there was the matter of "military appearance," including the relative position of the shoulders and the spine. I've never been able to think freely with my throat exposed. Whenever real problems arise, my chin and shoulders tend to huddle together in conference. This isn't the posture recommended at West Point, as I quickly learned. But there was little I could do about my mental habits by the time I entered the Academy. Either my chin went down when I thought or my chin stayed up and my mind went dead. My first year with this dilemma was difficult but eventually I found it possible to divide my energies between mental and physical exercise.

Also there was the matter of uniforms. At West Point there is a whole series of rules, regulations, flags, bells, messenger systems and God-knows-what-all to tell you what uniform is proper at any given second. One moment it's riding breeches with sweaters and the next minute it's white trousers with tailcoats. It took months to find out what the signals all meant, but eventually I caught on to that part of the problem. But what made the Officer of the Day fix his mind on one uniform or another remained a mystery till I graduated.

The closest we ever came to finding a real clue was the changing personalities of the various Officers of the Day.

"Pete Newby's on today," someone would hazard. "I guess that means white uniforms, provided it rains hard enough."

Or else, "Dapper Dan's on today. That means we'll be in full dress till Taps." *Chacún a son gout.*

And then there was the West Point fetish about neatness. Our ordinary uniforms had black braid down the front, which I am convinced was made out of chameleon skins. All an angry, red-faced inspector had to do was stare at my braid long enough and a great red spot would appear just as though I'd spilled some ketchup on it. The same with shoes, cap-visors, rifle barrels or anything else that they thought should be clean and shiny. Not that I objected particularly to the spots. It was the demerits that came with them that annoyed me. After you got a certain number of demerits, you'd have to spend your free afternoons walking back and forth across "the Area," working them off at the rate of one an hour-and that is a very slow rate in anybody's timetable. Although I never figured out how to avoid getting the demerits, I did eventually find a system for not "walking them off." There was a standing rule that anyone on a varsity athletic squad could postpone walking off his demerits until the end of the particular season for that sport. It so happened, however, that we played polo all the year round and I eventually managed to get permanent deferment from my company clerk who kept the demerit book. He thought it a little odd at first and tried to argue but as he was my roommate I had plenty of time to convince him. It all worked out beautifully until the day before we were to get our diplomas from General MacArthur. Some busybody over at Corps Headquarters began tallying up the scores and discovered I still owed the Academy some ninety-seven hours on the Area. I was called in and asked about this slight overdraft. I pointed out that we even had a polo game on Graduation Day. The season was therefore still on and the rules still stood. Besides, it was less than twenty-four hours till Graduation Ceremonies. How could I possibly squeeze ninety-seven hours into twenty-four or less? The busybody for once saw the logic of my argument but carefully registered the debt in my record. Presumably when I retire, I can go up to West Point, borrow a rifle, and square my account.

But for all the irritation there was always one great consolation: it wasn't going to last forever. Once I'd graduated, once I had left those "sacred walls," I promised myself repeatedly that I would never: shine my shoes, press my pants, square my shoulders, keep in step, take the spots off my braid (if I had any braid, which seemed unlikely) or be on time for a formation. My day would come.

It came about twelve years later in Vienna. The war was over but I was back in the Army, serving temporarily as General Mark Clark's interpreter. The Allied Marshals and Generals were fêting each other with Parades and Honor Guards and Banquets at a great rate.

Among my duties as interpreter was accompanying the General on all ceremonies at which his Russian colleagues were present. One day he, his Deputy, General Al Gruenther, his political advisor, Jack Erhardt, his aide, his photographer, his orderly and myself went to visit Marshal Konev at his Headquarters at Baden, Austria. Business was concluded with General Clark's usual dispatch and before we knew it we were in the middle of a standard inter-allied banquet. It was during that period just after the German surrender when every officer and soldier thought he could prove his role in the winning of the war by drinking his ally under the table. General Clark never subscribed to the theory that he had to be able to drink as much as anyone else at the table but he did believe in keeping up appearances. So it was my job to see to it that his vodka glass was filled with water at all times. I'm not particularly light with my fingers and the only method I could devise for keeping General Clark properly supplied with water was to drink up my glass of vodka as soon as it was poured, refill it with water, exchange it for Clark's vodka and drink it too, before some sharp-eyed Soviet General saw what was going on. We can skip the details of what went on that night at

Baden. In fact, we will have to skip them because my memory is a little hazy on the point.

The next morning at the crack of dawn I was pulled from my cot and told that General Clark had accepted a challenge to a swimming race with Marshal Konev's Deputy, General Zheltov. The race was to take place at Baden's bathing pool. Feeling like death, I crawled after Clark down to the pool which, the Soviet attendants proudly assured us, was one hundred meters long. The competing Generals were soon in their swimming trunks and pacing up and down the pool like two-year-olds in the paddock at Saratoga. Then Clark caught sight of me lurking in the background.

"Come on Thayer! For goodness' sakes, get into your trunks in a hurry." (Wrong uniform again.)

"But, General, I don't swim – at least this morning…"

"Damn it! Stop arguing. Didn't you hear what I said?"

I'm no better-probably a little worse – at swimming than I am at parachuting, football or skiing. They say my form with the breast stroke isn't bad but my speed is deplorable. However, General Clark is General Clark and nothing if not determined.

In a few seconds the three of us were lined up at the edge of the pool. Clark on one side, Zheltov on the other, and I in the middle. They agreed to race the length of the pool and back.

Someone said, "*Raz, dva, tri.*"

I translated, "One, two, three," and we all plunged in, more or less together.

At least, I thought, in a swimming race the Generals won't be able to talk. But I didn't know my Generals. They'd hardly hit the water when they started a running commentary on the event like a pair of sports announcers – the one in Russian, the other in English. I was already far behind both of them and could scarcely hear, let alone speak. But eventually I heard the purple words of General Clark asking what the hell I thought I was doing? Would I please tell General Zheltov that General Clark thinks he has a very fine crawl stroke. I opened my mouth to shout to Zheltov but the backwash of one of the Generals caught me in the face and the only thing I could get out was a mouthful of water. I tried again, "General Clark says..."

Then Zheltov got annoyed. "I've told you twice to tell General Clark his foot action is very good."

I shouted lustily at Clark, "The General says your feet..." but the backwash caught me again.

"What the hell's wrong with my feet?"

I gasped for breath. "General Zheltov says..."

"I don't give a damn what General Zheltov says. What was that crack you made about my feet?"

"It was General Zheltov..." But by this time they'd reached the end of the pool and were on their way back toward me. The night's activities were beginning to tell and they were saving their breath for more important matters. I struggled to the end of the pool, crawled out and lay exhausted, water-logged and thoroughly sick, on the cement edge. I never did find out who won. Frankly, I didn't care.

MY BIGGEST DIFFICULTY with General Clark was trying to be in the same sort of uniform as he at any given ceremony. It seemed like a repetition of my cadet days because I never quite succeeded. It didn't matter how often I'd call his aide and ask, "What's General Clark going to wear at the review?" Invariably when the time came, Clark had changed his mind or my breeches were at the cleaner or something. He'd give me one look, carefully examining whatever costume I had put on from shoes to cap and then shake his head wearily, "Thayer, will you ever, etc., etc., etc."

Not long after the swimming meet, Marshal Konev returned Clark's visit. The usual Guard of Honor was turned out and as usual I called Clark's aide: "What's the outfit for today's fiesta?"

"Battledress" was the reply. I always hated battledress because my Eisenhower jacket had a way of climbing up and bunching in a very unmilitary way above my belt, leaving a wide gap between it and my trousers. That day I took careful measures to have it well pressed and buckled tightly around me. Nevertheless even before I saw the General I felt it crawling up on me.

I was to meet Clark on the steps of his Headquarters three minutes before Konev was to arrive. General Clark was there before me, looking every inch a soldier but unfortunately dressed in tunic and pinks. My battle jacket took a further leap and ended up around my solar plexus.

"Thayer, for God's sake, can't you ever, etc., etc., etc."

It seemed like a long three minutes but eventually Konev showed up, General Clark stopped commenting on my costume, and we moved off toward where the Guard of Honor was drawn up, the Marshal and the General in front (I used to call them my minesweepers), their chests sparkling with medals and ribbons, I behind, my chest a wrinkled mass of Eisenhower jacket. We marched front and center. The Guard presented arms. The band struck up "The Star Spangled Banner." The General and the Marshal saluted and I followed suit. When the band had finished there was a pause. General Clark's hand began to come down from his overseas cap. From behind I could see him cast a sidelong glance at Konev who remained saluting. Quickly Clark's hand went back. The pause continued and Konev's hand began to fall toward his side. Then he sneaked a glance at the rigid Clark and back his arm came. Still nothing happened and the two hands sawed up and down alternately. Finally General Clark's six-foot-four figure swayed back on its heels toward me.

"Thayer, God-damn it," he growled out of the side of his mouth. "Thayer, God-damn it. Tell them music, God-damn it. Music."

As he spoke I leaned forward and whispered, "Yes, sir," in my most military manner. And then leaning back myself, to where a group of staff officers were watching the performance, whispered:

"General Clark says, 'Music, God-damn it, music.' "

I could hear the command being passed down the line to where the bandmaster stood. Then at last the band blared out. As the sound reached him, Clark finally made up his mind and his hand came briskly down to his side. I was about to follow suit, for I had been religiously imitating my front rank as I'd been taught at West Point. But this time my turn at last had come and my hand shot back to my cap.

Clark saw the motion out of the corner of his eye. Thoroughly confused he again rocked back on his heels:

"Thayer, God-damn it, Thayer. What the hell are they playing?"

"It's the Soviet National Anthem, sir," I replied as diffidently as I possibly could. This time Clark's arm followed mine to the cap. There are some military matters that can be difficult even for Generals.

2

GETTING RUSSIAN

Perhaps it was Beast Barracks. Perhaps it was the oppressive preoccupation of the military with polishing shoes that began to dim the glamor of an Army career. But gradually as I waded through the four years of West Point, it got to be fairly obvious that the U.S. Government would do better with me in some other form of public service, perhaps the Foreign Service.

I went down to the State Department to inquire. It was 1932 and the Economy Era was still on. The Department explained they were only recruiting people with special qualifications. Just what these special qualifications were they couldn't precisely explain. But Roosevelt had just won the election and had said he was going to recognize the Soviet Union. If I learned to speak Russian, I asked, would that be a "special qualification." The Department officials allowed as how it might be but that was a hypothetical question. We hadn't recognized Russia yet. The Department never answered hypothetical questions. However, they weren't entirely discouraging.

Then I went to see the Adjutant General, the personnel chief of the Army. The Army's share of the Economy Era was a severe scarcity of vacancies into which to commission graduates from West Point and the non-governmental military schools – the "Tin Schools" as we haughtily referred to them at West Point. That being the case, would the Army like me to resign my commission after graduation and transfer to the State Department, or did they insist I wait for the prescribed two years and then resign? Definitely, the Adjutant General would like me to resign as soon as possible. His definiteness was not very flattering but it suited me.

So after graduating I sent my resignation to the Colonel of the Cavalry regiment to which I had been assigned and bought a ticket to Moscow as a tourist, to learn the language and await Roosevelt's promised recognition of Russia. Everything seemed to be working out very nicely except that my regimental commander wouldn't reply to my request. As the days of my graduation leave were running out, I telegraphed him: what about my resignation.

No reply.

Then I telephoned his Adjutant.

"The Colonel says you should report for duty at once." I hurried to Fort Myer and reported to the Colonel. His name was vaguely familiar to me but his reputation didn't hit the headlines until much later. In 1933 George Patton was just an eccentric cavalryman.

He growled as I entered his office and saluted:

"What do you think you're trying to get away with, Lieutenant? The Army's just finished educating you and now you want to quit – to become a damned cookie-pushing diplomat – and in Russia of all places. Are you a Boleshevik?" he shouted.

I explained my plans in greater detail. I pointed out that it was after all the taxpayer who had educated me and, as I was going to continue to work for the Government, the matter of who paid for my education hardly arose.

The Colonel shouted louder:

"Well, the Army has something to say. The Adjutant General wouldn't even consider your resigning. I'm going to turn it down right now. Report for work in the morning."

"But the Adjutant General suggested my resigning. I talked to him personally a couple of months ago and he was unusually enthusiastic."

The good Colonel seemed a little startled. His tone changed.

"Didn't you play Number One on the Army polo team?"

I admitted I had.

"Well, we've lost our Number One on the Fort Myer team and we sort of planned to have you take his place. I was just thinking we needed a Number One badly," he added quite candidly.

I told him I didn't want to play polo any more and I was set on going to Moscow.

"Well, then! Go ahead, God-damn it! If you don't know what's good for you, I can't teach you. Damned cookie-pushing instead of good decent polo. And Russia on top of that! It's damned nonsense, I say. God-damned nonsense!"

A few days later I was sitting in a dreary airport at Konigsberg in East Prussia. It was part of Germany then and the jumping-off place for air travelers to the Soviet Union.

Out on the airfield a half dozen clumsy old Junker passenger planes squatted in the mud and weeds. Through the mist I could just make out the futuristic eagle painted on their fuselages, the symbol of the Lufthansa. On the other side of the field, far enough away to avoid contamination with these Nazi beasts, was a group of smaller single-motored planes carrying the star of the Soviet Civil Air Fleet. Beyond the field the drab farmlands of East Prussia stretched away to a misty horizon. Here and there a few gaunt poplars peered gloomily through the fog. By counting the number I could see from time to time, I tried to guess whether the fog was lifting or closing in.

Inside the airport things were hardly less cheerful than on the field. A few stolid travelers sat about staring at their feet, waiting patiently for their planes to be announced. At an unpainted wooden counter two bespectacled German clerks bustled about officiously. Behind them on a large blackboard were listed scheduled flights to Berlin, Warsaw, Danzig, Riga, Moscow and Leningrad. It was this last flight to Leningrad that interested me. I'd decided to do a bit of sightseeing in the old capital before settling down in Moscow. Besides, there was a little job involving some buried treasure in a Leningrad suburb that I'd promised to do for an old Russian friend.

That morning Konigsberg was really a jumping-off place. As I paced restlessly around the waiting room, I couldn't help but think of George Patton's comment: "Damn nonsense – God-damned nonsense!" My plans had all sounded so eminently reasonable when I described them to friends at home. I would simply give up my military career, abandon my Peal boots, Sam Browne belt and uniforms and take on a much more glamorous diplomatic career. All I had to do was to go to Moscow, learn Russian, wait for Roosevelt to recognize the Soviet Government and then apply for a job in the Embassy. It was perfectly simple. But on that gloomy, foggy morning four thousand miles from home, it began to seem far more nebulous. Suppose Roosevelt changed his mind? Suppose I couldn't learn Russian? Suppose they threw me out before an Ambassador arrived? (I only had a tourist visa good for a month.) The longer I stared at the bleak East Prussian landscape, the madder the whole scheme seemed. Perhaps I ought to reconsider. Maybe Colonel Patton would be forgiving and take me back if I promised to try hard to be a good polo player.

My morale was at rock bottom when one of the airport clerks announced the immediate departure of the plane for Leningrad. It was too late then to turn back. I grabbed my suitcase and started toward the field. One other passenger joined me. He was an old professorial-looking type with a shiny bald head, thick pince-nez and a rather shabby suit of knickerbockers. Together we were escorted to one of the Soviet planes. Beside it we found the pilot, a blond, tubby young fellow with an enormous grin.

The plane was a single-engined monoplane. Its paint was chipped and faded, its wings patched and dented. My fellow passenger and I clambered up the ladder into a diminutive cabin, stowed our suitcases on a rack over our heads and fastened our seat belts. A moment later the pilot darted up the ladder, hesitated at the top long enough to pat the fuselage affectionately, and bellowed something in Russian. I looked inquiringly at my fellow traveler who evidently had spotted my nationality for he interpreted readily enough into English:

"He says it's 'Old Granny's' last trip."

With this reassuring bit of news, they slammed shut "Old Granny's" door and a couple of mechanics gave the propeller a spin. A moment later we were bumping across the field, the throttle wide open. Before I had time to realize it, we had bounced into the air, circled the airport and were leveling off for the East. No warm-up, no preliminary tinkering with the controls, no last minute check-in with the tower. We were still flying at about tree-top level when the pilot peered back at us and waved gaily to indicate we were all set. I wondered when, if ever, he was going to get some altitude? just a little altitude. From where I sat it looked as though one extra big pine tree would be enough to sweep off our landing gear. I soon learned, however, that Soviet pilots prefer, in fact they insist on, what they rather aptly call "contact-flying" – if not with the wheels actually touching the tree-tops, at least close enough so you don't get dizzy or lose your way in a low fog. It took a little getting used to but I had insisted to myself that I was going to Russia (like everyone else) with an "open mind" and I wasn't going to start carping before I even crossed the border.

Other foreigners whose "open minds" didn't hamper their judgment as much have found this low-flying habit harder to get used to. On one occasion during the early part of the war – seven years after my first flight in a Russian plane – I had gone up to Archangel to meet Lord Beaverbrook[2] and the Lend-Lease Mission. They had arrived by sea and were being flown from Archangel to Moscow in a fleet of Soviet DC-3's. Just before the take-off Lord Beaverbrook sent for me.

"Harry Hopkins tells me these fellows never fly higher than fifty or a hundred feet. You tell them that while I'm aboard they're to stay above a thousand feet."

I started to argue, "But, Lord Beaverbrook, it's the way they've always flown. Isn't it just a little late to try and change their habits?

---

2. Lord Beaverbrook (1879-1964) was a charismatic, self-made tycoon, politician and writer, who at this time was a political ally of Winston Churchill.

It might even be a little risky. They might get dizzy way up at a thousand feet."

But Beaverbrook was unamused.

"You tell 'em what I said and no back talk from you either!"

So I relayed his message, translated verbatim, to the chief pilot. He was obviously annoyed but I warned him he'd be better off to do what Beaverbrook said. The old man had a reputation for getting his own way. At first all went well on the flight, despite my worry. It wasn't until we got to Moscow and were spotted by a Soviet anti-aircraft battery that the trouble began. From the ground, any formation flying so high above the usual ceiling was bound to attract attention. Apparently to the Battery Commander's still inexperienced eye, we must have been a formation of Germans. Whatever he was thinking, the first notice we got of it was a little white puff of smoke about fifty feet to the right of the formation. A second little puff blossomed a few feet astern. A moment later a whole salvo went off all around us. I wasn't in the same plane as Beaverbrook, but several others who were told me later what happened. When the salvo went off, His Lordship jumped from his seat and bolted toward the pilot's cabin. Just as he got there the pilot, who was undoubtedly just as aware of what was going on as Beaverbrook, decided he'd better get down where the anti-aircraft guns could see our Soviet markings. So he turned the nose down and dove straight for the earth. Beaverbrook landed on his bottom with a bang and, as the plane dove, he slid unceremoniously up the aisle until he was stopped by the lavatory door. When we got back down to "contact level," the pilot straightened out and Beaverbrook, grinning like a monkey, walked gingerly back to his seat. So far as I know he never gave any more flying instructions to Soviet pilots.

A few months after the Beaverbrook incident, another occurrence shook up a couple of young American naval officers who were flying in the "meat-can" nose of a Soviet bomber from Kuibyshev to Moscow. As usual the ceiling was "treetop." Unfortunately there were no trees along one part of the course and the pilots apparently had nothing to judge their altitude by until they came to one of the rare railroad tracks crossing the Volga plain. A freight train was crawling along the track just as the plane crossed it. One of the freight cars clipped the undercarriage and wrenched open the bomb-bay doors, spilling all the passengers' baggage onto the track. A second later the plane lurched onto the snow, skidded about a thousand yards, and stopped none the worse for its brief experience. But a party of peasants near by had seen the baggage tumbling from the bomb-bay and concluded naturally enough that some nervy German was bombing their railroads. Whereupon they grabbed their pitchforks and surrounded the somewhat stunned occupants of the plane as they climbed out of the wreck. Fortunately a Soviet General was among the passengers and he managed to hold the angry peasants at bay with a revolver while he explained the slightly unusual operation. Afterward the rumor went around that an order had been issued to the Soviet Air Force requiring all pilots to look both ways before crossing railroad tracks. The truth of the rumor was never confirmed.

But to get back to 1933 and the single-engine job from Konigsberg. In a limited sort of way, I was beginning to enjoy the tree-top flying because I could get a much better look at the countryside. It was easy to make out what the farmers were doing in their fields, what the great East Prussian farm carts were carrying along the roads and even what luck the occasional fisherman was having beside the lakes and streams we flew over.

Just as I was getting back into a fairly normal frame of mind, I heard a muffled explosion up front. Through the door to the pilot's cabin, I could see that the windshield was covered with a rusty-brown opaque film. The pilot was rocking agitatedly from one side window to the other, obviously trying to find out where he was going. His grin, however, was still as big as ever. Like all good airplane passengers who know nothing about flying, I began to look around anxiously for a landing place. But I was still a beginner at Soviet flying and didn't yet know one of the cardinal facts about the business: whenever a Soviet plane gets into trouble, there's always a perfectly satisfactory strip of ground right below. (I've dropped into beet fields in the Ukraine, corn fields in the Volga, wheat fields in the Kuban. Whenever there was trouble, there was always something flat enough – or nearly flat enough – to land on.) The engine was still sputtering when the pilot brought the plane to a slightly bumpy landing somewhere in East Prussia.

All this time my companion had been sitting on the end of his spine, hugging his briefcase, his eyes bulging almost out of his head. As the engine died, he turned to me: "Ach! It's enough. I leave."

The pilot emerged from his cabin and announced as nonchalantly as a conductor on the Paoli Local: "Tilsit."

The old man got out, dragging his suitcase after him, and started marching solemnly off across the field. I clambered after him and stood hesitantly trying to make up my mind what to do. After all, there was a good deal to what the old fellow had said.

But my trouble was a certain haziness about where on God's green earth we were. It's all very well to know that Tilsit is where Napoleon made a deal with a Czar on a raft. But when you're trying to get to Leningrad in a worn-out airplane and land in a field that the pilot says is Tilsit, that interesting historical fact is relatively useless. What I wanted to know was: how did the Czar get there, or better still, how did he get back? From where I stood there was no road, no river, not even a raft in sight. Except for a dilapidated wooden shack a hundred yards away, there was nothing to be seen but the muddy field surrounded by a high, unkempt hedge.

As I looked around at this forlorn landscape, the pilot was keeping up a steady flow of Russian accompanied by the grin and a good deal of back-slapping – evidently designed to restore my spirits. They needed restoring. I gave a last wistful glance at the gap in the hedge through which my fellow traveler had disappeared, sat down in the grass, pulled out my Russian grammar and began to memorize the forty-two case-endings of a Russian adjective.

While I struggled with the case-endings, the pilot began tinkering around the radiator of the engine which had obviously blown a gasket or something. Eventually a truck appeared out of nowhere and two mechanics joined the pilot in the tinkering. Now and then I looked up from the grammar book at sick Old Granny and thought again of Colonel Patton: "God-damned nonsense" was the word for it.

Two hours went by and then there was a shout and a grunt and someone spun the propeller. The engine took hold and began to purr a little hoarsely but fairly persistently. In a couple of minutes I was back in the cabin and Old Granny was gathering speed in great bounds across the bumpy field.

The weather hadn't improved any all day. It was still foggy and a gusty wind had sprung up which kept the airplane constantly bouncing and swaying around in a way that wasn't good for airplanes – or their passengers either. Then suddenly the sky cleared and as we headed north into Latvia a bright sun lit up the neat dairy farms a few, a very few, feet below. But with the sun the wind grew stronger and the plane slipped and slid and bounced about in a most disconcerting manner.

Suddenly the engine coughed and spluttered again. For a moment I shuddered, and then, as I should have known all along, a fine big airfield appeared below and we swooped in to a gentle landing.

"Riga," shouted the pilot as the engine died.

Riga airport was a bustling Grand Central Terminus compared to Tilsit. We'd hardly crawled from the cabin before we were surrounded by mechanics, officials and stray spectators. The pilot disappeared into the control room and came out a few minutes later with a very smartly uniformed official of some sort. The pilot started shouting Russian at me and pointing at his watch.

"Four-thirty," I said obligingly.

"Nyet, nyet," replied the pilot.

"Yes, yes," I came back, getting into the swing of the thing. The smart official joined the chorus with some broken English:

"Flyman say engine a little kaput."

"Again?" I asked.

"Flyman say wind very big."

"He hardly has to tell me that," I replied a little petulantly.

"Flyman say still plenty hours to Leningrad and darkness comes soon in northlands."

"And so?"

"Flyman says you spend night here. Tomorrow is all right to fly Leningrad."

The first part of the suggestion sounded reasonable enough. But as to the second, I reserved judgment.

A few minutes later a diminutive little car appeared. The pilot and I were stuffed inside and we flew off in a slightly modified version of our recent airplane ride. The car stayed a little closer to the ground and went a little bit slower – though not much. But its engine was made of sterner stuff and was still intact when we were deposited at the Roma Hotel.

That night the guests of the Roma bar could hardly have missed a rather noisy but lively pantomime as the pilot and I sat down for dinner. We both started talking at once and neither of us stopped, except for an occasional mouthful of food or liquor, until well after midnight.

The pilot pointed to the snack tray and said, "Zakuski."

"Hors d'oeuvre," I corrected.

"Riba," said the pilot.

"Fish," I retorted.

"Vodka," said the pilot.

"Vodka," I repeated and we both roared approval at our agreement.

The conversation from then on picked up both in tempo and volume. For some strange reason whenever people can't make others understand their language, they think it's because they're not talking loudly enough. Eventually even the orchestra at the Roma gave up the competition and left us shouting at each other until far too late in the evening.

As I was going to bed that night, I decided that if all Russians were as cheerful as the pilot, it might not turn out as badly as Colonel Patton had predicted.

The next morning, early, we found the engine repaired by an efficient team of Latvian mechanics and we were soon on our way. The weather had cleared. The wind had died and the air was as smooth as you could want it.

And then the motor coughed again, shaking me abruptly from my daydreams. The pilot turned around, grinned and shrugged his shoulders as usual. The motor spluttered and died. This time I was hardly surprised when I saw a landing field unrolling underneath us. This time it was Tallinn at the northern tip of the Baltic states. It turned out that the motor had developed some new and rather minor flaw. While a crew of mechanics swarmed over the plane, the pilot and I lay in the grass and exchanged shouts. When the job was finished, a local official appeared to speed us on our way. The pilot shouted a final word as we walked to the plane. The official interpreted:

"He says this is your last stop till Leningrad."

"How does he know?" I asked, a little sarcastically.

The pilot replied with a grin wider and more mischievous than ever.

"He says there can't be," explained the interpreter. "There aren't any more landing places – just swamps."

With that cheerful bit of information, I climbed aboard and strapped myself in while the pilot swung Old Granny onto the field and bounced her back into the air.

For an hour or more all went well. The air was smooth. The radiator somehow held together and the engine throbbed conscientiously. Below to our left we could see the gray, white-capped waters of the Gulf of Finland. To our right were the forests and lakes of Estonia. We passed the spires of the great Narva Cathedral at almost wing level. I figured the frontier of the Soviet Union must be just ahead. Imperceptibly the pilot had climbed a few hundred feet without my noticing it until we flashed past a double line of barbed-wire barriers. Suddenly the plane dove toward the ground. Through the pilot's windshield I could see the roof of a little farmhouse rushing up at us.

Then just as we seemed about to hit it, the pilot pulled u p with a jerk, peered back at me, and yelled, "Sovietski Soyuz."

At the same time my suitcase hurtled out of the rack above me and landed on my head. Like Queen Victoria, I was not amused.

A few minutes later we were circling what seemed to be a large muddy lake. Here and there I could see strips of mud poking up from the brown water, but for the most part it was just a liquid mass.

"Leningrad Airport," the pilot shouted to me and gestured to make fast my seat belt. The plane swung down as gradually as the pilot could bring it. As the wheels touched the mud, great tongues of brown water shot up past the cabin window. We rolled for a few yards as the weight of the plane settled on the undercarriage. Then there was a loud crack just below my feet. The plane stopped with a jerk that almost knocked my wind out against the safety belt. The tail flew up nearly to the perpendicular and then settled gently back into the mud. The pilot pointed to the undercarriage and yelled (a little unnecessarily, I thought), "Kaput."

An Intourist girl in high rubber boots waded out from the airport building to greet us while we waited marooned by the side of Old Granny, now lying ignominiously on her belly in the mud and water. The pilot grabbed my hand and squeezed it in his great paw and let out one final shout of Russian. The Intourist girl interpreted: "He wants to know how you enjoyed the trip."

It was my turn to grin.

3

LENINGRAD TREASURE HUNT

Sir Walter Citrine began a book about his tour of the Soviet Union with the fact that there was no stopper in the bathtub at his hotel in Leningrad. Because of that observation, he continued, some people would now call him unobjective. But the fact of the matter was, he insisted, that the missing bathtub stopper was the symbol of everything else he saw in Russia.

With me, I'm afraid it was the mud at the airport – and the ubiquitous Intourist guide. Probably the guide was no more ubiquitous than the mud but at least you could scrape the mud off.

Together we did the sights: the Winter Palace, the Hermitage Museum, the Ballet, Tsarskoe Selo, Peterhof. For three days she was by my side explaining everything in profound Marxian terms. Even the fact that the fountains weren't working at Peterhof:

"It's to give the workers more water during the week. On Sundays when the workers are free [and presumably didn't wash] the fountains work beautifully."

Leningrad depressed me. Great yellow stone palaces lined the major streets, their uncurtained windows staring accusingly or resentfully. The streets were half empty and the few people that one talked to seemed to be thinking back, not forward. It reminded me of the old story of the worker who was applying for a job at the Soviet Labor Office.

Undated photo of Charles Thayer. Likely in the 1930s, about the time of his arrival in Russia.

"Where were you born?" they asked him.

"St. Petersburg."

"Where were you educated?"

"Petrograd."

"Where do you live?"

"Leningrad."

"Where do you want to work?"

"St. Petersburg," he answered woefully.

As we met each morning, the Intourist guide would tell me what she had planned for us to do. Any suggestions from me were met with disapproval and insurmountable objections. She always got her way – almost always. In the evenings when she turned me over to the solicitous care of the hotel concierge, she gave him a look that indicated clearly enough that he was responsible for my being a good boy till morning.

We'd finished the rounds of everything I had the vaguest desire to see and I still had one more day on my itinerary before I was to go to Moscow. The guide suggested a bread factory, a textile mill, a prophylactorium, a creche. I turned them all down.

"Well," she asked sullenly, "what do you want to do tomorrow?"

"Nothing," I replied just as sullenly.

"All right then," she said as she started out the hotel door, "but I'll call in the morning anyway to see if you've changed your mind."

The fact of the matter was had something I very much wanted to do before I left Leningrad, but not with an Intourist guide.

Before I had left home an old family friend, the daughter of a Russian Czarist Admiral, had asked me whether I wouldn't take a look at her family's old villa at Tarkhovka out on the Gulf of Finland, about twenty miles north of Leningrad. She'd asked me at a cocktail party and, like most cocktail party requests, it was granted with a flourish and a bow.

"I'll draw you a sketch showing where it is," she added, reaching for a cocktail napkin and her lipstick. "And while you're there you might look into the root cellar to see if the family silver's okay. We buried it the day we escaped to Finland."

I explained that I was going to Russia in search of a diplomatic career, not buried treasures, but I'd be delighted to see what I could find out about the silver too.

I hadn't been ten minutes in Leningrad before I realized that I'd made a dreadful mistake. Ordinarily I'd be only too glad to look over a bit of real estate for a friend. Nothing would seem more natural than driving out to examine the condition of the house where Friend X or Friend Y had been born. But in Russia it was different. There was a way about the place, about the Intourist guide, the hotel concierge, the plainclothes men who filled the lobbies, that indicated any straying from the Intourist reservation was *verboten*.

I wasn't the only one who had got the hint. One of the first American Ministers in St. Petersburg had reported in a dispatch to the State Department:

"Nothing is more striking to an American on his first arrival here, than the rigor of the police. It would seem that the capital was in a state of siege."

That was in 1856.

So it wasn't a Soviet invention even though the Communists had certainly perfected it. And it had nothing to do with the Russian soul either. Given an opportunity and perhaps a vodka or two, the average Russian will pour his heart out to you till you're drowning in woes. He'll tell you every detail of his life from the pedigree of his grandfather's horses to the sex life of his girlfriend. Perhaps the xenophobia is a calculated compensation of a paternalistic Government, Czarist or Bolshevik. Perhaps it was decided that if the average Russian wouldn't keep his mouth shut, the Government should see to it that too many outsiders weren't around to listen to all the intimate details of Russian life.

But this didn't solve my real estate problem. That night, after the Intourist guide had left in a huff, I sat in my hotel bedroom and stared glumly at the paper napkin, trying to figure out what to do. I had already found out that there was a local train from Leningrad to the Finnish frontier which stopped at Tarkhovka and that it left from the Finland Station. But how was I to get a ticket? How was I even to get out of the hotel? Suppose the concierge spied me and phoned the Intourist guide? Suppose some railroad policeman asked me my business? Was I going to say that I was going to check into some buried treasure? Even a Pennsylvania Railroad conductor would find that a little peculiar. On the other hand, what was I going to say if, as seemed all too probable that evening, I returned home in a few months or weeks and the Admiral's daughter asked what I'd done about her villa? I couldn't tell her I hadn't even tried. After twenty years in America, what was she going to remember about the functionings of police states, about state xenophobia or whatever it was that made foreigners feel so far from home in Russia?

The next morning I was still asleep when the phone rang. It was the Intourist guide asking whether I hadn't changed my mind. Wouldn't I like to see the prophylactorium where the Government was stamping out venereal diseases? Or the creche where the Government was raising better babies? Or the bread factory where the Government was making better bread? I snapped an angry "no" at each suggestion and told the guide I proposed to stay in bed all day and let God and some sleep make me better without any outside help. When I hung up I was firmly resolved to go to Tarkhovka just to spite the guide and even dig the silver out of the root cellar, if possible. I'd like to see the guide's face next evening when I showed her a bagful of silver and jewels and told her it was just something I'd picked up around town, or found under my bed.

Down in the lobby, the concierge was having a row with some slightly drunk young sailors who were apparently demanding a room. I slipped quietly out the door without being seen.

At the Finland Station, there was a big, swarming mass of people milling about in every direction. They were, most of them, peasants with great sacks over their shoulders, bast boots, heavy greasy overcoats, shawls and fur caps with ear tabs tied up over the crown. It was my first look at a Russian railroad station and it left me bewildered. Somehow or another I found the ticket window and stood in line for about an hour telling myself that the smell wasn't half as bad as it smelled, and that after all it was just a combination of cheap tobacco and a little sweat not quite yet washed away by that water that used to be used in the Peterhof fountains before the Revolution. The ticket seller gave me a ticket without asking any questions and eventually I found the train just as the gates were opened. All the time I'd been looking anxiously around wondering how long it would take the Intourist guide to check up on my day-in-bed story, guess that I was going treasure hunting, and catch me at the station. I found an inconspicuous corner on the train and sat down. The conductor came by. I passed him my ticket and waited, trembling with fear he might ask me something and discover I was a foreigner. But he only took the ticket and nodded silently.

A small beggar boy in tattered clothes ten times too big for him came into the car, took off his peakless cap and announced he was ready to entertain anyone who wanted entertainment with a song or a dance. (At least that's what I thought he should have said even though I could hardly understand a word.) He started a wailing peasant melody, rolling his big blue eyes all over his enormous, grinning, dirty face and shaking his long, yellow, greasy hair rhythmically about his shoulders as he sang. Then he went into a livelier number and began a sort of jig. My fellow passengers were unimpressed though one or two passed him some kopeks. Then suddenly he spied my hat in the corner. Until then it hadn't occurred to me that my hat had long since told everyoe that I was a foreigner. The boy pointed to it and shouted "*inostranyets*" which I knew meant "foreigner." Everyone looked my way. I began to sweat. Surely someone would point me out to the railroad police at the next station and I'd be arrested and thrown out of the Soviet Union as a spy. The only thing to do was bribe the little beggar to go away. I gave him a handful of rubles and motioned for him to move on. Apparently my gesture was the wrong one because he started in again at the beginning of his repertoire and was only half way through it when I saw a sign "Tarkhovka" at one of the stops. I slipped off the train, across the track and up a little road that had been lipsticked to my napkin.

It ran along the Gulf of Finland, separated from it only by the railroad I'd just come on. Across the road were a row of very much run-down villas. They seemed to be occupied, but the number of glassless windows, the total lack of paint and the general state of confusion indicated that their owners or tenants were spending their incomes otherwise than on upkeep. A half mile up the road I found what I was looking for. It was a rather larger villa than the rest, trimmed from roof to foundations with the remnants of what was once very intricate and doubtless ugly gingerbread, a stone well in the front garden, a broken-down gingerbread gate – the Admiral's daughter had described every detail except the twenty years of wear and tear.

As I stood and stared at it, my early morning courage deserted me. Now what? It was obviously occupied and I had still thought of no practical way of getting into the house, let alone the root cellar. Suppose I told the occupant I was coming on behalf of the previous owners from whom he'd doubtless "liberated" it? Even if I got away with that and he'd hospitably shown me around, was I going to say: "And now would you mind letting me have a look at the root cellar – my friends left a few trifles buried there and asked me to fetch them?" And if I wanted to say all that, how was he going to understand my English?

Just then a group of peasants came around a corner of the road a hundred yards ahead of me. Something had to be done quickly. I couldn't let them find a suspicious-looking foreigner just standing with his thumb in his mouth on the edge of the Gulf of Finland looking wistfully over the water at the super-secret naval base on the island of Kronstadt. There was nothing for it but to walk up the path and into the house as though I belonged there.

I was greeted, not as I half-expected by a swarm of Pinkerton operatives or their Russian GPU equivalents, but by a small child busily at play on the floor with a toy dog. I haven't twenty-one nieces and nephews for nothing and before anyone, including the child or myself, knew what it was about, we were busily playing on the floor. The child pushed the toy dog at my face and growled. I shook my head, growled and retreated into a far corner. I'm not sure how long this went on but eventually I found myself at the kitchen door. I'd been vaguely conscious of some hammering coming from that direction but my one purpose had been to keep the child contented while I could figure out my next move. As I looked through the door, I caught sight of someone putting the finishing touches to a new floor. (Just where the door to the root cellar should have been, I reflected.) But this was no time to worry about root cellars. My predicament was complicated enough. The man rose to his feet. I rose to mine. He was what you might call an outsize man – or at least he seemed so to me. His face was large, red and heavily bearded. He approached me swinging his hammer beside him and said something rather briefly in Russian. I said, "Hello." (It was all there was to say under the circumstances.) He repeated his first words and was obviously expecting some sort of an answer. I said, "Hello," again. He stepped closer to me, the hammer still swinging carelessly by his side. Again he said something, this time just a little annoyed, I thought. I said, "How d'you do?" thinking to change the subject, but I could see at once that it didn't work. I glanced out of the corner of my eye at the hammer.

He was about to take the final step which separated us when suddenly the child burst in from the next room, toddled in between us and pushed the toy dog into my stomach with a loud childish bark. As quickly as I could, I retreated into the front room, not forgetting to growl at the toy dog. The child ran after me as I backed toward the front door still barking. The man followed, but the frown on his face had seemed to relax a bit. I got to the door, opened it and was down and out the garden gate before you could say "Joe Stalin."

When I finally got back to my hotel, I wrote a note to the Admiral's daughter, telling her that the house needed a slight paint job but that so far as I could tell the family silver was doing nicely.

That night I took the train to Moscow.

4

MOSCOW

In Moscow, Intourist took me in hand and put me in the Metropole Hotel. The only place I've ever seen that even slightly resembled the Metropole was the big glass passenger-shed of the Broad Street Station in Philadelphia. The station burned down nearly thirty years ago but, alas, there seems to be little likelihood that the Metropole will enjoy the same happy end. Intourist in Moscow was different from Leningrad's – more sophisticated, not quite so worried about your ideological education. They liked to know where you were and what you were up to, but they weren't quite so insistent that you tell them your innermost thoughts. Perhaps it was because they had more contact with foreigners. Perhaps, too, it was because Roosevelt hadn't yet recognized the Soviet Government and all the minor officials, at least, felt they'd better be on their good behavior.

Thanks to a few friends I met through relatives abroad and through the good offices of the American correspondents, I was soon out of the Metropole and in a Russian family. I was lucky enough to get a whole room to myself in an apartment of four rooms and a kitchen. The rest of the family included the landlady, her daughter, her sister, a maid and a little girl whose exact status I never did make out. The story was that she was the maid's daughter by the landlady's brother. But that's a mere rumor. The fact that the child was very bright and the maid was sub-moronic, would tend to disprove it. Of the three rooms other than mine, one was a living room-dining room where we gathered at mealtimes and in the evenings to discuss such affairs of the world as penetrated the Soviet frontiers – or originated within them. The daughter of the house had a tiny room to herself and the other four occupants, in some way I never found out, fitted themselves into the last room or into the various nooks in the hallway.

But by far the most important room was the kitchen, which tripled in brass as cookery, laundry and bathroom. It had the only washbasin in the place. Several large wooden planks on top of the bath tub served as the kitchen table. The result was that the washing schedule had to be dovetailed with the greatest care into the eating schedule. Obviously you couldn't bathe on baking or washing day nor could you wash when any meal was in process of preparation or liquidation.

Months later when the Ambassador insisted that I move into his palatial residence, I remonstrated that it would cut me off from my local contacts. He was adamant, however, arguing that it would be much more convenient to live where I was working. Besides, he added, it was obvious to anyone who had any contact with me that the Russian apartment was somewhat short on bathing facilities. He may have been right, though I tried as well as I could to worm my way into a bath at least once a week. Whenever that was impossible, I went to the public baths at what was once the Nobles' Club. There, after a careful inspection by a government doctor to make sure you had no contagious skin diseases, you could get a sort of mass production Turkish bath and even a swim in a heated swimming pool. "Swim" is probably the wrong word because it was always so jam-packed with people that all you could do was squeeze your way in, stand among a solid mass of naked bodies for a few minutes and then try to get out.

Besides a room to live in (I was one of the last foreigners to get one before the purges brought xenophobia to a new pitch), I found myself a Russian teacher, an old lady with a consumptive husband who used to lie in the room next to where I took my lessons and cough agonizingly while I recited my verbs. He died while I was still on the second conjugation.

Even before I'd found the room in the Russian family, I'd been awakened one night by the hotel night porter who told me with pathetic excitement that the radio had just announced that Roosevelt had written a letter to Kalinin hinting at reestablishment of relations. It was obvious, therefore, that an Embassy was soon going to be set up and if I was going to speak enough Russian to get a job there was no time to lose. So, I spent about eight hours a day in my room studying, memorizing conjugations, declensions, vocabulary and pronunciation. I spent two hours each afternoon with the teacher and then each evening I'd go down to a local bar for a couple of hours, limber my tongue up with a few glasses of vodka and practice what I'd learned during the day on the bartenders and bar girls. It's the second best way I know of learning a foreign language.

Another excellent way of learning is by talking to children. The landlady had an endless stream of nieces and nephews visiting her and they took special delight in hearing my lessons and conversing with me about America. One little fellow, Zhenia his name was, took it as a social obligation to teach me not only Russian but all about the Soviet Union and particularly about the Pioneers or junior Soviet Boy Scouts, of which he was a prominent member. He'd heard about the capitalist Boy Scouts and didn't think they were much good at first, but I think that in the course of our conversations he became rather more tolerant of them. Zhenia was especially anxious that I visit the school he went to. One day he came to tell me that he'd arranged with the Director for me to see the school in action. They would expect me on November 6.

November 6 is the day before the Soviet Fourth of July – and when I got to the school I found that instead of the regular routine there was a rather elaborate celebration on the program. Zhenia had met me at the door and taken me to the Director's office where I was welcomed very enthusiastically. I began to wonder just what sort of an explanation Zhenia had given about his American friend. The celebration started promptly after my arrival in the school auditorium. On the stage sat the Praesidium composed of the head of the student body (who naturally doubled in brass as the head of the Komsomols or junior Communist Party), the school Director and a handful of other dignitaries.

The Komsomol chief, a young man about sixteen years old with a very earnest and determined manner, opened the meeting by making some sort of a proposal which I didn't quite understand but which was obviously directed at me. Zhenia, who was sitting beside me and with whom I'd already developed a certain facility for talking, giggled delightedly. There was a vote and the proposal was, as is the custom in some countries, carried unanimously.

"Now you've been elected to the Praesidium," Zhenia whispered. "Up you go and sit on the stage."

Horror-struck, stage-struck and thoroughly embarrassed, I took a seat on the stage but not before I'd arranged to have Zhenia right behind me to explain in our private dialect what was going on.

The Komsomol speaker then made his big speech. It was short according to Russian standards – about half an hour. There seemed to be several references to the international situation in general and to America in particular and each time I caught the word, "United States," he turned to me and everyone clapped uproariously.

Zhenia began to translate:

"He says soon revolution in America and people like you, Communist teachers and students, will lead it."

"Zhenia, have you been telling them I'm a Communist?"

Zhenia reddened.

"Well, not exactly," he said. "I just said you were a 'progressive student.'"

That mollified me for a minute but I began to wonder what would happen (a) if the Komsomol found I came from good old capitalist stock, and (b) the future Embassy got wind of my wandering around Moscow posing as a Party member. I was extremely uncomfortable.

Eventually the Komsomol leader finished and the school Director began. The Komsomol came back to where I was sitting and said that according to the rules it would be necessary for me to make a speech – in Russian. I explained politely that I couldn't speak Russian and anyway I'd come here to see the school and not to get involved in any political celebrations. I was very sorry but as firm as I could be.

The Komsomol leader looked rather astonished and stared at Zhenia.

"I hadn't understood the circumstances," he said rather coldly. "Zhenia here told us you were a progressive student, and of course all progressive students in America would like to congratulate us on our national holiday."

Zhenia flushed again and looked as though he were going to cry. His enthusiasm had obviously got him into a nice pickle and the pathetic expression on his face appealed for any assistance I could give him. I remembered that it was the custom for Governments to greet other Governments on their national holidays, whatever their political complexion. We'd even sent congratulations to Hitler not so long ago. So I agreed to make a speech, provided it was very short and written out for me phonetically in Latin letters. One of the teachers, Zhenia and I retired into the wings to begin the drafting. During the course of my subsequent activities I've drafted a good many speeches and negotiated a number of agreements but that drafting and negotiating were as tedious, considering the length of the document, as any I've gone through.

The teacher came up with a first draft:

"Comrades," it read, "on this occasion of the sixteenth anniversary of the Great October Revolution, I bring you the flaming greetings of all progressive teachers and students in America. Hail to the World Revolution!"

I read it and winced. As a starter, I said that it was too long. "Let's cut out one sentence – particularly the second sentence."

They agreed a little reluctantly. Then I explained that as I didn't have any formal mandate I had no right to speak for any particular group in America. "Let's just say 'Greetings from America' – and cut out that flaming stuff. It isn't typically American," I explained. After a good deal of argument it was agreed to on parliamentary grounds.

"And now about this word 'comrades,'" I said. "After all I'm not a Communist Party member and it would be most presumptuous of me to use an expression that at least in America is reserved exclusively for fellow Party members." The teacher and Zhenia stiffened.

"But you can't begin a speech without 'comrades,'" they said. "Not in the Soviet Union."

I stood firm and insisted it must be deleted. They stood firm and insisted it stay in. We reached a deadlock and sent for the Komsomol leader. He argued. I argued.

"A speech isn't a speech in the Soviet Union without 'comrades,'" he said.

"That isn't so in America," I retorted.

"But you've recognized us now," he said, "and anyway when in Rome do as the Romans do."

"President Roosevelt wrote 'friend' to Kalinin," I replied, "and President Roosevelt always says 'friends' when he makes a speech."

The name of Roosevelt obviously impressed the Komsomol and at last he agreed to replace "comrades" with "friends."

By now the Director of the school had finished his hour's oration and it was my turn.

Trembling in every joint, I reached the rostrum and clutched the stand firmly in both hands. I looked at the scratched and rumpled piece of paper in my hand and started:

"Comrades…"

The thousand children in front of me howled with delight at the strange accent. The Komsomol leader laughed merrily that after all my fuss I'd used his word after all. I turned purple.

"Friends," I began again, "on this occasion of the sixteenth…" I looked down at the hieroglyphics on the paper in my hand to find the next word. (It was a hard one in Russian: "*Godovshchina*.") Before I could get it out a thousand prompters shouted in chorus:

"*Godovshchina*"

"*Godovshchina*," I repeated and continued, "of the great October Revolution, I bring you greetings from America." I sat down.

The roar was deafening. The children screamed for more. The Director shook my hand as though I'd just established a new world's record for the pole vault. The Komsomol grinned delightedly at his political triumph. I began to think of the Logan Act or whatever it is that makes it a crime for private American citizens to interfere in foreign relations.

But eventually the uproar died down. The Praesidium left the stage and a series of little plays and songs by the students followed and wound up the proceedings. Afterward everyone had a bowl of soup and we all went home. Zhenia, by now the hero of the hour, escorted me proudly down the street, his little fist firmly holding mine. If I hadn't actually seen the Soviet educational system at work, I'd had a first lesson in international oratory. There was going to be an awful lot more of it before I was done.

Aside from the school children, I soon made quite a number of friends among the fellow University students of the landlady's daughter. Frequently, beaus came to call on her and share the hospitality of the house, which had become rather affluent under the influence of the thirty dollars of *valuta* (or foreign currency) I contributed each month. Together we went to the theater and ballet, the Park of Culture and Rest for skating, and occasionally I was even asked to visit in their tiny and rather uncomfortable quarters. The curiosity they showed for everything to do with America helped to break down that fear of foreigners the police had been instilling in Russians for many a generation. Besides, now that Roosevelt had called Kalinin a "friend" and now that we were going to reestablish relations, they felt there was a good excuse for showing their natural friendliness and open-handed hospitality.

Russian hospitality is a curious thing. Perhaps because for so long there has been little stability in their political and economic lives, with the police, Czarist and Bolshevik, confiscating and arresting at pleasure, they've come to look on possessions as rather transitory things and when they have a bit of good luck they try to share it as quickly as possible with their friends before someone comes along and takes it from them. What is more, they expect any temporarily affluent friend to do exactly the same thing with them.

Once, perhaps a year after my arrival in Moscow, an acquaintance of mine, a young actor at the Moscow Art Theater, was promoted from third-class actor to second-class and his pay correspondingly increased from one hundred and fifty to two hundred and fifty rubles a month. Naturally that called for a celebration. He called me up and said he was giving a small "evening" for some thirty friends of the Art Theater. Wouldn't I come along? I would be the only foreigner but still I knew most of the guests and it wouldn't be awkward for me. I accepted at once. Just before he hung up the phone, he added:

"I'm going to have only a few simple things to eat and drink and I know you like whiskey which I can't get. So, maybe you 'll bring your own."

"How much should I bring?" I asked.

"Well," he said, "there'll be about thirty guests."

I caught the hint and said I'd bring enough and rang off. Two days later the actor called again:

"Have you some of that French champagne I tasted once at your apartment?"

I said I had a little.

"Do you suppose you could bring some to the party. Some of the guests don't like vodka... or whiskey," he added hastily.

"How much?" I asked.

"Well, as I said, there'll be about thirty people."

Again I told him I'd bring enough for the occasion and hung up.

The day of the party he telephoned once more.

"You won't forget about tonight?" he reminded me. "Ten-thirty at my mother's apartment – don't be too late."

I told him I'd be there promptly.

"And just one more little thing," he went on. "Do you know that wonderful Latvian vodka I tasted once at your place? 'Krystal' I think it's called. Do you happen to have any?"

I said I had a few bottles, how many would he like? "Well, you know there'll be about thirty guests tonight." That evening I turned up with a large and varied assortment of whiskey, champagne and vodka. The dining room table was already loaded with every available *zakuski* in Moscow: hard-boiled eggs, ham, red caviar, black caviar, cucumbers, radishes, sardines, herrings and huge stacks of white and black bread, and even butter. I wondered how in the world a student actor making two hundred and fifty rubles a month could swing it. But after the proper compliments, I handed over my little contribution and set about enjoying myself.

Like all unofficial Russian parties, the guests were in the mood almost before they arrived, and they needed no prodding to make their individual contributions to the general entertainment. In fact, hardly had one guest sat down than another was on his feet to do his favorite part. Old Kachalov, the senior actor of the Art Theater, recited a story of Chekhov's. Tarasova acted out part of her role as Anna Karenina. Angelina Stepanova, also of the Art Theater, did her bit as the younger daughter in *The Cherry Orchard*. Several ballerinas were constantly jumping to their feet, calling for a particular piece of music and flying about the air in their favorite dances.[3]

And, of course, everyone ate and drank without much restraint. Russian night life starts late and usually ends early the next day. It was eight-thirty in the morning before I realized it was almost time for the office to open. I was working then under Angus Ward, of Mukden fame,[4] in the Consular Section of the Embassy and Ward has always been known for his discipline. I said some hurried good-byes and lit out at a dog trot for the Embassy. I just managed to get to my desk in the reception room before Ward strolled in.

---

3. Vasily Kachalov (1875-1948), Alla Tarasova (1898-1973) and Angelina Stepanova (1905-2000) were leading actors in Stanislavsky's MKhAT.

4. In 1948-9 Angus Ward was Consul General in China and he and his staff were kept under house arrest by Mao's Liberation Party for nearly a year, causing a diplomatic crisis.

Somehow or other I got through that day, though I think if you looked at the record of business for the Moscow Consulate for that date you'd see a rather sharp slump in its activities.

Toward the end of the afternoon, when my resistance had reached zero and my eyes wouldn't stay off the office clock, the phone rang. It was my host of the night before:

"How did you like my party?"

"Just a little too good for my health," I groaned. "Otherwise, it was swell. I don't see how you managed it."

"I hope it was all right," he said. "It cost me all of my next month's salary," he added ruefully and hesitated a moment. "Charlie, do you suppose you could lend me two hundred and fifty rubles till my next pay check?"

It's all very well to bury yourself on the Left Bank in Paris or in the heart of the Himalayas or in Central Africa, but every now and then you have to come up for air. During those early days when I was spending practically all my time trying to memorize those adjective endings, I used to allow myself one afternoon a week with the American colony. Generally, I went to tea at the William Henry Chamberlins' where Mrs. Chamberlin put out a very good spread every Friday afternoon. While she served tea, William Henry, then correspondent for the Christian Science Monitor, would hold forth on some abstruse question of Russian history or politics. The 1932-1933 famine was just coming to a close and most of the journalists were fretting and fuming at not being allowed to visit the famine areas.

"I was reading a little history book today about the Ukrainian famine of 1732," I remember him saying, "and do you know that no foreigners were permitted to live anywhere but in Petersburg for a whole year?"

A fellow traveler from the *Moscow Daily News* protested that the present prohibition was different from those of the Czars. You couldn't compare the Czars with what happened after the Revolution.

Chamberlin turned to an American engineer present:

"Brown, what's the engineering definition of a revolution?"

"Well, one way we'd describe it is when something describes a complete circle and comes back to where it started from."

"I thought it was something like that," said William Henry. Then he changed the subject with a mischievous grin while the *Moscow News* man sulked.

Ralph Barnes of the *Herald Tribune*, Stanley Richardson of the A.P., Eugene Lyons of U.P., Bill Stoneman of the *Chicago Daily News*, and of course, Walter Duranty of the *New York Times*, were regular visitors at those Friday gatherings. Barnes was killed during the war on a bombing raid over the Balkans. I was to have many dealings with Stan Richardson fifteen years later when he was with the NBC. Eugene Lyons was the first of the correspondents to ignore the risks of being refused a Soviet re-entry permit when he wrote *Assignment in Utopia*. Bill Stoneman later became an assistant of Trygvie Lie in the U.N. but eventually returned to the *News*.

Of them all, I suppose Walter Duranty was then the most famous.[5] His great journalistic coup had been to pick Stalin as the winner against Trotsky for successor to Lenin. Always witty, always ready to take any side of an argument, he usually kept every party he was at in an uproar of argument and vituperation.

When I first got to Moscow, Duranty was the first person I called on and it was through him I found myself an apartment and a teacher. I'd hardly been there a day when Duranty gave me one word of caution:

"If you're here to write a book about Russia, do it in the next ten days. Otherwise, it'll take you ten years to figure out what it's all about." (That was only seventeen years ago but I've always thought Duranty was inclined to be a little optimistic.)

---

5. Walter Durante was bureau chief of the *New York Times* in Moscow from 1922-1936. He won a Pulitzer for a series on the USSR in 1932, but later his work came to be derided for being too uncritical of the Soviet Union. In 1990, the *Times* itself called his articles "some of the worst reporting to appear in this newspaper."

At my weekly vacations with the Americans, I generally sat and listened or asked questions about what was going on at home. (My only other source of news was the *Moscow Daily News* then edited by Anna Louise Strong and I always had the feeling that not all the news fit to print found space on its pages.)[6] But once I did enter the discussion with nearly fatal consequences. It was just before the big November 7 celebration when the workers parade through Red Square. "Every May Day and every November Seventh," I said one afternoon, "I seem to remember that the correspondents have always reported a million workers marching through Red Square in a five-hour parade. How is that estimated?" Several of the correspondents looked at me and then at one another: "Well, we've just estimated as best we can and we've all agreed that a million is a good round number and probably about right."

"I was walking through there this afternoon," I went on, "and it struck me that a million was awfully high. I paced off the narrowest approach and according to the way they taught us to estimate at West Point you couldn't possibly get more than five or six hundred thousand through in five hours. They'd have to run like rabbits to get through anywhere near a million."

It wasn't a very serious point, but it started a good hot argument. How fast did they march, how close was one rank to another, how many marched abreast, etc., etc. Like every argument in Moscow about things Russian there was no agreement reached but each of us decided to try to count the various elements that went into the calculations and compare notes after the parade.

November 7 duly arrived and through Intourist I managed to get a seat on the Square not too far from the Mausoleum where Stalin and the Politburo stood. Like all sections of the spectators' stands, mine was well guarded with NKVD soldiers who constantly walked up and down the aisles watching everyone.

---

6. Anna Louise Strong (1885-1970) was an American journalist who staunchly supported the communist cause in the USSR and China. She helped found the *Moscow News* in 1930.

As the Parade of the Proletariat started, I got out a little scratch pad and began my counting and calculating. I'd already surreptitiously paced off a couple of fixed points on the Square and occasionally I would time the marchers and write the results in my little book. I was thoroughly engrossed in my mathematics when a large and rather sullen NKVD policeman appeared beside me and demanded I turn over my scratch pad. I tried to argue but my Russian wasn't good enough and, anyway, he said he just wanted to examine it for a few minutes and then he'd give it back. So I gave it up and started to memorize the figures I'd computed. A few minutes later the soldier appeared at the end of the row I was in and beckoned me to come out and follow him. I was led to an officer of unknown rank who with an interpreter began to ask me what the figures were all about. I explained exactly what I was trying to do and showed him my computations. Unfortunately, they were mostly in feet and inches which thoroughly confused him. But, anyway, I proceeded with a detailed recitation just as though I were back at the blackboard at West Point. When I got to the Q.E.D. he shook his head unconvinced, stuffed the pad into his pocket and said very curtly:

"You can read how many marched tomorrow in *Pravda*."

Pravda announced the usual million the next day but I was proud to find the foreign correspondents reported only 700,000 that year.

After a month in Russia my visa expired, but with only a little difficulty I got it renewed for one more month. As the end of the second month approached, I asked for another extension but was told "nothing doing." Two months was the limit. I tried to get myself made Moscow correspondent of a small Texas newspaper, the publisher of which was the father of a fellow cadet. I showed the Foreign Commissariat a letter from the publisher, appointing me to the job. They looked up the paper in some sort of a register, smiled and returned the letter – still nothing doing. I asked Duranty and the other correspondents what to do. Roosevelt would be sending someone to Moscow soon and it was absolutely essential for me to be there when he came, otherwise my hopes for a job in the new

Embassy were nil. Duranty took the matter up with his contacts but without results. Only five days now remained. At the end of it I was supposed to be out of the country.

Then *Pravda* announced that Ambassador Bullitt was on his way to Moscow for a preliminary visit and would arrive in another ten days' time. I decided the best thing to do was stop seeing people about my visa and just drop out of sight for a while.

"Going underground" in Moscow is not particularly easy to do, especially if you have to show your passport every other minute. (Lenin had promised that one of the good things the Bolsheviks were going to do was to abolish passports, but they just hadn't gotten around to it yet after sixteen years.) For several days, I had no trouble. I just kept away from the police registration office, the bank, Intourist or any other place they might suddenly ask for my "documents." After five or six days, I figured the police would start looking for me, so I spent a few more days "visiting" with friends. But the police seemed to have forgotten me.

Finally, with a flourish and bands and newspaper headlines, Bullitt arrived and put up at the National Hotel. The papers were full of his pictures visiting this Commissariat, that factory and another ballet. Editorials proclaimed the new lasting friendship between America and the Soviet Union. I felt a little safer after that and moved back into my room. I figured they weren't going to spoil Bullitt's visit by any unseemly inhospitality to a fellow American who had let it be known he was an intimate friend of Bullitt. (As a matter of fact, I did know his brother slightly.)

But having Bullitt in Moscow and getting to see him were two different things. Years before, when I'd first gone abroad, an uncle of mine had instructed me carefully how to call on an Ambassador. I had no right, he explained, to request an audience, as Ambassadors represented heads of states before other heads of states. not individual citizens – that was a Consul's function. (If only more Americans knew that!) So the proper thing to do was to go to his hotel and leave a visiting card with your name and address and let him decide whether he wanted to see you. The first day of Bullitt's visit, I stopped at the National Hotel, left a card with the concierge, and left. Two days went by without a word, then three days and four and still no word. I had been sticking very close to home all this time waiting for the expected call, but still none came.

There were only two or three days left before Bullitt was to leave when Duranty called me on the phone. "I thought you wanted to see Bill Bullitt about your visa and a possible job?"

I said I wanted to see Mr. Bullitt very much indeed and had left a card with the concierge and had been hoping the Ambassador would send for me. "He hasn't as yet and I guess he doesn't want to."

"Don't be an ass," Duranty said. "This is 1933, not 1820. Visiting cards get lost and anyway Bullitt's too busy a man to go calling people up on the Moscow phone system. Go and call on him yourself."

But I was as stuffy and dignified as my old uncle:

"The Ambassador knows where I am. He knows I want to see him and if he wants to and has the time he can send for me. I'm not going to bother him any more." Duranty laughed at my stubbornness and hung up.

The next morning he called me up again. "So long as you weren't going to bother Bullitt I decided I'd better do it for you. Otherwise when he left you'd be in a nice pickle with that expired visa. I talked to him last night about you and he said he knew you were here and had been expecting you to call. He asked me to tell you to be at his hotel this evening at seven."

At six-thirty I pushed the door of the little apartment house open and went out into the dark street. It was snowing a little as I set out toward the National Hotel, about a mile away. I thought the fresh air would do me good. After all the fatal moment had arrived. Now I was going to find out whether my nebulous schemes were "damn nonsense," as colonel Patton had said. In another hour I'd know whether I had a job in the Foreign Service or whether I was going home to join the millions of other unemployed. I admit I was a little nervous.

At the National Hotel I talked and pushed my way through a few roadblocks in the lobby and upstairs in the hall, and knocked on the Ambassador's door. A very bald, very pink head peered out:

"You're Thayer? Come on in."

The Ambassador was dressed in a gaudy silk kimono – not exactly the sort of diplomatic costume I'd expected. But then, who was I to talk? My coat, a moth-eaten old piece of fur, had come from a second-hand store in Philadelphia and my sealskin cap, acquired in Petersburg in 1901 by my father, was so grotesque that even my not-very-fashion-conscious Russian friends found it peculiar. From both coat and cap melted snow was dripping into a rapidly growing puddle on the floor. I realized that I wasn't putting my best foot forward. But when it comes to matters of dress I've never been too good anyway. I threw the cap and coat into a corner as the Ambassador started:

"Duranty tells me you want a job with the Embassy. He says you're studying Russian. How much do you know?"

I admitted I didn't know much yet but that I was learning.

The Ambassador picked up a thick sheaf of papers in front of him:

"Here's the script of the play I'm to see tonight. Read it to me."

He tossed the script across the table. I missed it and the loose sheets scattered all over the floor. I'd like to be able to say I dropped it on purpose to gain a little time but I'm afraid it was just a repetition of all those forward passes I'd dropped during my sad football career. By the time I'd gathered up the pages I had made two important discoveries:

(a) the script was in Russian manuscript which I could barely decipher (I was still working in big block letters), and (b) the play was Bulgakov's *Days of the Turbins* which I'd already seen several times at the Art Theater.

"It's pretty long," I said when I'd got the papers back together again, "and you haven't much time. Why don't I just summarize it as I go along?"

The Ambassador agreed. I flipped the pages mechanically while I gave a short synopsis of what I remembered of the play. When it was all over the Ambassador smiled:

"I guess you'll do. I'll be needing someone like you as a personal interpreter. Keep on studying and when I get back in February I'll take you on."

A minute later I was walking back down the hall in a slightly dazed condition. When I got to the concierge's desk I was regaining consciousness.

"Get me an Intourist taxi, please," I said expansively.

I decided to call on Duranty at once to thank him for his help. Besides, he had some good Scotch whiskey which I suddenly needed very badly.

5

HOW TO ORGANIZE AN EMBASSY

A day or so later, Ambassador Bullitt went back to Washington, leaving behind George Kennan, then a Third Secretary in the Foreign Service, to arrange quarters for the new Embassy which was to open in February.

I went on with my Russian, working ten to twelve hours a day with my teacher and at home. By Christmastime, my head was swimming with case-endings, irregular verbs and a confused jumble of vocabulary. It seemed to me it was time for a rest. Besides, the weather in Moscow was foul with rain and snow and fog.

So I took off on a short trip to the Caucasus – this time without an Intourist chaperone. I wanted to go to Sochi, a summer resort on the Black Sea. But at that time of year there were no through trains and I had to change at a little town called Armavir. As usual in Russia, the train from Moscow was late. So I missed the connection out of Armavir and had to wait over for a day. Armavir is in the Kuban region, where the famine of the year before had been pretty severe. To kill time I took a *droshky* – a four-wheel carriage – driven by a bearded old peasant, and pulled by a very jaded and skinny mare. I told the driver to take me out through some of the villages in the neighborhood.

"I'll show you some villages," he said sourly, "villages the like of which you've never seen in your life." And he did.

The first village we came to consisted of about twenty or thirty peasant huts. Possibly a third were occupied, another third were burned to the ground, and the remainder were abandoned and falling apart of themselves. One or two children, their bellies puffed and round from lack of nourishment, were playing listlessly in the streets. A few old peasants were shuffling about the yards behind their huts.

The *droshky* driver waved at them as we passed and they waved drearily back. "This is my village," he explained. "Only I took my horse and went to town before the collectivization started. Collectivization!" he spat out the word with disgust. "Collectivization, hell! It's hunger they gave us."

The next village was smaller, only ten or twelve huts. Several of them were burned down and the rest were empty. Not a soul stirred. Not even a dog barked. It was dead. The driver drove through it without a word of comment. Several miles further we came to a third village. It was no bigger than the last one we'd passed through but in the fields behind it we could see a few men and women scratching at the earth with hoes. In the village itself there were no children, no one, in fact, except one decrepit old hag sitting on the doorstep of a dilapidated hut munching something from an earthenware mug. We stopped and I got out and went over to where she was sitting.

"Where is everyone?"

"Gone," she said dismally. "Everyone's gone. They took my two boys. They burned down my house." She pointed to the charred remains of a building next door.

"My man, they shot. The rest ran away to the city-children and all. But there are still a few people left and they give me something to eat. I'm too old for work." She held up the mug and showed me a mush of water and chaff which she was scooping out with her fingers. "That's my three meals for today."

I got back into the *droshky* and told the driver to head back to town. I'd seen all the famine I needed for a long time to come.

There was no hotel room to be had in Armavir, but the station master saw I was a foreigner and invited me to stow my things in his office and sleep beside his stove.

It didn't look as though it was going to be a very comfortable night. So I took a stroll through the town before turning in, hoping to get tired enough to be able to sleep on the hard floor. I'd hardly gone a hundred yards from the station and was just passing a lighted street lamp when a wagon loaded with firewood appeared out of the darkness coming toward me. The driver, sitting on the front of the pile, was sleeping peacefully. Suddenly about twenty yards down the street a pack of little creatures swarmed out of an alleyway and ran toward me. I thought at first they must be wild dogs or even wolves as they raced along close to the ground. Then, as they got closer, I realized they were children. Their faces looked like those of tired old men; their clothes, far too big for them, trailed in the dirt behind them as they ran. The leader must have been about twelve or fourteen. Behind, there were fifteen or more others. At the rear of the pack came the smaller ones who couldn't keep up. Seven or eight years old, I would have guessed them to be, from their small faces which were yet strangely old and haggard. I'd heard of the homeless waifs who'd been starved out of their villages by the famine and had banded together in the towns where they lived on what they could beg, borrow or steal. Despite their age, they had rapidly acquired a reputation for violence and murder any Sicilian brigand would have been proud of. This was my first personal encounter with them and there's no use denying I was properly terrified.

I stopped by the lamp and leaned against it. In my pocket I had a small Derringer pistol no bigger than the palm of my hand, which I'd always carried in Russia. For the first and only time in my life I took it in my hand and cocked it. The mere thought of having to shoot at a gang of children was horrifying, but the prospect of being knifed to death was even less agreeable. I just stood and waited. The leader of the pack came closer. He – or she – you couldn't tell from the clothing or the taut little face – was about ten feet away. I wondered whether to shoot through my pocket and try to scare him away. But the leader didn't seem to be heading for me at all. He – or she – came abreast of the lamppost and ran on past toward the woodcart. The wild little shining eyes were fixed on the firewood. The rest of the pack streamed past, brushing me with their long filthy coats, the sleeves of which dangled far below their little hands.

Not till they had reached the cart did I realize what it was all about. I've played jackstraws as a child but I've never seen as good a job as those children did on that firewood. In a few moments the pack had disappeared up an alleyway each carrying as much wood as he could manage. The driver was still sleeping on just about the bare minimum of logs that held him up on his high perch.

Many years later, I was interviewing a young Russian D.P. [displaced person] for a job with the Voice of America. He told me he came from the Kuban and had been orphaned by a combination of famine, which killed his mother, and deportation, which took his father. I asked him how he'd managed to pull through.

"I joined a band of waifs," he answered, "and we got through somehow."

"Where was that?" I asked.

"Armavir."

He didn't remember stealing that particular load of wood. But he admitted he'd stolen a good many.

I couldn't give him the job, but he's got another good one, and is married and living very happily in Long Island now.

I slept even worse than I'd expected that night in Armavir. The next morning I caught the train to Sochi.

Sochi was cold and gloomy – as everyone had told me it would be in December. So I took a Soviet steamer to Batum stopping at Poti for a few hours while we unloaded some cargo. In the harbor, a number of foreign ships, chiefly Turkish and Greek, were loading grain. I asked a sailor where they were taking the grain.

"Abroad – for *valuta*," he answered. But the way he said it showed clearly enough that he too was thinking of the famine not very far to the north.

Batum was warm and semi-tropical and I took advantage of the weather to go for a hike in the hills behind the town. I wasn't in too good condition and overestimated my endurance. By the time I was half way home my feet were blistered, my legs ached, and I was thoroughly tired. A Georgian peasant overtook me in his cart drawn by a couple of little mountain ponies. He evidently noticed how tired I was and offered me a lift into town. I accepted gratefully and soon we were busily chatting in broken Russian. I asked him if the ponies belonged to a collective. He smiled and said no, they were still his own and were going to stay that way. He'd already lost three others to the neighboring collective but that's as far as they were going to force him. He made a gesture that indicated what he would do to anyone who tried to press him any more. I asked him why he didn't join. Wasn't it better nowadays and didn't they give you more bread if you joined? What was wrong with the collective? For an answer he passed me one rein of the pair he was driving with.

"So you want to go to the left and you pull your rein. And I want to go to the right so I pull my rein. What happens? See, we stop. That's what happens on the collective – everyone is boss and you stop."

It seemed as good an explanation as any.

After a day or two, I moved on to Tiflis, which to my mind is the most attractive town in the Soviet Union. Whether it's because the tough-headed Georgians don't like to have their habits and homes and towns Sovietized – even if done by another Georgian – or whether it's because of the climate and landscape, I don't know. But Tiflis with its winding, narrow streets, its wrought-iron trellis balconies, its gardens and parks, has kept its own character more than any other town in the Soviet Union.

But I was in a hurry to get back to Moscow. There were rumors in the local papers that Bullitt was coming back sooner than he'd expected and I didn't want to be away when he arrived. After a day or so of meandering through the old sections of the town and climbing the nearby mountains, I took a train to Baku.

I traveled in a second-class sleeper with three Russian Party workers who had found time to pick up several liters of vodka before they caught the train. It was a gay, noisy and rather sleepless night as we drank the vodka and asked each other questions about Russia and America.

The next day we arrived in Baku at about five in the morning. My Party friends had suggested I go to the Europa Hotel. "It's where all the foreigners stay," they assured me. The Europa was full up, but one room was to be vacated during the day and the night clerk promised to fix me up later if I waited. So I sat in the lobby and waited. (It's a national pastime of Russia – waiting.)

While I sat there nursing the after-effects of my night on the train, the hotel bootblack came along and started to pass the time of day. He found my Russian not good enough for him so he switched to Turkish and then to German. Finally he tried English. We chatted for a few minutes and I remarked that his accent was definitely American rather than English.

"It should be," he said. "I learned it in America."

"What were you doing over there?"

"I was in the Czarist Navy in those days – twenty years ago – at the beginning of the first war, and the Russian Navy bought some battleships in America. I was in one of the crews that went to fetch them."

I pricked up my ears for I'd heard a lot about those battleships when I was a child.

"Where did you pick up the ships?"

"In Philadelphia," he answered. "They were built at the Cramp's Shipyards. We had a wonderful time in Philadelphia while we waited to take over. They're good people over there. They gave parties and took us around to see the sights – not just the officers, the way they do in most ports you stop in, but the sailors too. Why, I remember the manager of the shipyard – or maybe he was the assistant manager – anyway the one who handled the business with us. He took us out – some of the crew – one day to his home in the country and gave us a banquet I'll never forget. He had tables out on the lawn under a big oak tree by the side of his house and he served us a lot of Russian dishes we hadn't seen since we left home. Yes, they treated us well, those Americans."

I was pleased to be able to tell him that the oak tree he remembered so well was still flourishing. His host, it happened, was my father, and the house was the one I was born in. The ex-sailor was far too much a man of the world to make any trite remarks about small worlds. He just laughed and thanked me again for the good time he'd had in America.

In twenty-four hours I'd seen enough of Baku to last me a lifetime. It was damp, cold and very, very smelly. It had all the characteristics of a big oil town and I don't like oil towns. There were some old buildings that looked as though they had once been very livable, but since the big international oil companies had discovered Baku at the beginning of the century they had been swallowed up by the oil and the smoke and the dirt. So I left Baku in a hurry and took the "Express" back to Moscow.

When I got back there, I called on George Kennan, who was still at the National Hotel. In the hall outside his room was a long line of people. I pushed my way through, Moscow streetcar-fashion, and went into Kennan's room. He was sitting at a desk surrounded by papers, maps, blueprints and God-knows-what-all-else. He looked rather tired and harassed and I told him so.

Kennan smiled wearily: "Yes, there's plenty to do. I have to check the blueprints of the new Embassy buildings; I have to draft the leases and get Washington's permission to sign them. Those people outside are all applicants for jobs and have to be interviewed. I have to answer inquiries every day. After fifteen years without an Embassy there is bound to be a backlog of business. And some of it is urgent. At least it seems urgent to the individuals involved."

"Isn't there any way I could help?" I asked.

"We're not authorized by the State Department to employ anyone yet. Thank you just the same."

"I didn't mean a regular job. It just looked as though you could do with help."

"The regulations don't allow me to take on volunteers, but—" he thought for a moment, "what do you know about Customs House procedures here in Moscow?"

"I got a trunk of my own through Customs," I answered. "It took almost two months and I think I met everyone in Moscow who ever had anything to do with the Customs House. There may have been a few clerks who escaped me. But I got the trunk."

Kennan hesitated for a moment: "The trouble is we have about forty carloads of equipment on its way from America for the Embassy. Washington told me simply to turn the whole matter over to the Moscow equivalent of the Railway Express. But there isn't any such thing. The Department doesn't seem to realize things are a little different in a Soviet state. They'll catch on all right in the end," he added with slightly forced cheerfulness. "But it's the beginning that's a little tough for us on the spot."

"Forty carloads," I repeated, a little overwhelmed. "Forty carloads of what?"

"Forty carloads of furniture for the Embassy and for the staff apartments, and all the office equipment for the Chancery as well."

"Chancery? – what's that?"

"The Chancery is the office of an Embassy. Ours is going to be in the building they're finishing next door."

"But the building next door hasn't even got the roof on it yet. Where is the stuff to be stored?"

"Well, that's one of the things we have to attend to, find storage space in the Customs House. Maybe you could look into the matter and let me know what procedure we have to follow, what papers we have to prepare and so forth. I'll give you a letter saying you represent me. It's against regulations, but what the devil!"

Kazan Station platform, 1930s

A few minutes later, I hurried off on my first official mission for the Embassy.

The Chief of the Customs House received me in the bright whitewashed office of the Customs Office on Station Square where the Leningrad and North Stations stood side by side. Across the Square stood the big red-brick Kazan Station. (Eight years later on a gloomy, rainy night, I was going to leave Moscow for the last time from the Kazan Station, while German planes dropped bombs in that same Square.)

The Customs Chief was an enormous old gentleman six foot four or five tall and almost as big around. His gray beard reached half way down to his expansive waist. He was as affable as his figure was imposing. He treated me with the charm of an Old World diplomat and listened intently to my problem which I explained as best I could in my not-very-grammatical Russian.

When I got to the forty carloads, the Chief relaxed a bit and smiled. "Forty days, you say? Why worry till then? There's plenty of time? When your baggage arrives, we'll let you know and you send a messenger with the necessary papers."

"Not forty days, forty carloads," I said.

"Forty cars? An awful lot of cars for one Embassy – but then we know you Americans. You don't like to walk. If the Foreign Commissariat says it's okay, it's all right with us.

"When they come, you send us the chauffeurs. There'll be no trouble."

"No! No! Not cars, not automobiles, but railroad cars. Wagons, you call them."

The Customs Chief got a little impatient: "What in the devil does an Embassy want with forty railroad cars? Are you going to build your own railroad? Or are they a gift to the Transport Commissariat? If that's the case the Commissariat will take care of the Customs formalities."

I tried to find some way to explain in Russian "forty freight cars full of furniture." During my weeks of study, the phrase hadn't appeared once in my lessons. I pointed to the Customs Chief's desk, his chair, the couch, the table and all the other furniture in the room.

"Five times all this is about one carload. Tomorrow, next day or soon, the Embassy will have two hundred times all this furniture – forty carloads arriving here in the Customs House."

The Chief stopped smiling. He asked me to wait a moment and sent for his Assistant. The Assistant, a younger man, tall, thin and tired-looking, came in and sat down beside his Chief. The Chief asked me to repeat what I just said.

When I got done, there was a long silence during which the Chief stared at the Assistant Chief and the latter stared back.

The Assistant was the first to speak. "This is a rather new problem for us. We handle only small lots here. Small shipments to private individuals. We've never had a whole Embassy come all at once. Big shipments are always for a trust or a Commissariat – a part of our Government. They are sent directly to the plants and factories. All we see are the papers. But this is different. Everything must be inspected here, of course. But forty carloads! Why, a shipment like that would block up the Customs House for weeks. We'll have to work some special procedure." He looked at the Chief and said something under his breath. The Chief implied approval.

"Yes, that's it!" Turning to me, he explained: "Come back tomorrow and maybe we'll have figured something out by then."

"But the forty cars may be in your yard by tomorrow, and then what?"

The old Chief nodded, a little resignedly: "Yes. You're right. We must make a plan, and make it at once."

In a moment he was all energy and bustle. "A plan of campaign! Not a moment to lose or the enemy will be upon us," he shouted good-humoredly. "Why, it's like the Civil War all over again."

Our three heads went together and the Customs House Forty-Car-Plan took shape:

One car would be unloaded at a time. Otherwise the siding would be blocked for normal work. The Railroad would have to hold the remaining thirty-nine in the yards. The Customs Chief would arrange that.

Guards for the thirty-nine would be needed. The Assistant Chief would see to that.

Trucks? Ten a day at least would be necessary. That would be for me to work out. Maybe the Moving Trust would help, the Chief suggested.

Porters, at least eight per truck, would be needed. Perhaps I would contact the Labor Union Council?

Storage? "My God!" said the Customs Chief. "Haven't you even got a building?" A little sheepishly I explained that angle of the problem. Well, that was for me to worry about, but perhaps the Chief could give me a tip. He'd heard from his brother-in-law that the Artificial Rubber Trust was moving to Vladimir. Perhaps there'd be a bit of room in their old building for a few weeks till the Chancery got its roof.

Finally, the Chief pointed out, it would probably take a little time to coordinate the Railroad, the Moving Trust, the Labor Union Council, the porters, the warehouse, etc. He would instruct his agents at the frontier to wire him as soon as any shipments for the American Embassy crossed the border. That would give us a few hours' warning at least.

Eventually the Plan was completed and I took off on a round of the Trusts to work out the details.

The Moving Trust was housed in what looked like an old Palace. There was a little tussle with the guard at the gate but eventually I was ushered through a series of ancient ballrooms now overflowing with cupboards from which spilled bundles of paper. In a corner, a charwoman was making tea. Twenty-odd clerks were busily scribbling away at their desks or clicking out computations on their abacuses.

I found the Director in a tiny room in what had apparently been a part of the servants' quarters. With silver-rimmed pince-nez, pointed ears, and a trim little blond goatee, he looked more like a rabbit, I thought, than the head of a gang of movers. He received me courteously enough and asked what he could do for the newly arrived Americans. Everyone in Moscow, he said, was anxious to help their newest guests.

I had hardly started my stammering explanation when a secretary appeared at the door and shouted that the Comrade Director was due at a meeting in ten minutes at the Transport Commissariat. The Director smiled wearily in reply and asked me to go on with my story. I had just reached the point about the forty carloads when the phone rang. The Director picked up the receiver impatiently:

"Yes, this is Comrade Ostrovsky! What do you want? Listen, Comrade Ivanov, I told you when you left this morning that you were not to move the linoleum from the Blood Transfusion Institute. Do you understand? I don't care what the Meteorological Institute people say. Those are my orders from above and they're your orders. The linoleum is to remain in the Blood Transfusion Institute." He slammed the receiver a little irritated.

"We all have our troubles," he explained apologetically. "But that was a rather complicated case. The Blood Transfusion Institute, the Meteorological Institute and the French Embassy are exchanging buildings in a three-way shift. They're all trying to take with them as much of the building as they can lift. Yes, even to a certain extent, the French of all people! But go on with your story. I'm sure you won't be trying to do anything like that – not you Americans." He smiled again and sighed.

I was about to begin again but the door of the office opened and the old charwoman entered carrying a glass of tea on a tray. "Now, Sergei Dimitrich, you must take your tea. It's after twelve already."

Thank you, Anna Pavlovna, but I sent word I didn't want any tea. I haven't time."

"Now! Now! Time? What's that? Everyone has time for his tea or else his doctor makes time – later," she added ominously with a coy look at the elderly Director. She put a steaming hot glass in front of him and paddled ducklike out of the room.

"Sorry," said the Director. "Please continue."

"The point is, we have a large amount of furniture arriving in a few days for the Embassy. Forty carloads in all. And we have to move it…"

"Forty carloads seems an awful lot…" But the telephone cut him short.

"The devil!" he exclaimed, lifting the receiver in annoyance. "Yes. This is Serge Dimitrich. What? The Meteorological Institute wants to take the door hinges? No, absolutely not! Hinges belong to the building. Without them the doors would fall off!… I don't care whether the French Embassy is taking doorknobs or not. Maybe they're special doorknobs – for security. They can be replaced by regular ones easily. Anyway, the Meteorological Institute doesn't need security – except from the weather! They can take locks but no hinges, or doorknobs! Understand?… What? They took the linoleum after all? Who did?… The French Embassy? Damn it, they promised me they wouldn't!… Who said the Blood Transfusion

Institute's linoleum was all bloody?... Well! What the devil can they expect? You can't make omelets without breaking eggs – even French chefs!... Hello! Hello! Can you hear me? Operator, I've been cut off. Reconnect me at once!... What number was I speaking to? I don't know – the French Embassy probably. No, it was the Blood Transfusion or maybe it was the Meteorological – Oh hell, I don't know!" The Director slammed the receiver and turned to me.

"Yes, you want to move the Embassy? The American Embassy? But, my friend, it's not even here yet and you say it wants to move already? Oh dear! I hope you're not going to be as troublesome as the French." The office door opened and the secretary poked her head in.

"Sergei Dimitrich, you have just two minutes to get to the office of the Commissar..."

"Yes, yes, I know, I'll be there at once."

Slipping past the secretary, the charwoman paddled back into the room:

"Sergei Dimitrich! Your tea's getting cold..."

"Good God, can't you see I'm busy, woman? – comrade, I mean." He struggled to regain his composure. "Please, Anna Pavlovna, leave me alone! I don't want any tea!"

The charwoman, a little less coy, beat a silent retreat. "Yes, you Americans want to move before you get here, you say? Funny, but still, tell me from where, to where and on what date. We're booked up, of course, for the next three months."

Exasperation was beginning to get the better of me, too. "No!" I shouted, "we're moving from America."

From America? Oh! We can't handle anything like that! Nothing outside Moscow."

"But we're simply moving in our furniture from the Customs House..."

"Moving in? Oh, no! We're a Moving Trust – not a Moving-In Trust. We can't handle anything from the Customs House! Never did such a thing in our lives!"

"But who will do it then if you won't?"

"Ah – well, let's think that one over! Who will move you in from the Customs House? Now, let me see... Who was it telling me last night? Oh, yes! My daughter – she works in the Transport Section of the Soft Coal Trust. She said they were having a slack time. Perhaps the Director – a nice fellow – Posvolsky, I think his name is. Perhaps if you went to see him. Let me see, his address is Gertzena Street forty-four or forty-five – something like that."

The Director got up: "And now I'm sure you'll excuse me. I'm ten minutes late already and the Commissar for Transport – he's a bear for punctuality... ." The little goatee disappeared out the door.

Gertsena Street, Pokrovsky Lane, Pushkin Square, "A" Boulevard, "B" Boulevard. I slid along slippery snow-packed sidewalks and wrestled my way through streetcars from one end of Moscow to the other. The Soft Coal Trust, the Labor Union Council, the Artificial Rubber Trust and a dozen more.

But eventually the details of the Plan were worked out and I reported back to Kennan.

"It's a little complicated," I admitted, "but it ought to work. This is how it will be," I began enthusiastically. "When the shipment crosses the frontier, they'll wire the Customs Chief. He'll notify the Railroad Guards and the Freight Yards. His Assistant will notify me. I'll call the Protocol Division of the Foreign Commissariat which has promised to send a special man with the documents. I'll call the Soft Coal Trust..."

"The Soft Coal Trust," Kennan interrupted. "What the hell do they have to do with it?"

"Oh, they've promised to supply ten five-ton trucks every day till the operation is finished! And after the Soft Coal Trust I call the Assistant Chief of the Labor Union Council. He supplies the porters. Eight for each truck – eighty in all. Then, on the way to the Customs House, I call at the Artificial Rubber Trust. Their telephone's been disconnected since they moved to Vladimir."

As Kennan's eyes narrowed again, I quickly explained. "The Director of the Artificial Rubber Trust is still here in Moscow. He has agreed to rent to us their empty warehouse for two months. After that they have to turn it over to the South Ukrainian Sugar Beet Trust or something like that... But we're all right for two months," I concluded.

Kennan stared unenthusiastically at me:

"I suppose you know you have to get three competitive bids for each of these operations you've planned? Otherwise the General Accounting Office in Washington won't let us pay their bills."

"Competitive bids?" I moaned. "But this is Russia – Soviet Russia – You can't get competitive anything here!"

"Skip it," Kennan said wearily. "Of course, I know. But I wonder if G.A.O. does. I'll wire the Ambassador. Maybe he can explain. Anyway, I think your plan is splendid – if it works. Except," and he hesitated a moment, "suppose the forty carloads don't all come at once?"

DAYS ELAPSED AND no word came from the Customs House. Twice I called to review the procedure with the genial Chief of Customs.

Don't worry," he told me. "As soon as anything crosses the border, I'll let you know – day or night."

Finally, very early one morning, the telephone at the apartment rang.

"Karl Georgovich," roared the voice of the Customs Chief. "A shipment for the American Embassy passed the frontier at Negoreloye early yesterday evening. It's due in the Customs any minute. I'll call my people – and don't you forget to call yours. I'll see you in a little while."

I called Kennan at the National Hotel and told him the news. "I'll go straight to the Customs and report what the shipment contains as soon as the operation is under way." I've always liked the word "operation." It sounds so efficient and military.

Then I called a friend, a beau of the landlady's daughter, who worked in a nearby garage and had a motorcycle at his disposal.

Could he come at once to take me on a government mission to the Customs House? It was very urgent – and official – I added.

Then the Foreign Commissariat.

Yes, they'd send a man from the Protocol Section at once with all the necessary documents.

The Soft Coal Trust and the Labor Union Council were quickly alerted.

The sputtering of a motorcycle on the street announced the arrival of the landlady's daughter's beau. In a few minutes we were skidding over icy streets toward the Artificial Rubber Trust's warehouse and then on to Station Square. As we drew up in front of the Customs House, I noticed ten large trucks pulling into the yards, each with eight husky porters aboard.

Inside the building, the Customs Chief, his Assistant and a dapper little man from the Foreign Office were waiting. They appeared in the best of spirits – especially the hulking Chief, whose eyes were twinkling unusually brightly for that early hour. Together we went out through the yards to the Customs shed, the Chief leading, I, now almost bursting with self-importance, immediately behind him.

Halfway through the shed, the Chief stopped:

"Karl Georgovich," he announced with heavily accentuated solemnity, "the first of your forty carloads has been unloaded and lies before you!" He pointed to a small wooden crate at his feet.

It was marked "Pilsner Beer – 12 quarts. Compliments of the Brewery."

6

THE WAR OF THE TRUSTS

Eventually the furniture and the desks and the typewriters all arrived – in driblets, needless to say. And eventually we got them into the buildings and the rooms where they belonged. Late one evening George Kennan, "Pinky" Daves, a State Department architect, and myself carried an enormous bed upstairs into the master bedroom of Spaso House, the Ambassador's residence. The next morning early we hurried to the station to meet the Ambassador and his household. There was a slight confusion at the station, I remember, because the train carrying Bullitt also had a large contingent of female Communists coming to the annual Women's Day Celebration in Moscow. For several exciting minutes it looked as though Bullitt were going to get the bouquets and the band, and the women were going to get a bow and a handshake from the Chief of Protocol, who as Chief Ceremonial Officer had the job of welcoming new Ambassadors. But somehow or other, things got sorted out at the last moment and everyone was happy.

Along with Bullitt came his French cook, Louise, a highly competent and determined professional. The last car of the cavalcade from the station had hardly reached Spaso House when Louise started on a quick but comprehensive survey of her new bailiwick. A few minutes later she stormed into the dining room where the Ambassador was having breakfast:

"But Your Excellency, there is nothing in the house! Nothing! I assure you."

I looked at Kennan and growled under my breath: What did she mean nothing? I'd been carrying things into the house for days and now I was being told it was still empty.

"In the kitchen, there is nothing, no spices, not even red pepper. In the bedrooms there is nothing, not even coat hangers."

Bullitt laughed and turned to Chip Bohlen who had arrived with him from Paris. Chip had been preparing for his Moscow assignment for two years at the School for Oriental Languages in Paris. At last the time had come to put his learning to use.

"Chip, do you suppose you could take Louise downtown and help her buy whatever seems to be missing?"

The School for Oriental Languages had not specialized in terms for obscure French spices. Besides, Chip's chief effort all his life has been to keep as far away from kitchens as possible.

Several hours later he returned from his first assignment looking a little dazed.

"How did it go?" I asked him.

"Not as badly as I expected. The stores didn't have any of the spices and I knew the Russian word for 'coat hanger.'" I remember wondering at the time whether it was really worth the trouble trying to acclimatize a French chef to Moscow conditions, but several months later something happened that tended to change my mind. Another Foreign Service Officer, Eddy Page, who had been studying with Chip in Paris, arrived in Moscow with his bride, Terry. Terry, by then, had heard a good deal about what to expect in Moscow and was well on her guard against mishaps. We'd arranged everything in their new apartment as best we could, in advance, including a local cook straight off a collective farm. By that time we had an Embassy commissary set up with a few American groceries for sale. The Pages had hardly unpacked before they hurried down to the commissary to get the wherewithal for a model newlywed household. Terry bought the spices and the canned foods. Eddy got the cocktail fixings and some tennis balls. Within an hour or so they were sitting down for their first meal in their new home. Some canned soup was produced and eaten. Then there was a long pause. While the Pages waited for their next course, they could hear the cook muttering away in the kitchen. Eventually she burst into the dining room brandishing a saucepan in one hand and a fork in the other.

"They won't cook, I tell you, these darned American potatoes won't cook!"

She poked the saucepan under Terry's nose and stabbed at the "potatoes" with the fork. Bobbing about in the boiling water were a couple of Eddy's tennis balls.

But to get back to Spaso House where the Ambassador was wrestling with Muscovite housekeeping. Once we got the hang of things, we found it pretty simple to pick up a few "black workers," as the day laborers are called in Moscow, and got them to lug the furniture and office equipment around. But then an enormous safe arrived. Some black workers were mobilized and the safe was pulled and tugged from the railroad car onto a truck and then to Spaso House. There we managed to get it off the truck without damaging more than a toe or two and even succeeded in getting it through the front door. By that time it was late in the day and the black workers took a look at the dull light in the sky that passes for a sun in Moscow in winter.

"Time to quit," they announced stubbornly.

"But you can't leave the safe right in the front door. The Ambassador is having people to dinner and they won't even be able to get by."

"Time to quit," they repeated with a shrug of their shoulders, indicating that the Ambassador's guests were his problem. Then they turned and marched off down the driveway. In those situations there was only one thing to do: call the Chief of Protocol who besides being the Grover Whalen of Russia also was responsible for the welfare, such as it was, of the whole Diplomatic Corps. He said he was sorry but he wasn't much good at moving safes and neither were any of his colleagues. However, he'd try to find someone in the morning.

We held a council of war and took the only decision available: the Ambassador, the Counselor, two Second Secretaries, three Third Secretaries and the Private Secretary put their shoulders to the safe and shoved. Bit by bit we got it moved to a point where only half the door was blocked. It would take a very fat guest, indeed, to get stuck on the way in.

The next morning the Chief of Protocol sent word he was still wrestling with the problem but he didn't sound very hopeful. The black workmen turned up, but when they saw where we wanted the safe put, they sighed deeply and said it was beyond their powers. We'd have to get the Heavy-Weight-Lifting Trust.

"Where is the Heavy-Weight-Lifting Trust?" we asked anxiously. Four or five addresses were produced.

"It can be they're still living on the Tverskoi Boulevard."

"I heard someone say they'd moved to Zamoskvarechia."

"I'm not sure they don't still work across from Kazan Station."

A few minutes later four cars roared out of the American Embassy in search of the Heavy-Weight-Lifters. Back and forth across Moscow we dashed to Tverskoi, to Zamoskvarechia, around the Arbat, to the Kazan Station. We called at the Post Office, at the Telephone Exchange, at the Customs House. Did anyone know here the Heavy-Weight-Lifters hung out? We stopped trucks carrying Heavy Weights in the hope they might know. Some people seemed to think they might once have heard of them, but the great majority were firmly convinced they'd never heard of them and that it was doubtful whether they existed at all. But eventually in one office an old janitress came to the rescue. Of course, she knew all about the Heavy-Weight-Lifters. Her husband was one of them. She gave us their address and we hurried off to find them.

The Heavy-Weight-Lifters were a rather aristocratic outfit. They wouldn't take on any job until they'd seen it. So we loaded them into our cars and hustled back to the Embassy. They studied the terrain carefully, pushed the safe a couple of times and decided it could be moved. But they weren't going to do it for any chicken feed or rocksalt. How much would we give them?

I mentioned a sum in rubles.

"Rubles?!" they muttered. "Why, we thought you were foreigners and would give us *valuta* so we can buy in the special foreigners' store."

I suggested some Polish zlotys.

What kind of zlotys? Real silver zlotys?

Yes, I said, and produced a large silver coin as big as a dollar. "One for each of the five of you."

They snatched the zloty and fingered it.

"It's real, is it?"

I said I thought it was, though I knew there were plenty of fakes on the market.

"All right! We'll take your word for it. It's a deal." With that they unslung some old pieces of rope from around their middles, passed them under the safe and over their shoulders, gave a deep grunt and heaved. The safe rose like a feather and swayed precariously as they shuffled up the stairs and across the ballroom. In ten minutes it was in place. Chip Bohlen passed out five zlotys, and a couple of bottles of beer for good measure and the Heavy-Weight-Lifters stomped off down the drive.

We felt very pleased with ourselves and called the Chief of Protocol not to bother any more about our problem. We'd solved it ourselves to our entire satisfaction.

But unfortunately it wasn't quite so satisfactory to the Heavy-Weight-Lifters. The next day one of them, an enormous bearded old giant, lumbered up to the Embassy and demanded to see Chip. He was shown to Chip's office and swayed threateningly across the floor like a huge gorilla.

"It's no good. It broke," he muttered. "What broke?" Chip asked, puzzled. "The money broke."

"The money? How could the money break?"

"I hit it with a sledge hammer," the Weight-Lifter growled.

"Why in God's name should you hit it with a sledge hammer? It looked like a perfectly good zloty to me. Do you always hit your money with a sledge hammer?"

"Sometimes. I do when I figure it's fake. And this was a fake. Look!"

He held out two battered hunks of metal. "Look at that and tell me if a real silver coin breaks."

Chip confessed he'd never tried hitting a coin with a sledge hammer so he was no expert, but he admitted that the battered bits of metal didn't look like silver to him. He pulled out another zloty from his pocket and gave it to the Heavy-Weight-Lifter. "Here take this and try your sledge hammer on it. If it's no good, come back and tell me."

The Heavy-Weight-Lifter must have been satisfied for we never saw him again.

Whether the Chief of Protocol was annoyed by our obvious self-satisfaction over the weight-lifting episode or not, I'm not sure. But at any rate he called up a few days later in great distress and asked who lived in the second floor northwest corner bedroom of the Spaso House.

"Why do you want to know?" I asked him cautiously. "Because whoever does just threw a soda water bottle out the window at a policeman and badly wounded him. I just got an urgent phone call from the Special Police and they want an immediate report." The Chief of Protocol was obviously scared to death of the police and determined to get satisfaction for them as quickly as possible.

"I'm sure I don't know anything about any bottles," I answered. "But the northwest corner room is Ambassador Bullitt's bedroom and he's been taking a nap in there for the last hour and a half. I'll ask him if he threw the bottle at the policeman and call you back."

It was all very well for the Ambassador stoutly to deny that he threw any bottles during his nap. The policeman was produced and exhibited a large gash over his left eye and the broken soda water bottle which he insisted came over the Embassy wall and caught him on the forehead. Even in Russia bottles don't fly and there seemed no reason for the policeman to invent the story. Nevertheless, the Ambassador was just as convincing with his story. It may have been true that as an undergraduate at Yale he had bandied some milk bottles around, but for the last thirty years he insisted he hadn't thrown even a milk bottle let alone a pop bottle.

The Police Department was adamant in its demand for blood. "An eye for an eye" was their motto. The Chief of Protocol, who knew where his bread was buttered, backed them up. The Ambassador was just as stubborn. Stalemate.

And then my chauffeur, Grecia, a man of many parts, came forward.

"What's all this about the Ambassador throwing a pop bottle at a policeman?" he asked me with a huge grin all over his face.

"It's not so darn funny," I answered sourly. "Someone threw a bottle and the policeman got hit and now they say it must have come from a window in the Ambassador's bedroom where he was sleeping."

"That's a lot of baloney," Grecia retorted. "It didn't have to come from that bedroom at all."

"How do you know?" I asked.

"Because I threw it," Grecia replied, grinning more than ever.

"You threw the bottle at the policeman? What the devil do you think you were doing?"

"I didn't throw it at the policeman. I just threw it away. Someone left it in the backyard and I ran over it and cut a tire almost in two. I was so sore I just heaved it over the wall. Tough luck for the cop if he got in the way."

So Protocol was notified. The scarred and scared policeman was produced, Grecia made a very perfunctory apology. The Ambassador was officially absolved and the case of the pop bottle was closed.

But the next round with Protocol was ours – at least morally. The plan for a bigger and better Moscow called for blowing up a block of houses that stood between the Chancery and the Kremlin. (There has always been a difference of opinion as to whether the Kremlin is across the street from the American Embassy or vice versa. And it all started with fireworks.)

One day we got a very flowery note from the People's Commissariat for Foreign Affairs stating that a week hence at high noon a large quantity of dynamite was going to go off directly opposite our offices. Would we therefore mind opening our windows so as to avoid smashing all the glass in the building? It took several days for the note to get down the street to our Chancery from the Commissariat, but it got there in plenty of time to notify everyone to keep his windows open – and his eyes and ears shut – come high-noon Friday. So the windows were opened, the eyes and ears were shut, the dynamite went off with a bang, half a dozen old houses collapsed with a roar and everyone was very happy indeed.

About a week later the whole procedure was repeated except that it took the Chief of Protocol almost a week to get the note to us and it arrived at about H-hour minus ten minutes. Some fast footwork on the part of the Embassy messengers got the word around before it was too late and when the bang came, all the windows were open. So we were very happy once more and thanked Protocol for their courtesy and thoughtfulness.

Almost a week later at high noon, there was an explosion across the street that shook Moscow Oblast to its roots. A few windows happened to be open in the Chancery but the rest were blown to atoms – except where the catches on the windows were faulty so that the whole window blew open. About three days later the Chief of Protocol sent us a note asking us to be sure to have our windows open three days ago. Our reply was just a little tart.

Little by little we began to find our way around town and even have some time for some social life. There were two kinds of social life – the official kind newspaper correspondents write about and the kind nobody writes about. In the first category, my earliest recollection is of the party Litvinov[7] gave for Anthony Eden when he was deputy to Lord Simon in the Foreign Office. It was back in 1934 when various governments were beginning to say rather rude things about each other. Stalin put it bluntly when he told the world that he was having no other people's pig-snouts in his backyard. Hitler retorted with speeches about guns for butter. Litvinov put it a little more delicately when he suggested peace could only be global, or as he expressed it in his inimitable English, "Piz is indivisible."

The Eden dinner followed the usual pattern, except for one small incident. The Ambassadors were all invited to dinner (in tailcoats) at the official reception house, Spiridonovka Palace. (Litvinov, himself, lived in a small apartment above the garage of the palace.) We small fry were asked to attend at a somewhat later hour and were put into one of the outer reception rooms. There we got potato vodka as compared with the wheat vodka in the inner sanctum. We got gray rather than black caviar and only three kinds of smoked fish instead of the five or six the Ambassadors were served. But everyone was satisfied – particularly the small fry, and particularly that night. For it turned out that Litvinov's chef was as keen on politics as his boss, if not as subtle. At least so we gathered from what one of the Ambassadors told us when they all emerged from the inner sanctum. The table, he said, had been thoroughly decorated with flowers, crystal candlesticks, the best gold service that was left over from the last regime, and all sorts of very fancy platters of delicacies. Among the latter, the most conspicuous was the butter, served up in one large block a foot long and six inches thick. When the Ambassadors had settled themselves and the caviar and toast had been passed around, Eden leaned forward to snag a slice of butter from the huge block in front of him. Then he hesitated and seemed to change his mind for he put down his butter knife and ate his caviar on dry toast. A

---

7. Maxim Litvinov (1876-1951) headed up Russia's foreign affairs from 1930-1939, reputedly ousted from the post (in favor of Vyacheslav Molotov) so that Hitler – with whom the Soviets brokered a pact in 1939 – would not have to interact with a Russian Jewish diplomat. He narrowly escaped being purged before the war broke out, and he went on to serve as ambassador to the US and then Cuba.

careful examination showed that the chef had inscribed on the butter those winged words "Peace is Indivisible." It was not the policy of His Britannic Majesty's Government to demonstrate the fallacy of the doctrine even when the "peace" was made only of butter. That was left for Hitler to do several years later.

But others had their troubles with food in Moscow, especially Ambassador Bullitt's successor, Joseph E. Davies. Ambassador Davies, it seemed, had a very sensitive stomach that permitted him to eat only very special foods. In fact the entire time I served under him, I can't remember his ever having eaten anything outside his own house. (I admit that in the movie of his stay in Russia, *Mission to Moscow*, there are scenes of the Ambassador eating heartily at wayside buffets in Soviet railroad stations. However, as I never saw anything even remotely resembling the movie versions of these buffets, I dare say the sequences were the result of some over-enthusiastic producer.) Anyway, even before the Ambassador arrived, his coming was heralded by the arrival of twenty-five deep-freeze iceboxes which were duly installed in the basement of the Spaso House.

Then from Antwerp, or perhaps it was Bremen, two carloads of frozen foods carefully packed in dry ice set out for the long trek across northern Europe to Moscow. A young food engineer accompanied the precious shipment. Every day or two we would get a telegram from him describing his progress. The eyes of the whole Embassy were on the two freight cars. On a wall map in the Chancery, we marked its journey by means of a large red thumbtack.

"Arrive Berlin today. Hope to get away this evening."

"Passed the Oder safely."

"Arriving Soviet frontier in the morning."

There was a slight hitch at the Soviet frontier because the dry ice had evaporated out of several of the containers, leaving the containers empty. This puzzled the Soviet Customs authorities a good deal because, as they quite rightly explained, no one rents a freight car to carry empty boxes around. Besides, there was nothing in the Soviet Customs rule book about how to classify the contents of a box that has nothing in it. However, after a rather long lecture on the chemistry of dry ice, the food engineer managed to get his point across, and eventually the shipment arrived and was stored away in the twenty-five deep-freezes.

Everyone was delighted for several weeks. The delicious frozen steaks and vegetables were a welcome change for all of us who'd been accustomed for years to eating out of tin cans. There was even frozen cream, four hundred quarts of it, which those of us who were invited to the Embassy for meals lapped up with delight.

But then a small incident occurred which eventually put a serious crimp in our frozen meals. It all started when we discovered a microphone in the process of being installed in a ventilator shaft leading down from the attic of Spaso House through the wall of the Ambassador's office. The microphone, when we found it, was separated from the Ambassador's desk by only a thin layer of plaster. Whoever was putting it in had not quite finished the job and we could find no wires leading beyond the attic. So we photographed the mike, which had been made in Leningrad, and put it back where we found it, hoping to surprise the culprit when he came back to finish the job. Otherwise we would have no proof whatever as to who was being so curious about what our Ambassador had to say in his office. (He was more fortunate perhaps than another Ambassador who was embarrassed to find that a mike had been placed in the wall between his and his wife's beds. Moscow's Diplomatic Corps unanimously agreed that it had been a most delicate and deserved tribute to the dominating personality of the other Ambassador's wife.)

For several nights, George Kennan, Elbridge Durbrow, another Embassy Secretary, and myself took turns hiding in the dusty old attic with a revolver in one hand and a flashlight in the other. It wasn't exactly comfortable, because to stay hidden we had to lie on our bellies on the hard floor. Besides it was rather cold and the atmosphere was anything but gay. Every now and then a night owl or some other bird with insomnia would hop across the tin roof above and bring us to with a start. But in many ways it wasn't much worse than getting jacked up in a tailcoat and standing for half the night at some boring diplomatic reception. Besides, it was all in the diplomatic day's or night's work.

But eventually it began to tell on our nerves so we hooked up what seemed to be a very ingenious system of fine silk threads criss-crossed across the floor near the fatal ventilator shaft. The threads were attached to some homemade switches which in turn were connected to an alarm bell in one of the bedrooms where we took turns standing guard in a good deal more comfort than the attic provided. We thought it was a pretty foolproof system because there were so many threads and the attic was so dark that it was practically impossible to move without setting off the alarm – as we proved to ourselves on several occasions. I don't doubt that other amateur detectives would have thought of something better but then we were new at the game and working in a country where we couldn't be one hundred per cent sure of the cooperation of the local police.

But there was one flaw in the trap. The electricity on which it operated came off the regular house current. One morning when Durbrow, I think, was standing (or rather sleeping) watch, the Ambassador's English butler, Taylor, woke him to say that the main switch for the house had been pulled during the night. Realizing that the whole apparatus we'd set up was out of commission, Durbrow dashed upstairs to find practically every silk thread pulled and the mike gone. Naturally we were a little disappointed but we soon got over it and consoled ourselves with the thought that we hadn't been hired to be detectives anyway. (I was a little surprised some years later when I saw the film *Mission to Moscow* and heard the character representing the Ambassador chastising a junior Third Secretary – presumably myself – for insinuating that there might be a microphone in his office. But I guess that was a misunderstanding of the affair by one of the scenario writers. At any rate a photograph of the mike is on file in the State Department in case anyone in Hollywood is interested.)

But there were more serious results of the night of the big mike snatch that soon became very apparent. Two days after the current had been cut, the Ambassador's butler called me.

"Two of the deep-freezes seem to have failed to get back into action after we reconnected the current the night before last," he announced dolefully.

"What was in them?" I asked.

"The frozen cream," he replied, "and it's passed all saving."

This was serious business, I realized, not just because we wouldn't have any more frozen cream for a while. The Ambassador's frozen food supply had already become world news and if ever the Moscow correspondents of the American press got hold of the story, it was going to play hob with the frozen-food company's reputation.

But still there were four hundred quarts of rotten cream in the basement that had to be gotten out and quickly or else all Moscow could have smelled the story. There was no use relying on the Embassy's chauffeurs. They were all close friends of their colleagues who worked for the press corps. Besides, since the Embassy was swarming with people all day long, we couldn't remove the cream except at night. So that evening I got hold of a truck from a Russian trust, manned it with a couple of black workers I picked up in the market and stealthily drove into the backyard of Spaso House. While the workmen, a little reluctantly, loaded bucket after bucket of the stinking mess into the truck, I kept watch in front – largely in order to get away from the smell.

When it was all loaded, I climbed into the cab and we headed out into the open country. As we bounced along the cobblestone road, through the dark and deserted night, I couldn't help thinking of the lines I'd learned at school of the "Burial of Sir John Moore":

> Not a drum was heard not a funeral note.
> As his corpse to the rampart we hurried.

At last we came to a deserted stretch of road in a large pine forest. We backed the truck into the ditch and in a few minutes our job was done and we were headed back to Moscow.

BUT THE HARDEST thing to get used to in Moscow housekeeping was the trustification of every minor activity connected with running a house. While trying to get the Embassy set up, I'd already run into the Artificial Rubber Trust, the Soft Coal Trust, the Moving Trust and a dozen others. They were sometimes a little difficult to work with but at least they seemed to have a place in the national economy.

Then later I ran into the Green Trust that planned, built and tended your garden. There was the Entertainment Trust, set up to provide orchestras and dancers for entertainment. There was the Heavy-Weight-Lifters Trust which went around breaking zlotys. And then there was the Window-Washers Trust.

But worse than that, each trust had to have a Five-Year-Plan and a One-Year-Plan all prepared well in advance and approved by the upper levels of the economic hierarchy. For instance, if you went to the Entertainment Trust and asked for an orchestra, they'd tell you they had planned all their entertainments last June and were very sorry but they had made no provision for supplying music for a dance the Ambassador had decided to give six months later. However, if we wanted to give them our dance program for the fiscal year 1935, they'd be only too glad to consider any reasonable requirements we might have. I never revisited the Entertainment Trust. The Green Trust, too, was hipped on plans, but they consented to take over the job of landscaping the Embassy backyard and somehow shoehorn it into the current One-Year-Plan as a very special favor. However, that would require a plan in itself.

I asked them what they meant by that.

"It's quite simple. Until we have a plan for landscaping the garden, we can't integrate it with our One-Year-Plan or our Five-Year-Plan and, until it is integrated, we can't make a move."

"But the plan is obvious. I have a budget of six thousand rubles to landscape the garden. Now go ahead and give us six thousand rubles' worth of garden."

They shook their heads pityingly at the benighted child of capitalism.

"No, it's not as easy as you think. First, we must have a project of how to landscape the garden. Then we must have a plan of how to execute the project and how much it costs. Then we compose an overall plan and submit that to our Planning Board. If the board approves, we go ahead."

I saw I was licked and asked them to go ahead with the plan of the plan of the plan as quickly as possible. The only thing to remember was that I had six thousand rubles for the garden and no more.

Spring was upon us and soon the trees began to turn green and the flowers in others peoples' gardens began to bloom, but only a couple of surveyors showed up for a few hours at the Embassy and then disappeared.

The Ambassador began to complain about the garden. "Where is it? Why aren't they working? Where are the plants and the shrubbery?"

I explained the complexity of the problem and the Ambassador seemed to understand because he didn't grumble for another two weeks. But then he seemed so disturbed that I went around to the Green Trust and asked them what was going on.

"At this rate, there'll be snow on the ground before you plant a seed," I complained a little sourly.

"Don't you worry," they replied equally ill-humoredly. "We're the designated agency for making gardens and we'll do it the right way or not at all. The project for the plan is almost finished and when it's done, we'll show it to you." Another couple of weeks passed and then the architect of the Green Trust showed up with a huge roll of papers under his arm. He unfolded them on my desk with a gesture of pride.

"Here is how your garden is going to look," he said, and pointed to a beautiful painting in water colors of a splendid English garden. Little gravel paths wandered along lilac and jasmine and rhododendron bushes. Beds of annuals nestled cozily under the trees, and delicately espaliered fruit trees grew along the garden walls.

Then the architect unrolled another sheet which showed a vertical projection of the project which confused me a little but seemed to him just as magnificent as the water color. Next he showed me a horizontal projection which was a little clearer but still slightly technical. It all seemed highly satisfactory to me, even though a little elaborate for a half acre backyard.

I showed the water color to the Ambassador, who smiled skeptically but said that if they'd make the backyard look like that for six thousand rubles, he was satisfied.

I asked the architect about the cost.

"Oh, we haven't figured that yet," he replied. "You see, we can't estimate the cost of a project till we have the project. Now if the project is approved, we will give you a cost estimate and then turn the project over to the Operations Section of the Trust to execute. And, of course, we will bill you for the project." It seemed even more confusing than I'd thought at first but there were a lot of other things in the Embassy that needed attending to, like getting the windows in the Chancery washed and the flyscreens made, so I said, "Okay, but please hurry. The summer is half over already." Another two weeks went by and after several phone calls, the Accounting Division of the Green Trust turned up with a sheet full of figures. I looked quickly at the total at the bottom of the page:

"Rubles eleven thousand."

"But I told you in the first place I only had six thousand rubles to spend. That's all the money we can get out of Washington to fix the garden. We don't have eleven thousand rubles."

"Perhaps you told someone about it but no one ever said anything to us," the Accounting Division replied. "If you want to cut the plan down and do something cheaper, it will mean a new project and that will cost more money, too."

"What do you mean, that will cost more money? I have six thousand to make a garden with and that's all."

"But eleven thousand only includes making the garden," the Accountant explained. "The project costs separately." He fumbled in his pocket and pulled out another sheet of paper. "Here is the bill for the project – the design and the drawing. This bill is for seven thousand."

"You mean I owe you seven thousand rubles already without one shovelful of earth being moved?"

The Accountant Division shrugged their shoulders collectively.

"Sorry, but that's the way it is. We always do things like that in the Planned Economy."

In a way, the Window-Washers Trust was even worse. But they were funnier. For one thing they were newer. They'd just been organized a few months and hadn't yet worked out all their routines. Their approach, too, was a little fresher. Besides, they were younger than the Heavy-Weight-Lifters or the Green Trust or the Entertainment Trust. The President and the Treasurer who came to call on me were young Ukrainians in their early twenties. But they were as cocksure of themselves and as stubborn as all the rest.

I explained my problem: The Chancery had about 170 windows of various sizes. Six of them were...

But the President of the Window-Washers Trust had all the information he needed:

"We charge a flat rate of ten rubles a window, no matter what the size."

"But as I was saying," I broke in, "six of the windows are exceptionally large..."

"We don't care how big they are. Ten rubles apiece..."

"But these are double-sized studio windows and they're very hard to get at. You'll need special equipment..."

"If you don't mind not telling us how to wash windows, we won 't tell you your business," the President replied tartly. "We don't care how big they are: ten rubles apiece, no more and no less."

"All right. Have it your own way. But how long are you going to take? We have to have them finished quickly."

"We can easily do seventeen windows a day. Say ten days for the whole job."

But I knew better. I'd had the windows cleaned once before, when the Trust still didn't exist, and it took well over a month.

"I don't think you can get them done that quickly," I said, "but I'll tell you what I'll do. It's an old custom in America. If you do all the windows in ten days, I'll give you a bonus of two hundred rubles, and for every day under ten days it takes you I'll give you four hundred. But if you take longer than ten days, you have to forfeit a fine of two hundred rubles each day you're late."

The President looked at the Treasurer and the Treasurer looked at the President. Finally the latter broke into a wide grin:

"You Americans are the darnedest people! Always trying to make a game out of things. Always thinking up something funny and new. But – it's an idea," and he went into a whispered huddle with the Treasurer. Apparently the Treasurer was a little suspicious, but the President seemed enthusiastic. They argued for a few minutes. The President looked up:

"All right, we accept! If you Americans can do it that way, so can we Russians."

The next day they started work and each morning thereafter I made a little calculation on my calendar. About a week later they had reached the studio windows and I went up to see how they were doing.

They had rigged a rickety contraption of ropes and ladders and beams in the studios and were all perched up on it like a flock of crows in the Kremlin Park across the street. Even the President and the Treasurer were there rubbing away at the glass. When they saw me they looked down sullenly but said nothing. Obviously the facts of window-washing in the Chancery were beginning to sink in and weren't particularly agreeable.

The Chancery building at Mokhovaya 18 (above, in 1934), just across the street from the Kremlin, was designed and built by the neo-classical, Stalinist architect Ivan Zholtovsky in 1932-34 and was nicknamed "the nail in the coffin of Constructivism." It served as the US Embassy until 1953, when the building was given to Intourist. There have been so many reconstructions that only the facade remains from the original construction.

"Anything I can do for you?" I asked, smiling just a little. "No. Just go away and attend to your own business," the President growled.

Another week went by and the Window-Washing Trust was still rubbing away energetically. They even began to work at night on double shifts. Finally one evening rather late, the President and the Treasurer came back to my office.

"We're all through," they announced. They seemed a good deal meeker than they had been on their first visit.

"Well, let's see," I said, referring to my calendar. "That makes just twenty days since you started. Is that right?"

"I guess so," the President muttered disconsolately.

"Well then, I owe you seventeen hundred for washing the windows and you owe me ten times two hundred rubles for being ten days late. That's two thousand rubles. In other words, you owe me the difference, or three hundred rubles in all."

The President had evidently figured it all out before, because he reached into his pocket and tossed three hundred-ruble notes on my desk.

"There it is." His voice was low but he was obviously determined to hide any signs of emotion. The two of them got up and started for the door.

But their pathetic unhappiness was a little too much for me.

"Hey, wait a minute," I said. "Seeing as how this is the first time you tried a contract like this, let's call it an experiment and forget about the fine."

I counted out seventeen hundred rubles and handed them to the President.

"But next time, you might have a look at the windows before you start making bids."

The President took the money and thanked me. His grim expression had turned to a broad smile. As he shook my hand, the President laughed:

"But what all of us want to know is who the devil wants to live in those damn fishbowl studios upstairs?"

After they left, I wondered if I hadn't been a little soft on them. But I consoled myself with the fact we'd got the windows washed in record time.

7

SEALS IN THE KITCHEN

When the American Embassy arrived in Moscow in 1933, there was already a large colony of American newspapermen, engineers, students and fellow-traveling do-gooders. In those days Moscow provided plenty of attractions in the way of excellent theater, lush opera and ballet and even nightclubs of a peculiar Muscovite sort. It was easy to buy tickets to the Moscow Art Theater – one of the best of its kind in the world – or to the ballet – the only one of its kind in the world; and a good dinner at the Metropole or the Medved Restaurant was cheap enough. (Today, I'm told, theater tickets are distributed according to the rank of the prospective purchaser – Generals in the parterre, Colonels in the balconies, other ranks in the fresh air.) But there was no central meeting place for Americans like the Embassies of other foreigners.

So when Christmas, 1934, drew near, Ambassador Bullitt told me to arrange a party for the American colony.

"And make it good," he insisted. "They've been long enough without a real shindig."

Unfortunately, he was called back to Washington before the holiday for consultation with the President, and his Counselor, John Wiley, was to act as host instead.

So I went to work.

For all its theaters and ballets and operas, Moscow isn't exactly an Elsa Maxwell paradise.[8] Somehow or other, the State Planning Commission had overlooked the lighter side of social progress. There were a handful of jazz bands which were engaged by various hotels and they were rather reluctant to come to Embassies. There were no catering firms to prepare large dinners. There were no accessible theatrical agencies from where you could order u p a song-and-dance act. There wasn't even an Elsa Maxwell. Gradually we learned how to use a little ingenuity in getting around these omissions in the Socialist system. But this was our first attempt and I was starting from scratch.

I went to the wife of the Embassy's Counselor, Irena Wiley, and explained the problem.

"Let's glass over the big ballroom floor and make an aquarium we can dance on," she said.

As a first suggestion, it showed imagination, but I pointed out that plate glass had been somehow overlooked in both the First and Second Five-Year-Plans. Besides, what would we use for fish?

"Perhaps you're right. How about an animal act? Let's go to the Zoo and see what they have to offer," Irena said.

That sounded better and together we called on the Director of the Zoo. He was a nervous little man, obviously not entirely at his ease in talking to foreigners. You would have thought that directing a zoo would normally be considered a fairly safe non-political sort of job, even in the Soviet Union. However, I remembered that one of my few Russian friends had been Director of the Zoo during the Revolution and had been fired for letting the only elephant which survived the overthrow of the Czar die. (My friend was subsequently shot during the purges for crimes not specified.) Perhaps the present Director had some sick elephants. Or perhaps he was just reluctant to get involved in so hot a political issue as a foreign religious holiday. At any rate he was not enthusiastic and very little help.

---

8. Elsa Maxwell (1883-1963) was an American gossip columnist and professional host-ess. Her parties for royalty and the in set were renowned.

From the Zoo we went to the Durov Animal Museum. The Durovs were a well-known family of animal trainers for a generation or more before the Revolution. They had been famous all over Europe. In their honor the Soviet Government had established a museum of live and dead animals. One of the exhibits I remember very well. I had first visited the Museum with the daughter of a Scandinavian diplomat. An attendant pointed out a gaudy cockatoo sitting peacefully on a perch.

"You will notice that the bird isn't chained and yet it never tries to get off its perch," the attendant said. "The reason is that for twenty years the bird was chained to the perch and after the chain was taken off, she had lost any thought of leaving it."

"That's a hell of a thing to show a Soviet audience," my companion muttered. "How many years is it since the Revolution?"

Aside from the cockatoo there was not much material for a team of entertainers at the Museum.

As a last resort we went to the Circus. In Moscow the Circus is more like a theater. It has only one ring housed in a permanent building and operates all the year round. There we saw some trained horses (not very good for parquet floors), some trained dogs (not very original at best), some trained bears (a little lethargic, we decided, for a Christmas party and besides someone might try to make some political capital out of our replacing Santa Claus by a bear that walked like a man). And then we saw the seals. There were three of them – Misha, Shura and Lyuba. They did all the regular seal acts, bouncing balls on their noses, climbing ladders while balancing their little dunce caps, and even playing tunes on the harmonica (only instead of "The Stars and Stripes Forever" they played the "Internationale").

As soon as the act was over, we went down to see the seal trainer, a young man also of the Durov family, though, we gathered, not a direct descendant of the Great Durovs. He was still in his early twenties and free of most inhibitions.

At first he seemed a little reluctant.

"I've never had my seals in a ballroom."

Charles Thayer in his Moscow home, circa 1935.

I told him that so far as we knew, the ballroom had never had seals in it. But that was no way for a young Soviet citizen to talk. There were first times for everything – and this would be a double first. The argument impressed him.

"I suppose that if we can have two or three rehearsals at the Embassy, they might take to it all right."

They did. Late the next evening after the last performance at the Circus, Durov and his seals arrived in a truck for their first dress rehearsal. We built a sort of chute like a sheeprun from a side door into an unused service room which we set aside for the seals' dressing room. From it we arranged another chute into the big ballroom itself.

It's quite a sight to see three big black seals come prancing into a ballroom – particularly into the ballroom at Spaso House with its white polished marble pillars and equally white walls that sparkle like icebergs in the sun when the chandeliers are all on. Apparently, even the seals thought they were icebergs for they slithered across the floor to the nearest pillar, cuddled up beside it and acted as though they were coming out of their native rookeries for their morning toilette. It took several housemaids with mops to clean up after them while Durov tried to explain to them that they must act housebroken in the American Embassy. With that first lesson over, the seals went through the special routine we'd developed for them and eventually – in the early hours of the morning – they slithered back into their truck and went home to bed at the Circus.

For two more nights preceding Christmas Eve, the seals rehearsed their act at the Embassy, leaving themselves, the trainer and me completely exhausted. But by this time Durov was thoroughly enthusiastic about the whole idea. He even wanted to add a bear to the act. He explained he had two bears – one he'd had for several years, the other he had just bought in Siberia. He admitted the second was pretty wild and had developed a rather nasty habit of killing people. But he promised he'd only bring the nice bear. However, I figured three seals were enough for one party and suggested he bring the nice bear around another time.

On the night of the party, Durov and his seals arrived through a side gate and his seals were surreptitiously chuted into their dressing room till the moment for their show. What with having had no sleep for several nights and with all the excitement of his first Embassy appearance (it was his last too), Durov seemed to need a little stimulant to put him on his toes. So I took him out among the guests, introducing him as a newly arrived American engineer. (The fact that he spoke no English confused some of the guests but, on Christmas Eve in Moscow, things like that are apt to happen.) I poured a couple of whiskeys into him and when the time for his act came, he seemed thoroughly restored.

We collected the guests in one end of the large ballroom and turned out all the lights. Then through the little door at the far end of the room, a small Christmas tree with twelve lighted candles swayed precariously into the room to all appearances supported only by a large black mustache. Then a spotlight went on and revealed Lyuba hiding under the mustache and balancing the tree on her nose. Behind her pranced Misha and Shura, one carrying a tray of wine glasses and the other a bottle of champagne. Durov poured one or two glasses and distributed them among the guests. Then he lifted the champagne bottle to his mouth and drained it. This last piece of business hadn't been in the rehearsals, but I guessed he was still pretty tired and needed a pick-me-up. The seals then went through their more usual routine: balanced balls, climbed ladders and even played a Christmas carol on the harmonica.

The act was about over when I began to notice a little unsteadiness in Durov's gait. Then, just as the last trick was finished, he turned to the audience, made a handsome bow, sat down on a bench and quietly passed out. Lyuba, Misha and Shura waited a moment for their next cue then flopped across the floor to their master, took one good look at him and stampeded.

There are several versions of what happened during the next fifteen minutes. I can only tell what I saw. Misha disappeared into the audience. Lyuba bolted for the pantry where the smells of a fine supper were rising from the basement kitchen. I went for Shura (she was the only one who didn't bite) and managed after several minutes to herd her into the chute and back to the dressing room. As I locked her in, I heard a fine mixture of a seal barking, women screaming and German cursing coming up from the kitchen. I got down just in time to find the kitchenmaids scampering in all directions, and the newly arrived Austrian chef jumping up and down on the kitchen table while Lyuba circled around the table bellowing like an angry cow and upsetting coal scuttles, chairs, garbage cans and anything else that got in the way of her big flippers. The chef was holding a large frying pan and was trying very ineffectually to beat Lyuba on the nose. Just what he was hoping to accomplish, I don't know. But it seemed to amuse Lyuba, for every time he took a pass at her, she'd duck out of reach, bellowing with obvious delight. When the chef saw me standing in the doorway, he screamed:

"Do something, for the Gott's love. Do something! Is no use standing there like laughing jackass!"

While the chef screamed, Lyuba roared and the kitchen help twittered noisily.

Eventually the commotion attracted the attention of Durov's assistant, who had been having a little fun in the servants' hall. He immediately took charge of the situation like the traditional drummer boy in a military rout – which indeed it was. He dashed upstairs, dragged the limp Durov from the ballroom, fetched a pan of very smelly dead fish from his truck and proceeded to realign his forces. The formation he produced was almost as unique as the situation itself. I found myself holding Durov under the armpits in front of me while from behind me the assistant reached around in front of Durov, shook the fish in the direction of Lyuba and made noises presumably imitative of the semi-conscious trainer.

One sniff of the fish was enough for Lyuba. She stopped her wild dance around the kitchen table and slithered across the floor toward us while we slowly backed toward the stairs leading to the dressing room. We'd gotten halfway up to the first landing with Lyuba in pursuit when she suddenly suspected she was being tricked and paused. Relaxing on a stone staircase is not the easiest thing for a seal to do. As soon as she stopped climbing, she lost her hold and slid to the foot of the stairs. We followed after her. I shook Durov to try to make him look alive. The trainer shook the fish and made strange noises. Lyuba changed her mind and decided we were on the level and started after us again. But again she paused, slipped and ended at the foot of the stairs. While this was going on, the kitchen help, the yardman, the janitor and the chauffeurs had gathered around the foot of the stairs shouting encouragement and advice. Each time Lyuba slid back down toward them, they scattered in disorder.

"Get some brooms," I shouted at them. "When she begins to slide the next time, ram the brooms under her and hold her up. All she needs is a little support."

The brooms were quickly produced and three or four of the more courageous souls below followed gingerly after Lyuba as she started once again to clamber after the limp body of her master and – what was no doubt far more attractive – after the pan of very smelly fish. The next time she paused, the brooms held her in place until she could be inveigled into taking a few more steps.

Eventually we reached the head of the stairs and in a few moments she had joined Shura in their dressing room. Then we rounded up Misha who had been going through a series of unrehearsed acts among the guests. Finally the truck was backed up to the side door and the seals were carefully herded down the chute into the truck and off to the Circus. Later I found out that the journey hadn't been entirely without excitement. Halfway home, on a busy boulevard, Lyuba, still restless after her kitchen experience, had jumped over the side of the truck just as she'd leaped over the wall of the chute to the kitchen stairs. In winter the streets of Moscow are usually an icy composition of hard-packed snow as slippery as the best skating rink. Lyuba was in her element and took off down the boulevard at a mile a minute with the trainer's assistant sliding after her. Just how she was finally brought to heel I never discovered, but I do know that half the militia in the Arbat District chased her to the very edge of the Moscow River before they surrounded her.

Back at the Embassy, all that was left of the Circus was Durov. His assistant had promised to come back for him as soon as the seals were put to bed. By the time the assistant got back after Lyuba's second dash for freedom, Durov was again on his feet, not quite sober, but almost his old cheerful self. It took some talking to persuade him that his share of the party was over and that it was time to go home, but only after I'd promised to drive him in my new Ford convertible did he finally agree to go.

The three of us drew up to the Circus building well after three a.m. The trainer and I each gave Durov an arm and helped him into the building and across the ring to the big animal room beyond, where most of the animals were housed. Halfway across the ring a mysterious figure loomed out of the darkness. It was the night-watchman, muffled up in a huge hairy sheepskin overcoat, his rifle slung behind him, the barrel sticking up behind his head like a misplaced horn. "Sh-sh," he whispered out of the mass of fur that completely hid his face. "Go quietly, the elephant's asleep."

I almost dropped Durov in the tanbark. Had all of Moscow gone mad? I looked questioningly at the assistant. He apparently understood my feelings.

"It's all right," he said. "He just means the elephant is lying down. Elephants don't usually lie down to sleep. It's a rare sight."

We tiptoed silently across the ring. Why, I don't know. It was like everything else that night. If we'd had hobnailed boots on, we couldn't have made enough noise on the tanbark to scare a mouse.

In the animal-room we switched on one small light and there, sure enough, was the elephant comfortably stretched out on the straw, sleeping peacefully. The only sensible creature I'd seen all evening, I thought.

As we stood admiring him, there was a rattle of chains down at the far end of the animal-room. In the darkness I couldn't see what had made the noise. But Durov apparently recognized it.

"Dushka, my little soul," he shouted, tore himself from the assistant and dashed into the gloom, his assistant and I right behind him. When we reached the end of the room, I could just make out a huge brown bear standing on his hind legs and tugging at a chain by which he was fastened to the wall. He waved his two great paws petulantly about as he swayed and tugged against the chain.

"Dushka, my little pet," Durov yelled again, and stretched out his arms to hug the bear.

He had almost got his hands around the shaggy beast's neck when his assistant grabbed him by the scruff of his coat and pulled him back.

"You damn fool," he muttered. "It's the wrong bear."

8

POLO FOR THE PROLETARIAT

ASIDE from an occasional handshake and grunt, Genereralissimo Stalin and I have only once exchanged words. The experience was not particularly enlightening for either of us and, I'm afraid, gives me little reason to claim that I "understand the Russians." The occasion was a gala dinner in the Kremlin in September, 1941. The big banquet hall was brilliantly lighted by a half dozen pre-revolutionary candelabra. The main table, studded with carafes of vodka, stretched the length of the hall. Behind it a row of French windows, opening on to the Kremlin courtyard, were "blacked out" with heavy red curtains. Stalin sat at the center of the table dressed in a simple military tunic – the Order of Lenin was his only decoration. On his right sat peppery little Lord Beaverbrook, on his left the American Ambassador. My place as a junior interpreter was way down at the end of an offshoot to the main table.

The dinner started in good Moscow Art Theater style. A series of toasts had been proposed and drunk when the air-raid sirens began to wail. A moment later a battery of antiaircraft guns in the courtyard below opened fire. With each burst a brilliant red flame lit up the curtained windows. For a few moments there was silence throughout the hall, punctuated by the bark of the guns below. Then Stalin rose and raised his glass:

"Gentlemen: To the gunners!"

The firing soon subsided and the banquet progressed through the normal gamut of toasts: to Stalin, to Roosevelt, to Churchill, to Montgomery, to Voroshilov, to Marshall.

The Ambassador sent word to me to fetch some papers for him. As I was delivering them to him at the big table, Lord Beaverbrook suddenly exploded with a string of British vituperation at one of his compatriots sitting near by.

"You damn rum-nosed, straw-chewing vegetarian," he concluded. Stalin's eyebrows rose inquiringly and he turned to the only interpreter in sight:

"And what, may I ask, did Lord Beaverbrook say?"

President Roosevelt had only recently defined U.S. policy as "all-out aid to Britain." As an obedient civil servant, I could hardly ignore it.

"Lord Beaverbrook was commenting on Mr. X's taste in food, sir," I answered.

Stalin grinned skeptically. He never asked me to interpret again.

My interpreting experiences have not always been as fruitless. Nearly eight years before – just after the United States had recognized the Soviet Union – there had been a similar banquet in Moscow. Ambassador Bullitt was giving a dinner for the leading Generals in the Red Army. Our Embassy was not yet ready, so the Ambassador had engaged the banquet hall of the National Hotel. On his right was the War Commissar, Voroshilov, nattily dressed in a white summer tunic glittering with medals and ribbons, his round cherubic face bursting out of his high choke collar. On the Ambassador's left sat General Budyonny, the father of the Red Cavalry, his enormous black mustaches sprouting like outriggers from his upper lip. Around the table were all the leading Soviet military men of the thirties: Yegorov, Tukhachevsky, Khmelnitsky, and a dozen others.[9]

---

9. Semyon Budyonny (1883-1973) was a civil war cavalry general who sided with the Reds and was famous for his large mustache. Mikhail Tukhachevsky (1893-1937) was a Marshal of the Soviet Union and a decorated war hero, but later became a high-profile victim of Stalin's purges. Alexander Yegorov (1883-1939) was a close friend of Budyonny and Stalin but was caught up in the Tukhachevsky trial and died in prison.

It was a real banquet in the best Muscovite tradition. The table was heaped with caviar and foie gras, pheasant and duck. A squad of fast waiters ran around behind the guests filling glasses with half a dozen kinds of vodka, champagne and whiskey.

My post was on a little stool between the Ambassador and Voroshilov. Occasionally, when the current of conversation turned, I would dart around the Ambassador's chair, stool in hand, to interpret for Budyonny. It was a hot sticky evening. I was tired after a hard day's work in the office and I was frankly not happy over my evening assignment.

Interpreting at a banquet is about the most frustrating – and foodless – job I know of. Occasionally you can swallow a glass of vodka between sparks of wit from your interpretees. But eating is out of the question. A waiter puts a plate piled with caviar and toast in front of you. While your interpretees are warming up to the business of conversation, you gingerly pile a piece of toast with caviar... "Tell the General it's a hot night."... You translate and wait for another pause till you can squeeze some lemon on the caviar... More talk... A moment's silence and you sprinkle some chopped onion on the caviar... More talk... Another momentary pause and you raise the toast to your mouth... "Tell the General I like the ballet..." Your hand stops just short of its goal and you translate... A pause, and you raise the piece of toast... "Which ballet does the Ambassador like best?... You lower the toast and translate... The Ambassador hesitates a second, and you snatch at the caviar but... "I think Swan Lake is the best I've seen but of course *Giselle* is excellent too."... Translation... Quick with the caviar, but not quick enough... "And does the Ambassador like the theater too?"...

Eventually you give up, lay the toast untouched on your plate , gulp a glass of vodka – any pause is long enough for that – and resign yourself to a liquid diet.

The conversation purred on in low gear. My mind began to wander: why had I ever left the Army and got mixed up with all this "romance of diplomacy"? I might be at Fort Myer still escorting

The first marshalls of the Soviet Union, 1935. Rear, from left: Semyon Budyonny, Vasily Blyukher. Seated, from left, Mikhail Tukhachevsky, Kliment Voroshilov, Alexander Yegorov.

dead – and speechless – ambassadors to Arlington Cemetery, or even playing polo.

Why not polo here?

"Ask the Commissar where the best summer resorts are in Russia."

I began to translate: "The Ambassador wants to know – why you don't play polo in the Soviet Union." Now, what did I do that for?

VOROSHILOV: "What's polo? We never heard of it."

I turned to the Ambassador: "He says there are many good resorts all over the Soviet Union."

THE AMBASSADOR: "But which does he personally prefer?"

C.W.T. (in Russian): "It's a game you play on horses and it's very good training for cavalrymen."

VOROSHILOV: "How is it played?"

C.W.T. (in English): "The Commissar says he likes all the resorts in the USSR."

THE AMBASSADOR: "Ask him if he ever goes to the Crimea or the Caucasus."

C.W.T. (in Russian): "It's played by two teams of four each with long mallets and a small wooden ball."

VOROSHILOV: "It sounds as though it might be good fun." Turning to Budyonny, he added, "What do you think?"

Budyonny: "Very interesting but who could teach us?"

C.W.T. (in English): "The Commissar and General Budyonny go to both the Crimea and the Caucasus."

THE AMBASSADOR: "What's the best month to go?"

C.W.T. (in Russian): "The Ambasador used to play and so did I – we could teach you."

VOROSHILOV: "Well, if Budyonny agrees, it's okay with me."

C.W.T. (in English): "The Commissar says all the months in the Soviet Union are good, but he wants to know if you could teach the Red Army to play polo." At least we were all back together again.

The change of pace was a bit swift but the Ambassador hardly faltered: "Polo? I teach polo? Why I haven't played in forty years."

C.W.T. (in Russian): "The Ambassador says he's too old to play but he thinks he could referee."

VOROSHILOV: "Splendid. The Ambassador will be Chief Referee and you'll be Senior Polo Instructor to the Red Army. When do we start?"

C.W.T. (in English): "The Commissar suggests you be referee and I'll be instructor. He wants to know if we can begin on Monday."

The Ambassador turned on me. The top of his bald head began to get red. It was a danger signal I knew very well. "What's all this about? How did the subject of polo get started? Where did you come into this conversation? What have you been translating anyway?"

I began to stutter: "I'm sorry, sir, but the conversation sort of got off the rails a little—"

Abruptly the Ambassador's expression changed and he started to laugh: "Tell the Commissar we'll be ready to start as soon as we can get the equipment."

THAT NIGHT, AFTER the guests had gone, I sent a cable to a former teammate then stationed in Texas in the U.S. Cavalry :

"Please ship complete polo equipment less ponies for four teams."

Next day a reply came: "You're nuts."

A second telegram to a less skeptical friend in London soon produced a large case of assorted mallets and balls.

A few days later, the Ambassador and I reported for duty. For the first experiment in Soviet polo, a crack Cavalry regiment of the Moscow Garrison had been selected and twenty of its best horsemen were detailed for the course. As a playing ground we had found a large, gently rolling plain of pastureland, until then used only for sheep grazing. It lay across the Moscow River from Silver Forest, a favorite swimming resort which we frequently visited during the hot summer of 1934. At Silver Forest the river makes a sharp U-turn. Across the top of the U a high barbed-wire fence had been built, leaving the plain – about a mile square – surrounded by water on three sides and by the fence on the fourth.

We assembled at a nearby Cavalry camp and rode to the river, across a shallow ford and onto the plain. The cavalrymen were neatly turned out in regular Russian tunics belted around the waist, the skirts outside their breeches. Their military caps were perched very squarely on their heads. They watched politely as we demonstrated the various strokes of a polo mallet.

After a little while they were each given a ball and mallet and allowed to try for themselves. They were all superb horsemen; before very long, polo balls were flying in all directions. After one ball had hit him sharply on the shin, the Ambassador decided they'd practiced enough. He sorted them into two groups of ten. Then he pointed to a church steeple on the horizon and told one group to hit in that general direction. To the other group he indicated a factory chimney in the opposite direction. "But when you come to the river, stop," he urged them. He went on to explain a few of the rules of the game and told them that when he blew the whistle the game was over.

I tried to translate. None of the players, of course, had ever seen even a picture of a polo game. And the Russian vocabulary – or at least my Russian vocabulary – was anything but rich in polo terms and phrases. When I'd finished, I seriously doubted that they'd understood anything.

They all looked a little puzzled and bewildered as they squared off facing the Ambassador. He tossed the ball between the two teams and the fun began.

For a brief moment there was a dead silence as the ball rolled into the forest of a hundred horses' hooves and mallet heads. Then someone took a swing. There was a loud grunt and a curse as a mallet connected with someone's anatomy. For several minutes the scuffle continued; then the ball popped out of the melee and all twenty horsemen went in mad pursuit. A whirling mallet head hit it again and they galloped on. A series of savage thrusts missed it and the horde converged into another scrimmage. More grunting, more cursing and the agonizing sound of mallets beating against human and equine legs. The ball reappeared and the field strung out in full cry. The leading player swung viciously, missed and pulled up abruptly. The next man behind crashed into him, almost throwing them both. In a moment the ball had again disappeared among the horses' legs.

They were warming up fast. At first the Ambassador galloped along beside the mob warning them of fouls, but it soon was obvious that no one was paying attention to anything but the ball. One of the keenest of the twenty was a little Mongol from Central Asia. At first he plunged furiously into every scrimmage, twirling his mallet and letting out strange war whoops. Then I caught sight of him lurking away from the mob. At that moment the ball shot out of the scrimmage with the rest of the players in pursuit. The Mongol drove his spurs into his horse and flew at the ball at right angles to the charging crowd. It was obvious that if something didn't give way, there was going to be a collision. The Mongol let out an exultant scream. Perhaps he thought he could frighten the rest away. But everyone held to his course. There was a dull thud and a cry of pain as three horses galloped full speed into each other. The Mongol's horse staggered and fell. The two others stumbled and came down on top of him. Placidly the ball rolled on down the meadow, with the rest of the players in mad pursuit.

"That was a foul," I said to the Ambassador as we hurried to the spot where the horses had fallen. "Foul – hell," said the Ambassador. "That was murder."

Even before we reached them, the horses had staggered to their feet, and their riders were walking about slightly dazed, but otherwise apparently all right. The little Mongol had a gash on his closely shaved scalp and his tunic was in shreds. But in another second he'd mounted his horse and was galloping off after the other players, still yelling at the top of his voice.

The game had been going for about fifteen minutes when the Ambassador pulled up, announced that it was enough for the first chukker and solemnly blew his whistle. The horde continued to gallop and shout and strike out viciously at the ball. He blew again. Several of the players looked at him with uncomprehending glances. One or two grinned, obviously amused at the sight of His Excellency sitting majestically on his horse and piping shrilly on a little whistle.

As I went by, the Ambassador shouted, "Did you explain to them to stop when I blew the whistle?" Taking my cue from the players, I pretended not to hear and hurried on. The Ambassador took off after me.

Another ten minutes went by. By this time, the Ambassador was beginning to get a little annoyed at his inability to stop the charge he had set in motion. He eventually cornered me by the riverbank.

"Did you or did you not tell them to stop when I blew my whistle?" he shouted angrily.

"I'm sorry – I guess maybe – I don't remember."

The Ambassador was roaring now: "Did you or—"

"I must have skipped that part, sir. I'm very sorry." "Well, damn it! Then you stop them! I can't. They'll die of apoplexy if they go on much longer – or their horses will."

I nodded respectfully to the Ambassador and stared helplessly at the cloud of dust half a mile down the meadow. "I'll try," I murmured meekly and spurred my horse toward the horde, shouting: "*Stoi! Stoi!*" A few sweaty, blood-smeared cavalrymen stared at me for a second, grinned maliciously and rushed on after the ball.

Snatching up an extra mallet, I decided to join the scramble and see if I couldn't break it up. The next time the ball darted from the scrimmage, I dashed at it at right angles to the charging crowd. I swung mightily, missed, and spurred on as twenty horses, bug-eyed with excitement, skimmed past my horse's tail at a dead run. I tried again, this time more successfully. The ball sailed into the air for a hundred yards, I after it, still shouting over my shoulder: "Stop! Stop! His Excellency wants you to stop."

The troop turned toward the ball and galloped on. I could almost feel the eighty hooves on my neck as I steadied the horse for another shot. Ordinarily there's a big thrill to carrying the ball out in front of a polo game. But there also is a certain amount of orderliness to the game – some rules and a referee. This time there was nothing but a wild, bloodthirsty and sweat-grimed horde to deal with. The frustrated Ambassador had long since lost his grip as referee. There was not even a goal post or a backline to stop them. Just the river and the fence – for whatever they were worth.

I hit again and the ball bounced on. Several hundred yards beyond lay the river. If I could only get that far and send the ball into the water...

I dug my spurs in and struck again. The ball swerved to the side. I nearly threw my horse turning to it, but too late. My quick-eyed pupils had cut across to the ball and were already laying about themselves with their mallets.

They had stopped shouting now and merely grunted thunderously as they lurched at the little ball. The horses, white with lather, were breathing heavily. Steam and dust arose in clouds from the tight knot. Once more the ball came out of the pack. I lunged madly and got it moving toward the river. A challenging shout rose from the galloping riders behind. There was no longer any doubt as to who was on whose side. It was twenty to one and the river was nearly two hundred yards away. Out of the corner of my eye I caught sight of the Ambassador trotting leisurely along at one side. He seemed to be laughing.

I struck savagely at the ball. It bounced into the air a few feet in front. I swung the mallet again and caught the ball a few inches off the ground. This time I connected and the ball sailed over the remaining yards and landed with a splash in the Moscow River.

I pulled up my horse and slumped exhausted in the saddle. Right behind me the charging mob pulled up and glared first at me and then at the river. Then one of them drove his spurs into his horse, leaped down the bank into the shallow stream and disappeared in a shower of water. Before I could collect my wits, he emerged ball in hand, and hurled it back onto the field. The roaring mob were on it in a flash, and galloping away down the field in triumph.

I stared at the sight and groaned helplessly. But the Ambassador was at me in a second:

"Get on with you, damn it! They'll kill themselves if you don't stop them soon."

By the time I caught up with the melee, they were well in the middle of the meadow. Another run to the river was beyond my strength, to say nothing of my exhausted horse. We had been galloping ceaselessly for nearly an hour.

The next time the ball came out of the whirling mass, I darted at it and swung the mallet as hard as I could. The ball spurted forward fifty yards. I slipped my feet from the stirrups and steadied my pony. There was just a chance I could fall on the ball before the crowd reached me.

From where he was standing, the Ambassador told me later, all he could see was his Secretary roll from his saddle in front of the charging mob. Then the milling horses shut off his view. When eventually the Ambassador forced his way through the crowd, I was lying huddled on the ground, the polo ball tucked under my arm like a fumbled football. Twenty faces black with dust and sweat looked down at me, half-angry, half-amused.

I looked up: "Please," I panted. "Enough! Promise?" A roar of laughter greeted my appeal.

The Camp Commander, coming out of his tent, stopped dead in his tracks and stared down the road leading to the river. The neat platoon of horsemen he'd dispatched earlier on Budyonny's orders for some sort of diplomatic folderol looked as though they were returning from the Civil War. A few still wore their tunics – sleeves torn and buttons gone, but most were stripped to the waist. Several had handkerchiefs tied around their heads. Little trickles of blood oozed down their cheeks. One had improvised an arm sling from which a bloody fist protruded. At the rear of the column two troopers walked, leading a pair of limping mounts beside them.

At the head of the column, in slightly better shape, rode the American Ambassador and beside him, hunched in his saddle, the remnants of his Private Secretary.

The Ambassador grinned down at me m grandfatherly fashion:

"Of course, it may be difficult at first to remember to translate everything I say, but with a little practice, you'll catch on."

'I'll try," I replied humbly.

THE FOLLOWING DAY Budyonny telephoned:

"Sorry I couldn't make it to your first tryouts yesterday, but according to reports from the Cavalry camp, it seems to have been a great success. The only complaint is they don't seem to have the right sort of horses. Could you describe what kind of horses you use for polo in America?"

The Ambassador explained that it would be better if they could get a few young, three-quarter bred animals, five or six years old, around fifteen hands high. They should be broken, but not schooled. The players and I would do the schooling ourselves.

"How many do you need?" Budyonny asked.

"Well, in America, each player has three, sometimes four for a game, but that many isn't necessary here."

"We'll see what can be done," Budyonny answered and rang off.

Three weeks went by without word about polo ponies. But we kept on with our polo practice almost every day after office hours. It became a little more restrained than the first attempt, and gradually the players began to catch on to some of the rules and penalties. Then we got a call from Cavalry Headquarters:

"Comrade Budyonny would like to know whether the Ambassador could meet him at the Cavalry Barracks this afternoon at three. He has a few of those polo ponies he'd like to show you."

We found Budyonny on the parade ground with his aides and the Garrison Cavalry Commander. At a nod from Budyonny, soldiers began to lead the ponies from the stables past our little group.

The first horse was a little bay gelding with the fine legs of a thoroughbred and the round lines of a Cossack pony. The Garrison Commander explained: "Five years old; three-quarter thoroughbred; one-quarter Kuban; fifteen hands high. He's been broken but not schooled."

"Exactly the type we need," the Ambassador commented enthusiastically .

The second horse, except for his sleek chestnut coat, was almost identical with the first.

"Five and one-half years; three-quarter bred from the Don country; broken but not schooled."

"Superb!" the Ambassador said.

A third, a bay mare from western Siberia answered the same description.

I began to figure that they were putting their best foot forward, so to speak, and showing us a few prize selections to start with. But as the line from the stable grew longer my eyes began to pop out.

Every animal they led out was as good as the one before. This was a collection that even the U.S. Cavalry could hardly have produced.

After fifteen or twenty had passed by, the Ambassador, obviously as amazed as I was, asked: "But how many are there?"

"Sixty-four," replied the Garrison Commander in a flat, matter-of-fact tone.

"Good Lord! This *is* a polo string!"

"But that's what you told us, isn't it?" Budyonny said. "Four horses for each player – four teams makes sixteen players. I guess we can afford as many as you Americans."

As the last of the sixty-four went by, a big chestnut charger was led up, saddled and bridled :

"And this is the sixty-fifth – for His Excellency, the referee. Would you like to try him out?"

While the Ambassador mounted his horse, I sidled up to one of the aides and asked:

"How did you ever manage to get this collection together?"

"Easy," he said. "Budyonny just sent a telegram to all the horse farms in the Union and told them to report what horses they had that met your specifications. Then he ordered the best ones shipped to Moscow."

Several more weeks went by while we schooled the ponies and taught the players the game. Then finally the day arrived for the first formal polo match in the Soviet Union.

It was a hot September afternoon and the beach by the ford was crowded with swimmers. It was still before the days when nude bathing was decreed uncultured in the Soviet Union, and the only compromise that they'd made so far was a board fence between the women's beach and the men's. The ford from the camp to the "polo field" crossed the women's beach. But by this time they were so used to seeing us ride by each day that they didn't even turn their heads as we passed – even though we were all decked out in bright blue and red polo shirts provided for the occasion by one of the Moscow Sports Clubs.

Earlier in the day a regiment of foot soldiers had marched down the beach and splashed across the river to the plain. On the other side they had deployed, and standing at about arm's length apart, had formed a giant circle almost a mile in diameter. They were, in fact, so far from the actual field, and so well concealed by the folds in the ground that they were practically out of sight of the spectators.

Even this had not caused much notice among the bathers. People are accustomed to all kinds of military maneuvers in the Soviet Union.

What did bring the naked ladies to their feet was a convoy of long black limousines which plowed across the sand, through the ford and disappeared on the plain beyond.

I imagine some of the bathers found out what it was all about the next day when they read in *Pravda* about the polo game at Silver Forest. Only very few people actually watched the match – the circle of soldiers saw to that. But the audience, though small, was about as select as any that ever collected at Meadowbrook. Litvinov, the Foreign Commissar; Voroshilov, the War Commissar; several members of the Politburo, Ambassador Bullitt with a few of his staff, and a handful of carefully chosen Soviet and American newspaper correspondents.

The Ambassador's Private Secretary was on the blue team. The game itself probably didn't approach Meadowbrook standards but it was exciting enough and hard enough for anyone's taste. My team was beaten. (Later I was undeservedly complimented for my diplomacy in letting the other side win.)

After the game, players and spectators came to the Embassy for a party that lasted nearly till morning. The only thing that went wrong there was that Midget, my police dog puppy, misbehaved in the War Commissar's lap.

ALL THROUGH THE summer the polo continued. When the snow came, practice was transferred to a large riding hall in the city. Then gradually some of the best players began to drop out.

"Maneuvers," the Commander explained.

Elsewhere, other events were taking place that had little to do with polo. Goering announced that Germany was developing an Air Force.

At a parade in Berlin, the German Army unveiled a new mobile cannon.

The papers reported that the Reich was organizing new mechanized divisions.

You didn't hear much about the German Cavalry in those days, and nothing at all about German polo.

One day in the early spring, they telephoned from the Cavalry Barracks and said there would be no practice that day. All the troops were off on maneuvers.

"When they return," the Commander explained politely, "I'll let you know."

The troops were still on maneuvers, for all we know, when war broke out six years later.

But so far as I'm aware, I'm still Senior Polo Instructor to the Red Army.

9

A DIPLOMATIC KOLKHOZ

One day in a fit of exuberance, I slid down the banisters at the Embassy and sprained my ankle. The Embassy doctor ordered me to bed and Ambassador Bullitt bought a police dog puppy to keep me amused. John Wiley, the Embassy Counselor, usually referred to her as the "secret police" dog and I admit she didn't look exactly like the German police dogs I'd seen before. But when she eventually grew up, she turned out to be a black Belgian shepherd – a Grönendael, much to the surprise of all of us, especially myself as I'd never heard of a Groenendael before.

"Midget" (I named her after a minute Moscow ballerina) was a little smaller than the ordinary German police dog and much lighter. Her coat was jet black and long and silky – if and when I combed her. As a puppy she behaved no differently from any other dog and promptly destroyed all my shoes and most of the Ambassador's. She was still very young when she was introduced into Moscow Society. At the first party she was allowed to come to, as I've already described, she sat in Marshall Voroshilov's lap and succeeded in giving his breeches a slight wetting. But he took it well and after a sponging off took Midget back onto his lap.

As she grew, however, her ability to get into trouble got out of all proportion to her self-control and the damage she did increased correspondingly. So I started looking for a trainer for her only to find that all the dog trainers in Moscow belonged to the GPU. However,

Charles Thayer (right) with Ambassador William Bullitt, examining a cup and saucer at a china factory in Moscow.

the GPU very kindly consented to take her on and for three months she went to boarding school with Stalin's secret police.

When she came back she was the proud possessor of the canine equivalent of a Soviet Ph.D, consisting of a large red and yellow enamel medal with her name and grade (Excellent) inscribed on the back.

Later the medal turned out to be quite useful. In 1939, just before the war broke out, I was stationed in Hamburg and living at the Atlantic Hotel there. One evening I came home tired and in a bad humor to find that Hermann Goering had moved into the hotel for the weekend. As a result I wasn't allowed to park my car where it usually stayed. I wasn't allowed in the front door until I'd been inspected by the police and then I could hardly squeeze through Goering's bemedaled and beribboned attendants to the elevator and upstairs. When I finally got to my room, I was so annoyed at Goering for all his ridiculous henchmen that, after I had dressed for dinner, I took the red silk sash off my bathrobe, tied it over one shoulder and across my chest as though it were the Order of St. George. Then I covered it with every pin I could lay hands on. There were tie pins, collar pins, safety pins, just plain pins and, in the middle, Midget's Soviet Ph.D. There was a good deal of curiosity as I got into the elevator. But when my fellow passengers got a closer look at my decorations, their reactions were, as I'd hoped, just about as hot as mine had been when I arrived at the hotel. However, they merely snarled at me and I managed to get out of the hotel in my own skin – sash and all.

Among the tricks the GPU had taught Midget was one that made her diplomatic career a success. If you put a piece of sugar in front of her and told her it was a present from Hitler (or John Jones for that matter) she would turn her nose up in disdain and not touch it. You could name half the world's population with the same reaction until you pointed at the sugar with just the slightest movement of a finger. Then she'd jump for it. I showed the trick to everyone from Kings to porters, always, of course, pointing when I called the name of the person I was showing it to. I never found one whose ego didn't expand like a rubber balloon when Midget jumped for the sugar. They seemed to think I'd sat up half the night teaching Midget their name. I'm inclined to think most people would rather have a good reputation with a dog than with the majority of their fellowmen.

About a year after we got to Moscow, several of us Embassy bachelors got ourselves a dacha, which, in Russian, means a country bungalow. Midget was moved out there to the great relief of the Ambassador and spent the rest of her Moscow tour there.

Some time later she was joined by another dog, a Japanese spaniel, which was given to me by the daughter of the Japanese Ambassador, Togo. Just to show I wasn't anti-Japanese, I named the spaniel Togo.

It was a good name, I thought, until one day when the entire Togo family came out to the dacha for tea.

At the time, the dacha was under the slightly erratic care of an old Russian servant called George. George had had a distinguished career of making the wrong decision every time in his life he'd been confronted with a choice. Before the Revolution, he'd been a pants-presser and somehow or other had managed to establish himself in London. When the Revolution broke out, he decided revolutions were a very good thing and came home via Siberia to help the Soviets along. But then by chance he met Kolchak's troops in Siberia and spent the rest of the Civil War fighting against the Soviets. After a brief stay in the salt mines, he came back and decided to join up with the American concessionaires who were being tolerated by the Soviets so they could get a little badly needed foreign cash. As soon as there was enough cash, the concessions were liquidated and George was sent for three years to the notorious prison at Solovetski in the White Sea to think things over. After that he decided to join forces with Trotsky until the latter got into trouble with Stalin and George spent a year or so in Central Asia. When he got through with that, he concluded that the Americans were pretty good people even though they might get you into trouble. So he joined u p with Hearst's International News Service, then about the most unpopular institution in all Russia. Not long after he joined up, the INS was liquidated just as Kolchak, the concessionaires and Trotsky had been. This time, however, George was getting old and decided he didn't want to go away again so he appealed to us to take him to the dacha where he remained for the rest of his useful life as butler and pants-presser.

All of which has only a faint connection with the spaniel or the time the Togas came to tea. It was a most unfortunate coincidence that teatime was also feed-time for the dogs. As we sat under the trees making polite conversation with the Japanese Ambassador and his family, George appeared from the house with a bowl of slops and walked across the lawn calling plaintively for the spaniel, "Togo, Togo, Togo." There was an embarrassed silence at the tea. Suddenly

George realized, a little late, what he'd done and ran like a jackrabbit back into the house.

The next day the Dean of the Diplomatic Corps, the German Ambassador, Count von der Schulenburg, sent for me. "Is it true," he said, "that one of your dogs is named after the Japanese Ambassador?"

I said it was and that it was an old American custom to show your affection for a friend by naming a dog after him. Schulenburg frowned skeptically.

"Well, it's obviously not an old Japanese custom and the Japanese Ambassador is hopping mad."

I said I was sorry but that after all I couldn't be expected to know every old Japanese folkway. Besides, the dog was young and undisciplined and if I changed her name now she'd not only be impossible to manage but might get some incurable psychological complex. But Schulenburg was firm and after considerable dickering I agreed, for the sake of good relations, to change the dog's name to Hobo. Perhaps the spaniel wouldn't notice it or at least would not get too upset over two new consonants.

The day Ambassador Togo left for Tokyo, where he later became Foreign Minister, I asked Schulenburg on the station platform if he didn't think it would be all right now to change Hobo back to Togo. Schulenburg thought it over and said he guessed it would be all right if I didn't tell too many people.

Some years later, when Sir Stafford Cripps arrived in Moscow as British Ambassador, he asked me to help find him a police dog. I looked up my old dog-loving contacts and they promised to produce a few to choose from. Several days later they turned up with a pack of Airedales. "I said Sir Stafford wanted a police dog," I told them. "These are police dogs," they answered, "and damn good ones. Just because they aren't German shepherds doesn't mean they can't be police dogs. Besides, we hardly thought Sir Stafford would want a German police dog seeing as how he's at war with Hitler."

Sir Stafford appreciated their arguments and took one of the Airedales. He called it Joe and no one said anything. But then, he was an Ambassador and I was a Third Secretary.

Eventually, when the Germans attacked Russia and drove us out of Moscow I left Togo behind. I thought maybe the Germans would like a Japanese spaniel. But the Germans never got into the capital and I don't know to this day what became of the spaniel. Old Count Schulenburg was hanged for participating in the putsch to overthrow Hitler in 1944 and Ambassador Togo died in a Tokyo prison in 1950 while serving a long sentence as a war criminal. George died peacefully in a home for the aged near Moscow.

The dacha itself was nothing more than a slightly overgrown log cabin, but it had been "modernized" by a Lithuanian diplomat from whom we took it over. He had dug a well, installed a pump and tank, a bathroom and shower, a tennis court and garden, a duck pond and most important of all, a high wooden fence to separate the dacha from the nearby village. There was always something very comforting about driving through those big wooden gates after a long hard day trying to understand the Russians. When the gates closed behind you, the Soviet Union, the Five-Year-Plan and, best of all, the GPU, seemed to disappear from existence.

The garden stretched down the lawn in front of the house and beyond it all you saw were fields and woods. We had a little trouble with the garden from time to time. For one thing we discovered to our horror that there was no mint in it. But we telegraphed to Holland for some roots and straightened that situation out before the julep season opened. Then we got a gardener whose favorite flower was tobacco plant or nicotiana. It is the only plant I have any really strong dislike for. It has all the faults of a streetwalker and none of the advantages. It blooms only at night, has a very strong, disagreeable, pungent smell and has a way of turning up where you least want it. Eventually we fired the nicotiana gardener and got another one whose passion was roses. Once, when I went on home leave, he persuaded me to bring back from America a dozen tea-rose plants.

The Soviet Government had already accused a Japanese diplomat of distributing bouquets infested with Japanese beetles along the Trans-Siberian railroad and a strange "Mr. Brown" had been charged in *Pravda* with spreading "pink worms" among the Soviet cotton fields by means of some cuttings he had treacherously given to a Soviet cotton expert as a "gift." So when I brought back the rose bushes I took care to put them in a diplomatic pouch where they couldn't be seen and seized by Soviet Customs inspectors.

On my way back from leave I opened the rose-pouches in the Embassy at Paris to give them a breath of fresh air before they started off on the last lap of their trip. I was just a little bewildered when I discovered that they were already sprouting leaves and buds as though the diplomatic pouch were a greenhouse. I hurried on to Moscow and put them into the garden before their enthusiasm had carried them too far, and eventually they turned out to be quite a success. There was only one slight difficulty with them. Each tea rose had a label with its name conspicuously printed on it. One, I remember, was called Mrs. Franklin D. Roosevelt and another Herbert Hoover. Each spring regularly Herbert Hoover burst into bloom days and sometimes weeks before Mrs. Roosevelt even got started, to the acute embarrassment of ourselves, employees of a Democratic administration. After several years of worrying I finally solved the problem by switching the labels and from then on Mrs. Roosevelt did splendidly.

Our final addition to the dacha was a stable of three horses. It took months of searching, dickering, bribing and protesting before we finally got ourselves three so-called riding horses. They were in fact just undersized farm horses but we pretended not to know the difference and gradually by some sharp trading over a period of years managed to exchange them for some fairly reasonable horses.

But our biggest trouble was getting a decent groom. Either they promptly sold all the oats we bought to the local *droshky* drivers or else they installed themselves and several wives and children in the tiny stable and settled down to live off the land.

After we'd fired half a dozen we finally found Pantelemon, one of the outstanding grooms of the twentieth century. Pantelemon was a small bow-legged Cavalry soldier of the old school. He invariably wore an old Czarist Army cap and sported an elegant ivory cigarette holder which he manipulated with the same bravado as Franklin Roosevelt. Pantelemon assured us that above all his other virtues we could trust him absolutely implicitly as a gentleman of his Imperial Majesty's Cavalry. Furthermore, Pantelemon explained, he was so anxious to be in the company of other gentlemen, that he would work for practically nothing. He had, he explained, a particularly large soul even for a Russian and the narrow life he was being forced to lead among the proletariat was stifling him. Before he was through with us Pantelemon had bought himself the building rights on a plot of land adjoining the dacha, and had built himself a three-room bungalow. When we asked him how he'd managed it he explained he'd done it all with his own hands.

When he applied for the job he told us he was a bachelor and always had been, but within four days of his arrival we discovered an old woman later known as the *babushka* living in the feedbin. When we asked who she was, Pantelemon twirled his long gray Cavalry mustaches and explained she was just an old friend of the family who'd come to pay a call. She was still calling nearly five years later when the Germans chased us out of Moscow.

One day we invited an old German General to go riding with us and in the course of preparing the horses Pantelemon told him that he'd taken part in the battle of Tannenberg, the first great defeat of the Czarist armies in World War I. The German pricked up his ears and asked him what Russian division he'd been with, for he too had fought at Tannenberg.

"His Imperial Majesty's Fifth Household Cavalry Division," Pantelemon answered with a flourish of his cigarette holder.

"But how did you manage to get away then?" the General asked. "I happen to know that particular division was killed or captured to the last man."

"Sir," said Pantelemon, puffing out his chest and blowing a cloud of smoke from his cigarette, "my father brought me up to be a jockey."

When we first got the horses, we managed to convince the local authorities that we were a collective farm and consequently entitled to buy feed at the cheap Government price. The authorities had hesitated at first but when we asked them if they'd ever heard of a private stable in the Soviet Union they admitted they couldn't imagine such a phenomenon. Besides, we suggested, the Moscow Oblast agricultural statistics would look pretty funny if they could only report they were 99.9 per cent collectivized. So after scratching their heads a bit, they gave in and we got our grain at the Government price just like any other collective farm. The system worked for several years but then some snooping inspector began to study our legal status a little more carefully and got the lawyers reading the books and finally came out with a decision that we were really rich peasants or *kulaks* who'd managed to escape liquidation because of our diplomatic immunity. *Kulaks*, he decreed, could only buy oats on the open market.

By this time the dacha had become the central meeting place of most of the diplomats in Moscow. Two days a week we kept open house and our colleagues from half the countries of the world flocked out to play tennis in summer or ski and skate in winter. To take care of them we kept a staff of eight or ten servants and naturally our cellar always showed a rapid turnover. For all this, princely old Uncle Sam gave us a handsome sum of about a hundred dollars a year as an "entertainment allowance." It just about took care of one month's rent.

So when the Horse Feed Trust told us to go on to the open market for our hay and oats, where the prices were four times higher than in the Government stores, it looked as though we were going to be liquidated along with all the other *kulaks* after all. But then some of our colleagues came to the rescue. The British and the Germans each agreed to buy half a horse. The scheme worked beautifully until the war started in 1939. Immediately an argument began as to who owned which end of the horse. The fact that we sold our manure to the collective farm only added to the cost differential between the horse's head and the horse's tail. For weeks the argument raged back and forth, complicated by the fact that the Germans couldn't speak to their former English friends and the English were under instructions "to bow but not smile" when they met their enemy colleagues. (I always thought it would have been much more effective to smile but not bow, but the Foreign Office thought otherwise.) The argument was only settled when I issued an ultimatum that since I'd made the original sales I could decide that the horse was divided from stem to stern and not from side to side. The Germans and British admitted that was fair enough and things settled down to their normal routine until the Germans up and attacked the Russians in 1941. It was obvious that there wasn't going to be much more galloping around the Soviet countryside for pleasure from then on in, and that the only thing to do was get rid of the stable as quickly as possible.

I called the Chief of Cavalry of the Red Army, Marshall Budyonny, and told him that as a gesture of anti-Hitlerite solidarity I wanted to present my horses to the Red Army. He thanked me warmly but explained there was no procedure in the Red Army for accepting gifts. Would I be prepared to sell? I said I was very disappointed, but when I recalled what my bank balance was I agreed to the compromise. A day or two later an officer appeared at the dacha to "evaluate" the stable. Before showing him the horses I took him inside and offered him a glass or two of vodka. It was a long time before we managed to get him out into the stable-yard, but eventually he swayed out of the dacha and took a look through slightly glazed eyes at the three animals. Without a second's hesitation he said the Red Army would give me the equivalent of six hundred dollars for them – about double what I'd originally paid. That same afternoon some soldiers came to take the horses away. It was sad watching them prance out the gate for the last time after so many years but when I looked at the bundle of rubles in my hand I couldn't help wondering how many horses the officer thought he'd bought.

But then came the payoff. The English half-owner was still with us in Moscow and I gave him a share of the profits, but the German had been interned and shipped off the morning the war broke out. In 1950 when I was transferred to Germany I finally caught up with him in a nightclub in Düsseldorf. When I handed him a check for a hundred dollars, he seemed to have forgotten the half a horse he'd left behind in Moscow nine years before.

The collective farm across the fields from the dacha was in a sense our nearest neighbor for the high wooden fence shut us off completely from the village behind us. In front of the garden the land dropped off sharply into a little valley of scrub ash. Beyond, it rose again into the fields of the collective farm. To the left you could see the forest that stretched off to the west as far as Stalin's dacha, just six miles beyond us. We often rode through those woods but never quite as far as Stalin's home because, for some reason or other, as we got close to it, little leather-coated men would spring out from behind the trees and ask for our documents. I'm afraid we gave the little men a good deal of trouble because our standard reply was "Where are *your* documents?"

This always annoyed them and they would stamp up and down and insist it was none of our business who they were.

"Well, obviously if you're just some curious Soviet citizen who wants to look at documents, go climb a tree. Prove you have a right to see my documents and I'd be only too glad to show them to you."

Eventually they broke down and showed us their documents and our little game lost its point. But later on I got from home a cellophane passholder. In it I put my diplomatic card folded so that the photograph was on the inside. Then I got a postcard of Comrade Stalin taken a good many years ago when his mustaches were large and flowing and inserted it, face out, behind the diplomatic card. Each time I presented the holder the little men would read it carefully, and then solemnly turn it over to find Stalin's beaming face staring at them. It was always a pleasure to watch their faces.

But to return to the collective farm across the hill. Our relations with it from the first had been excellent. They sold us some straw and hay, on the side, and we sold them our manure. Sometimes we went over there on holidays and joined them in their dances and celebrations – usually with a couple of bottles of vodka in our pockets to add to the gaiety. We had several rather special friends in the collective. There was Peter, who delivered the straw to us, and his daughter Anna, a short stout red-faced girl of about twenty, who was the leading young Communist among the farmers and the only one who could drive the farm tractor. Then there was the President of the farm who was forever showing us the latest improvements they'd made. Whenever they built a new cow barn or a tractor shed or a beet cellar he'd insist on our coming over to admire it. We didn't know much about cows or tractors and nothing at all about beet cellars so it was always a little hard to know just what to say but evidently our "oh's" and "ah's" were good enough because he always came back for more.

One day I was riding through the fields by the collective village when the President caught sight of me and called me. I trotted over.

"Karl Georgovitch," he shouted, "we've just bought a new potato-planter that's perfectly wonderful. It does the work of six men. We're just trying it out now in the field beyond the stream. Come down with me and see how it works."

We went down across the stream where half the village was gathered for the great tryout. Anna and some of the younger fry were still busily trying to attach the tongue of the brand new, bright red potato-planter to the tractor. At the edge of the fields, half a dozen old men were sitting in a group chewing grass and watching the proceedings with obvious amusement. They were the old timers of the village who had never thought much of the collective and even less of the innovations it was trying to introduce. But there was nothing they could do about it all except sneer and do as little work as possible.

Eventually the potato-planter was attached to the tractor with the aid of a certain amount of old rope and baling wire. Anna got on the tractor and someone started to crank it up. But for some reason it wouldn't start until a small boy jiggled the carburetor to keep the gas flowing. Whenever he got tired and stopped jiggling the engine died, so he climbed up under Anna's feet, flattened himself out on the chassis and settled down to become a permanent part of the machinery.

Anna put the tractor in gear, raced the motor, and started off with a flourish – backward. Before she could stop, the potato-planter had backed in the ditch and the tongue had snapped neatly in two. After a good deal of consultation, with the old men contributing some rather cutting comment on collectivization in general and machines in particular, they eventually managed to fix the broken tongue and within another half hour they were ready to go.

But in the meantime a connecting bolt in the tractor tread had come loose, so that another young man with a hammer was obliged to trot along beside it, hitting the bolt back into place every time it came around.

When everything was ready again, Anna took a little more care with the gear shift and this time started off with a roar down the field, the potato-planter bobbing nicely behind.

"Wonderful, isn't it?" said the President who had been watching the proceedings beside my horse. "Wonderful how one machine does the work of so many people."

Then one of the old men who'd been sitting by jeering went out into the field and began to grub in the tracks left by the planter.

"That's a fine planter," he shouted to his cronies, "but I'd like it better if it planted."

The younger set looked worried and began grubbing in the field too, but no seedlings could be found.

By this time Anna had turned around and was roaring back to home plate. When she came to a stop another period of consultation and examination took perhaps another half hour before it was decided that the potato seedlings were larger than the holes they were supposed to go through in the planter.

"Well, we'll just have to shove them through," said Anna. And in a few minutes three more women armed with broomsticks had perched themselves on the rear of the planter and by working the broomsticks like pistons managed to get the potatoes moving in the right way.

The tractor was brought up again to the starting line. Anna let out the clutch and off they went.

"Wonderful," said the President for the tenth time, "and to think it does the work of six."

The boy under Anna's feet jiggled the carburetor. The young man with the hammer trotted breathless beside the tread slamming periodically at the loose bolt. The three old women poked their broomsticks and Anna beamed proudly. There were exactly six of them.

10

HUNTING A LA RUSSE

Before the Revolution liquidated the upper classes and abolished privilege, hunting was one of the most popular sports in Russia. But after the Revolution, when permission to carry firearms was restricted to the police, the Army and a handful of the formerly underprivileged, there were only a few hunters still active.

However, once we got to know our way around, we in the Embassy were able to find ways and means of getting out into the villages to shoot at whatever game came our way. Not that I ever did much damage. In fact my hunting friends generally conceded that I was the best friend our feathered friends had ever had.

Some of my companions were more successful and every now and then even my gun brought down a partridge or a pheasant. But whether I hit anything or not, there were few pleasanter ways of spending an evening after a day of frustrating getting-along-with-the-Russians, than sitting in some birch forest just before the sun went down and waiting for a woodcock to come whistling through the red and gold foliage.

These expeditions had a dual purpose. In Moscow itself we were so cut off from the local population that we seldom had a chance to find out "what the Russian masses were thinking." Once out in the villages though, the peasants showed no such restraint and talked incessantly about their woes. I don't pretend it was exactly the most scientific way of testing public opinion, but it was the best we could do. If Gallup should smile at our amateur efforts, I'd be tempted to think of November, 1948, and smile right back.

Occasionally we even went as far as the Caucasus looking for game to shoot at and public opinion to report on. Chip Bohlen and I were setting out on an expedition to Baku one day when we discovered General Budyonny, the Chief of the Red Cavalry, on the train with us. On the station platform Budyonny greeted us rather curtly but once we were underway and out of sight of the Moscow plainclothes men, the old General got friendlier.

Trains in Russia are not particularly fast and we were still north of Rostov by the evening of the second day. Chip and I had had dinner and were reading in our compartment when the door opened and Budyonny's enormous mustaches appeared.

"Have you got any of that '*Amerikansky vino*' you gave me at the Embassy?" he asked.

"American wine? We didn't serve any wine, I don't think. What did it look like?"

"It was brown stuff," Budyonny explained, "and plenty strong. Vist... vistee? Viskee – yes, that's it. You call it viskee."

"Whiskey! Sure! We've got lots. Wouldn't you like a drink?"

"Not just now. We're coming into Rostov soon and I have to make a speech to some comrades on the platform there. But after Rostov I'll be along."

It must have been a fairly long speech because the train stood in Rostov for almost an hour and it was ten o'clock before Budyonny's mustaches appeared again in the doorway.

"I'm free now. Nothing to do till tomorrow morning when we get to Nalchik Junction. Stalin is going to meet me there for some boar shooting."

He sat down between us, poured himself a tumblerful of straight Scotch, knocked it back at one gulp and roared contentedly. He put an arm around each of us, told us he thought all Americans were wonderful and gave us each a loud wet kiss on the cheek, his bristling mustaches tickling us violently in the ear as he hugged us affectionately.

Then we settled down to some serious drinking. The trouble was there was no drinking water – or water of any kind for that matter – on the train. At Budyonny's suggestion we bought a watermelon at the next stop, cut a hole in it, poured a quart of whiskey in and drank the mixture that came out of the melon. I can't say it was an improvement over straight whiskey, but at least it was a little diluted.

Some thirteen hours later, two of our original stock of five quarts of Scotch were left but Budyonny was still going strong when the conductor came to remind him we were coming to Nalchik Junction in ten minutes. Budyonny tossed off one final tumbler of "*Amerikansky vino*" and got up to go.

"Stalin might be down to meet me and I wouldn't want him to catch me drunk and disorderly with a couple of young Americans," he explained as he disappeared into his compartment.

When the train came to a stop, he reappeared, shaven, brushed and looking as though he'd just waked up from a good night's sleep. It was all Chip and I could do to stumble onto the platform to say goodbye. Then we crawled into our berths and slept till they called us at Baku the next afternoon.

The next time I saw Budyonny in Moscow I asked him how he'd managed to get through the first day of his vacation. "shot five wild boar," he replied laconically. "Big ones, too."

The shooting in Baku was not all it was cracked up to be, but the local hospitality turned out to be well above normal. We took a train up to Daghestan, where the North Caucasus Mountains butt into the Caspian Sea. But the pheasants had apparently got word of our plans and disappeared. Then we went down to shoot some duck in the marshes near Baku. There were some duck there, but not enough to hold us for long. So finally we arranged an expedition to shoot gazelle in the desert, along the banks of the Kura River. Our host, Comrade Babaev, was the local head of Intourist and had orders from Moscow to give us the works – it was 1934 and still the honeymoon period of Soviet-American relations and nothing was too good for us – or too expensive. Babaev was a man of big ideas with a passion for shooting. Everything he did, he did in a big way. In fact, shortly after our visit we found out that he had sold the new Intourist Hotel in Baku to the Oil Workers' Union as a clubhouse, pocketing the money. I understand it was his last really big deal. There's not much money in the Siberian salt mines.

Except for this habit of embezzling, Babaev was a good Party man. But he didn't let his Marxian ideology get in the way of his comfort. The Intourist Hotel was run largely to meet the needs of its boss. The menus were selected for his palate. The meal hours were timed to his appetite, and the rooming arrangements so made as to provide him with the bridal suite. Babaev also had a personal bodyguard, Karkadaev, a muscular, swarthy Georgian with not much brain but plenty of devotion. Karkadaev carried Babaev's gun, served him his meals, mixed him his drinks, and even pulled off his boots at the end of a day's hunting.

So when we set off early one morning to go gazelle shooting we weren't surprised to find Babaev had arranged for a truck to follow our open Ford and carry our food, camping equipment and the beer. Besides the driver, there were four of us in the car, Babaev, Karkadaev, Chip and myself. The road ran south along the shore of the Caspian. The countryide was dry and sandy and by the time we'd been gone an hour the sun and glare from the desert had us both hot and thirsty. A small boy by the side of the road waved a string of red objects at us as we passed.

"*Raki*," shouted Babaev. "Karkadaev get us each a string and be sure they're all females – they're tenderer."

The raki turned out to be a cross between crayfish and shrimp. They'd been boiled in the salt water of the Caspian and though they tasted very good they didn't help our thirst. But Babaev fixed that, too. He motioned the truck to pull alongside. "A pitcher of beer, quick," he yelled. A foaming pitcher was passed across to us and we drove off.

But one pitcher of beer among four thirsty men didn't last very long. Babaev waved again to the truck to pull alongside. The driver slowed down as we passed the pitcher across to be refilled and we resumed our way. Before we reached the hunting grounds we had stopped several more times for more *raki* and had slowed down a good deal oftener to get our beer pitcher refueled.

Babaev, sitting in front, explained as we drove that we would shoot the gazelles from the car. "You can't stalk them," he explained. "And they run too fast to get them any other way." Shooting from a car wasn't exactly our idea of sport, but we figured we ought to try everything once.

"The only difficulty is that unless you obey the rules very carefully someone may get shot," Babaev went on to explain. "The important thing is to shoot one at a time. When we get within range I'll get up, take one shot and sit down. Then the man behind me gets up, shoots and sits down, then the man in the middle of the back seat, and finally the man behind the driver. Now, remember, don't take more than one shot, keep in turn, and don't shoot forward. You may hit the engine."

We'd been cruising along the desert for about ten minutes when we spotted a white speck bobbing up and down ahead of us. Babaev pointed it out to the driver and in a second we were flying across the sand at seventy miles an hour. Suddenly a deep gully appeared dead ahead. The driver, an expert at the game, spun the car sidewise and we skidded down the slope. At the bottom he stepped on the accelerator and we climbed diagonally back onto the desert floor. A few minutes later we were right behind the unfortunate gazelle. It zigzagged and twisted and put on all the speed it could but eventually we drew alongside it and Babaev killed it with a single shot. In a second Karkadaev had seized the dying animal and cut its throat with a long ugly knife he'd produced from his pocket.

"Moslem law," Babaev explained. "Can't eat meat that hasn't been bled at the throat." Chip and I exchanged smiles. Hadn't we heard

something about religion being the opium of the people? Apparently
Leninism had still a few addicts to convert in Baku.

A few minutes later we were off again. For half an hour we saw
nothing but the shimmering heat waves of the desert and the blinding
sun in a clear yellow sky. Then suddenly a whole mass of white spots
started bobbing up in front of us. The driver pressed down on the
accelerator and we were off again. This time though it wasn't just one
poor gazelle but a herd of thirty or forty.

And that's basically what caused the ensuing trouble – that and the
beer Babaev had stowed away.

As we came alongside Babaev stood up and fired. I was next in
turn, as he'd described the rules. So I got to my feet, sighted down
the barrel and was about to fire when I realized the thing in front
looked less like a herd of gazelles than the back of Babaev's head.

"Hey sit down," I shouted but apparently there were too many
gazelles for the rules and Babaev fired again. So I leaned out beyond
his head and let go. At that moment Karkadaev beside me rested
the barrel of his gun on my shoulder and fired. By this time Chip
was apparently beginning to feel left out of things. I heard him yell,
"Duck, damn it, I'm going to shoot." I just managed to get my head
down before a charge of buckshot whizzed over me.

For the next ten minutes the Ford was turned into a pocket
battleship firing broadsides in all directions. At one point I remember
wheeling past the truck which was vainly trying to get out of range.
I heard some shot tinkle against the body but apparently no one got
hurt.

Eventually we ran out of ready ammunition and pulled up. Around
us in the desert were half a dozen dead gazelles and not far off four or
five more were standing wounded waiting for us to put them out of
their misery. Our own casualties were not serious. The radiator cap
was gone and one of the tires of the truck had been punctured, but
except for that we were in fairly good order.

"You see how it is," Babaev explained a bit pompously. "If you just
follow the rules and take turns, no one gets hurt."

WE RAN THROUGH quite a number of American Ambassadors during the years I was in Moscow but only one, Laurence Steinhardt, turned out to be fond of hunting. Taking the Ambassador along on a shooting trip added one slight complication – we had to take three or four GPU boys along too.

Every Ambassador in Moscow, except perhaps the Tanna Tuvan or the Outer Mongolian, always had a staff of GPU boys dressed in neat little double-breasted blue serge suits following him wherever he went. Although they were transferred now and then from one Embassy to another, they were almost always the same individuals and after seven years I got to know them fairly well. But the strange thing about them was that officially they simply didn't exist. Once, when a story came out in an American magazine quoting our Ambassador as saying that the GPU boys who followed him didn't cause him much inconvenience, the Soviet Foreign Office protested vigorously.

"There are no GPU boys following your Ambassador," they told us.

"But then who are those fellows who've been hanging around our boss for the past ten years?" we asked.

"The Soviet Government hasn't the slightest idea – except that they are not agents of the GPU," the Foreign Office replied stubbornly. "Perhaps they are just curious Soviet citizens," they added. From then on the "boys" were referred to in the Embassy simply as "Those Curious Citizens."

But when we went on a shooting trip with the Ambassador, whether they existed or not officially they did take up room, they did eat and they did require beds to sleep in.

Once the Foreign Office stuck its neck out and agreed to arrange an elk-hunting expedition for Ambassador Steinhardt.

When they asked us how many there would be on the party we told them, "Just two of us, but don't forget accommodations for your four curious citizens."

"We'll make all the necessary arrangements for as many people as you want to have along," they answered testily. "Just tell us how many there'll be."

"Just the two of us and the four GPU boys," I repeated. "You mean there'll be two only," they answered.

"No," I replied, "there'll be six."

When we got to the shooting lodge, there were beds for six. Presumably four of them were non-existent, but they were good enough for the curious citizenry.

Some of the boys hated going shooting and grumbled so about it that I made it a point to tip them off in advance, so that they could rearrange their shifts and eliminate the non-hunters. It was easy to do. While the Ambassador was working in his office, I would just walk out on the street and stick my head into the little Ford parked a few feet away from the Embassy.

"Shooting tomorrow," I'd announce. "Bring your guns but don't bring Sasha. He complains too much."

They'd smile and thank me and that was the end of it.

But the day we went elk shooting something went wrong with their arrangements and Sasha came along.

It was a fairly long drive to the elk-shooting preserve, and it was late in the evening before we found the hunting cabin and installed ourselves in the two tiny rooms. After a bite to eat and a couple of glasses of vodka, we discovered that the GPU boys had brought along birdshot instead of the solid slugs elk needed to get killed.

So when we finished eating I got out some extra slugs and we started reloading the boys' ammunition. It gives you a funny sort of sensation to find yourself sitting around a table with the Soviet Secret Police loading their ammunition for them. I think they were a little self-conscious about it too. Sasha began grumbling as usual, commenting on the cold and the fact that the cabin wasn't properly heated. It was a little irritating to find one of your guests, even if he wasn't invited, complaining about the hospitality. So I said:

"Sasha, what the devil are you always kicking about? Lots of the boys back in Moscow would give anything for a chance to go elk shooting."

Sasha grunted: "Huh. I spend my whole life in Moscow chasing two-legged beasts and then when we get a little excursion in the country, what do we do? Chase four-legged beasts!"

But Sasha didn't get much shooting that trip. The first day out we didn't see a thing and both the Ambassador and Sasha froze their feet so badly that they had to stay home the next day.

The second day the beaters found a herd of elk and drove them to the line of hunters, now dwindled to myself and three of the boys. Elk, apparently, aren't very high on the I.Q. list for animals. Besides, they don't see so well, can't smell, and at least from what I saw, can't even hear. At any rate, a large bull elk suddenly appeared out of the bushes in front of the snow-pit I was standing in and made straight for me. It was late in the season and some of the elk had already cast their antlers – including the bull who was advancing on me. At first I decided to be a good sportsman and let him go, but then it occurred to me that if we didn't shoot any elk, the Kremlin might liquidate all the elk in the Oblast which had cast their antlers before they were supposed to.

While I was turning the problem over in my mind, the deaf-dumb-blind bull continued to advance toward me. He was very big and rather heavy-looking and it struck me that if I went back to Moscow empty-handed but bruised and bleeding with the only explanation that I'd been run over by an elk, it would make me look a little silly. By this time the unfortunate beast was hardly fifteen yards away and blithely trotting ahead. So I raised my gun and let him have it. By the time he stopped, his front feet were sticking into my snow-pit.

11

BEARS IN THE BALLROOM

During the early thirties, and right up until the purges of 1937-1939, Intourist carried on a brisk trade with Americans in search of adventure, paradise or emancipation. It was mostly women who came for emancipation, after reading the books about free love in Russia. But they also came to see the abortion clinics (closed in 1936), the Kremlin Museum (closed to outsiders in 1937), or the University (closed to most foreigners by 1938). There were professors who came to study the new economies of planning; agriculturalists who wanted to see how the collective farm system worked; engineers who wanted to see the famous new subway. But usually they were just tourists who wanted to see what was going on in general and be able to tell their friends they'd been to Russia.

One of them, Mrs. Ned McLean of Washington, came on a bet that she would wear the Hope Diamond on the streets of Moscow. When we explained to her that the Hope Diamond had a relatively limited market in Russia and consequently was not very likely to be stolen, the novelty of the stunt rapidly wore off and she left the diamond in her hotel room. (Just to be on the safe side, however, we asked Intourist to station a couple of detectives in the hall outside Mrs. McLean's room.)

Norman Thomas and his wife turned up to see the difference between socialism and communism. They enjoyed themselves thoroughly, even when we got stuck in some collective farm mud and they had to get out of my car and push. It was the only time in my life I'd been pushed through the mud by a presidential candidate and I'm afraid the Thomases were as unsuccessful in getting me out of the bog as they were in getting into the White House. But they were very good sports and we always enjoyed their visits.[10]

Then there was Lawrence Tibbett,[11] who came to hear the Soviets sing. We took him and his wife on a picnic on a bluff overlooking the Moscow Valley – not far from the polo grounds. After supper we were sitting about the campfire talking about the Socialist experiment and its influence on the opera business. Below us in the valley several flocks of sheep were grazing. As it grew dark, the shepherds began to sing to each other. Since they were fairly widely separated from each other, they took turns, each singing a line or a stanza. After listening to them for a few minutes, Tibbett joined the chorus doing his part at the top of his voice. The peasants must have been a little puzzled by the unknown voice, for little by little their voices seemed to come closer. Then the singing stopped and we could hear the sound of scrambling feet on the steep bluff below us. A few moments later the inquisitive, shy faces of a hundred sheep poked diffidently into the firelight. Behind them came the shepherds with their dogs and sat down beside us.

"Who was that fellow with the voice?" one of them asked. Tibbett confessed it was he.

"You've a good, natural voice," they said, "but you need some training."

Through an interpreter, Tibbett asked if they couldn't give him some pointers. They quickly agreed and in a few minutes they were teaching him an ancient Russian peasant song. It wasn't too long before Tibbett had gotten the tune and was singing as lustily as any of them.

---

10. Norman Thomas (1884-1968) was an American Presbyterian minister, socialist, pacifist, and six-time presidential candidate for the Socialist Party of America.
11. Lawrence Tibbett (1896-1960) was a famous American baritone who was also a film actor and radio personality.

"He learns easily," one of the shepherds whispered to me.

"If he took a little trouble he could make something of that voice."

It was well after midnight and the sheep had long since curled up in a huge circle at the edge of the firelight, when Tibbett finally decided he'd had enough singing lessons for a day. We stamped out the fire as the shepherds raised their little round peakless caps and bowed themselves back in the darkness followed by their sleepy flocks.

THE SOCIAL SEASON among the diplomats in Moscow lasted from early autumn until late spring, with a few summer parties thrown in for good measure. The first time we Americans got into the social whirl was sometime after Ambassador Bullitt's arrival. He'd been the round of the other Embassies at soirees, concerts and dances, and was not particularly impressed by the originality of the entertainment. So, when he went to Washington on consultation at the end of the winter of 1934-1935, he left instructions that three days after his return he wanted a party laid on that would compete with anything Moscow had yet experienced, before or after the Revolution. "The sky's the limit," he told me, "just so long as it's good and different."

After my experience with the seals, I was a little wary about wild animals, but Irena Wiley, the Counselor's wife, insisted that there be some animals at least. No other Embassies ever had anything more lively as entertainment than a tenor. And our orders were to be different.

"Let's get some farm animals and make a miniature barnyard in a corner of the ballroom. We can call it a Spring Festival." I knew better than to argue.

It sounded easy enough. All we would need were some baby lambs and some wild flowers and a few little birch trees in pots. But we'd figured without the weather. Two weeks before the party was scheduled, it was still cold and miserable outside and the snow was still knee-deep in the forests. The birch trees and flowers hadn't even begun to think about blooming. Besides, we began to run into difficulties with the sheep. A collective farm had agreed to let us have

Inside Spaso House, then and now.

some, but when we tried them out at a dress rehearsal the smell they gave off was too much for any ballroom. We tried washing them, dipping them, perfuming them, but it was no good. Then we tried some young goats. Surprisingly enough they were better but the atmosphere was pretty heavy even with them. We went to our old friend the Director of the Zoo. He'd gotten more friendly now and a little less nervous about collaborating with foreigners. He suggested mountain goats. "They smell less than barnyard varieties and are even more of a novelty." So he loaned us half a dozen baby mountain goats and we rigged up a little barnyard for them on a platform at the head of the buffet table.

But Irena decided mountain goats weren't enough. No barnyard was complete without some roosters. We'd hang them in glass cages around the walls of the dining room, she explained. But Moscow was fresh out of glass cages big enough for roosters. So we dismantled the glass towel racks from the apartments of all the American Embassy staff, thereby stirring up a minor revolution, and set the carpenter to work to build the cages. We told the rack owners that, provided nothing went wrong, they'd have the towel racks back later. (All but one or two were, in fact, returned.)

Even a dozen white roosters still didn't satisfy Irena. "One small wild animal won't do any harm," she argued. "A baby bear, for instance."

So we got a baby bear from the Zoo and built him a little platform complete with a tree trunk to sleep on. The Director of the Zoo was reluctant to let us have him though and insisted that a properly trained nurse accompany him to the party. Remembering the seal trainer, I asked him to pick a teetotaler for a nurse and he promised he would.

That still didn't solve the problem of the late spring. There were only ten days till the ball and there wasn't a sign of a bud in the whole of Moscow Oblast. Then somebody thought it might be warmer in the south. So we chartered a plane and told the pilot to go to the Crimea and bring back whatever flowers he could find. The next day he telegraphed from Yalta:

"Spring late here too."

"Try the Caucasus," we wired back. Two days later he returned to Moscow with the news that it was even colder in Tiflis than in Moscow.

Two of our major problems were the birch forests for the ballroom and the green lawn which we planned to have on the dining room table. The table had been built for the occasion. It was about ten yards long and a yard and a half wide. Every two or three feet we'd built troughs running the width of the table. In the troughs, we planned to put flowers; but there weren't any flowers. Between the troughs, where the buffet platters would stand, we were going to have lawn grass; but there wasn't any grass. The ballroom was to have been a mass of wild flowers; but there weren't any wild flowers.

Just as we were really getting nervous, the Stage Director of the Kamerney Theater came to the rescue. We didn't need wild flowers at all. We could have them painted on glass slides and projected against the white marble walls.

"A little cold and dead," Irena commented.

"We can cheer it up with an aviary," the Director suggested.

"More wild life?" I asked dubiously. But there was nothing else to be done. So we got some out-of-work artist to paint the flowers and arranged to have the Kamerney Theater closed the evening of the party so we could use their projectors.

The aviary caused us a little trouble until someone suggested buying a fisherman's net, gilding it, and wrapping it between two large pillars in the ballroom. We tried it and it worked. I went to the Zoo Director and asked for some golden pheasants, paroquets, and whatever other feathered life he had a good supply of. He suggested a hundred zebra finches. "They're small but very pretty," he explained. They were pretty and small – a little too small for the fish net as it turned out.

But the grass and the flowers for the buffet table had us stumped until we asked the Department of Botany at the University for help.

"That's easy," they said. "You can grow some chicory on wet felt. It makes excellent lawn. As for the birch forest, just root up a few trees, put them in a hot room for a few days and they'll begin to get green."

So we covered the attic floor with wet felt and filled one bathroom with a dozen ten-foot birch trees and waited. The botany people turned out to be right and a day or so before D-Day the grass grew, the trees turned green, and we all heaved a sigh of relief. All we needed now were the flowers for the buffet table. We sent a courier to Helsinki, where they were capitalistic enough to have greenhouses for the bourgeoisie, and he brought back a thousand tulips. He'd got his orders a little confused though and brought them cut instead of in pots. But we put them in cold storage and they managed to stand up until the party was over.

For entertainment we got a Czech jazz band that was visiting Moscow and a gypsy orchestra complete with dancers. The latter held forth in my downstairs bedroom, fixed up to look like a gypsy camp.

On the second floor we set up a Caucasian *shashlik* restaurant where a Georgian band held forth and a Georgian sword-dancer performed. The Caucasian restaurant was a rather late idea and, by the time I'd had the garden furniture painted for the occasion there wasn't time for it to dry. The resulting green stripes on the dinner jackets of the Diplomatic Corps could be seen for months later. A certain coolness toward me on the part of the wearers was also discernible.

When the big night finally arrived, Ambassador Bullitt awaited his guests under the chandelier of the main ballroom. To his considerable annoyance, he was joined there by one of the zebra finches who had managed to get through the fish net. When I came upon the scene, Bullitt and his Counselor Wiley, complete with white tie, tails, and white gloves, were stealthily stalking the finch around the ballroom in a vain attempt to surround it.

Among the first guests to arrive were Foreign Minister Litvinov and his wife, Ivy. Ivy took one look at the barnyard scene in the dining room and decided it was a collective farm. We tried to explain it was a perfectly ordinary capitalistic barnyard, but she was not convinced and, to prove it, she expropriated one of the baby goats and held it in her arms throughout the evening.

In all, there were about five hundred people, including the Diplomatic Corps; most of the Politburo including Voroshilov, Kaganovich and Bukharin; the leading generals of the Red Army including Yegorov; the Chief of Staff, Tukhachevsky who was executed two years later after a court-martial by Yegorov, who himself was shot a year later. There was the old perennial Budyonny who managed to sit in judgment on both Yegorov and Tukhachevsky and is still alive. Radek, the leading Soviet political writer until his liquidation two years later, was also there with his strange fuzzy whiskers neatly trimmed around the edges of his jawbone. In fact, except for Stalin, practically everyone who mattered in Moscow turned up.

When all the guests had arrived, the lights in the ballroom were turned down, the flowers from the projector appeared on the walls, and on the high-domed ceiling a constellation of stars, complete with a bright moon turned up. This was a last minute addition from the Kamerny Theater Director's fund of bright ideas.

As time for supper approached, I took one last look at my roosters who lined the walls of the dining room in their glass towel-rack cages. They were still covered up in the hope that when the covers were taken off and the dining room lights turned up they might by chance think it was dawn. When I'd finally gotten the signal from the Ambassador and the chef that all was ready, only one of the twelve roosters was fooled, but he set up such a crowing that you could hear it all over the house. However, his good performance was spoiled a bit by another rooster who decided that sitting in a glass cage in an Embassy banquet hall was a lot of damn nonsense. He succeeded in kicking the bottom out of his cage and flew clumsily into a platter of pate de foie gras which we'd had sent all the way from Strasbourg for the occasion.

During the entire evening I was far too busy settling jurisdictional rows between the pastry chef and the meat cook over whose stove was whose, or seeing to it that the wine supply flowed in the right direction from the wine cellar to the dining room and not into the chauffeurs' lounge. So I missed it when Radek discovered the baby bear lying on his back with a bottle of milk in his arms. Radek took away the bottle, put the nipple over a bottle of champagne and replaced it in the bear's arms. The bear had two or three lusty sucks of Mumm's Cordon Rouge before he discovered his mistake and hurled the bottle on to the floor. Radek had disappeared by this time and Yegorov, the Chief of Staff, noticing how distressed the bear was, picked it up in his arms and put it over his shoulder as though he were burping a baby. He must have done it just a little too well because the baby bear burped most effectively all over Yegorov's brand-new bemedaled and beribboned tunic!

The first I knew about what was going on was when I heard the good General roar. By the time I got to the scene, a half dozen waiters were sponging him down with napkins and finger bowls. But the damage was far too great for halfway measures of that sort and the General was in a fine old military frenzy.

"What sort of place is this anyway?" he shouted at me. "Do the Americans invite guests just to have them messed up by wild animals? Is this an Embassy or a circus? Tell your Ambassador that Soviet Generals are not accustomed to being treated like clowns."

With that, he stalked out of the room toward the front door with me trotting along behind, trying unsuccessfully to explain it hadn't been planned that way. But Yegorov was still cursing and shouting as he stormed out the door. "This is the last time I ever go through this door," he concluded and marched out of the house.

I reported the incident to the Ambassador, caught another scolding from him, marked the whole business down to profit and loss and went about settling another argument in the kitchen as to who should have the honor of lighting the plum pudding.

About an hour later the head butler called me to the front door.

"There is another guest coming," he explained. I hurried down to the entrance just in time to see General Yegorov in another brand-new tunic come marching in.

"I decided it wasn't your fault after all. Babies will be babies even when they're bears," he laughed. "And I did want to have just one more dance."

At nine o'clock next morning there were still a handful of hardy souls keeping the orchestra busy. At ten, we wound up the party with Tukhachevsky doing a Georgian dance with Lolya Lepishinkaya, the new ballet star. It was Tukhachevsky's last appearance in the Embassy before he was shot. By ten-thirty, however, the remaining guests had gone.

Among the last were the Turkish Ambassador, Vassif Bey, an enormous gentleman sometimes referred to as Massive Bey, who died of a heart attack the next year, and Oumansky, who later was Soviet Ambassador in Washington and then in Mexico, where he was killed in an airplane accident. When the door closed on the last guest, I sat down and ordered a bottle of champagne. It was the first drink I'd had since the show started. When I'd finished it I started to clear up the shambles. The first thing to do was catch the birds in the aviary and put them back into their cages in which they came from the Zoo. I'd caught the pheasants and paroquets and was making some progress with the zebra finches when the champagne plus the evening's activities caught up with me and I decided to go to bed. Unfortunately though, I forgot to fasten the aviary door.

I'd hardly gotten into bed before the Ambassador's valet woke me. "The Ambassador wants to see you at once in the ballroom."

Sleepily I stumbled into some clothes and out onto the scene of the previous evening's battle. Under the chandelier stood the Ambassador looking more than a little annoyed. The cause of his bad humor was obvious enough when I looked up into the high dome of the room to see a flock of zebra finches merrily skimming through the air.

"Well," said the Ambassador, "stop staring and do something about those damn birds before they ruin every stick of furniture in the Embassy." With that he marched back into his study.

It was a nice problem – especially after a night like that. Obviously I was going to need some expert help, so I telephoned the Director of the Zoo and asked him to send his best bird catcher. The bird catcher trundled up the Embassy drive on his bicycle a few minutes later with a net and the disassembled sections of a long handle under his arms.

"It won't be any trouble at all," he said as he came into the house. "I can catch them in a minute."

"But wait till you see the room..." I began to explain.

"No, it won't be difficult...." He was screwing the sections of the net's handle together as he walked down the hall to the ballroom. We got to the door and he looked up at the sixty-foot ceiling and gaped. There was a moment of silence and then the direction of his hands as he wound the parts of the handle reversed.

"But why didn't you tell me it was like this?" he asked plaintively as he disassembled the rod.

When the bird catcher had left I wandered around from room to room, puzzled and disconsolate. By this time the flock of finches had split up into a number of sub-flocks which distributed themselves throughout the Embassy. Soon the whole house was filled with their chirpings and droppings.

From time to time the Ambassador appeared from his study and glared about him.

"Well," he would say, "whatever you're going to do, you'd better get started. Much more of this and we won't have a decent piece of furniture left."

It was well after dark when I suddenly got an idea. I asked the butler to round up the whole staff and soon every last kitchenmaid and yardboy was assembled in my bedroom while I explained the strategy. We turned out all the lights in the house and opened all the windows. On each window sill we put one bright lamp. Then armed with brooms, pillows, and any other throwable object we could find we went from room to room stirring up the birds till they flew toward the light. Once in the window we'd give them a final shoo and chase them into the night. I knew the Zoo Director wasn't going to enjoy losing his zebra finches, but I also knew he had a lot more of them – more at any rate than I had prospects of jobs. For three hours the house was a hubbub of rushing wings and pillows and people but in the end the finches were out and the Embassy liberated.

It was the last party the Ambassador ever asked me to organize – I like to think it was because I was getting too valuable in other lines of diplomatic work.

12

GPU OR GESTAPO

By 1937 the great Soviet purge trials were getting underway and the isolation of foreigners in Moscow was practically complete. One after another of my old friends either had disappeared or broken off all contact with us. It had never been easy to have friends among the Russians, and it hurt when the few who had been friendly with us began to turn their backs when they saw us in the street or in the foyer of the Opera House. Every two or three days we read in the papers the name of some acquaintance who had been convicted of espionage or had confessed to sabotage or had been denounced as a traitor: Tukhachevsky, Yegorov, Radek, Bukharin and the fabulous Baron Shteiger.

Shteiger came from an old Baltic family and at the time of the Revolution had thrown in his lot with the Soviets. Some people said that he did it to get permission for his father to emigrate to France. Whatever the reason, he seemed to have served the Soviets well. He was a cultured man with an excellent sense of humor and a fund of stories which he loved to tell in flawless French. He had some mysterious connections in the Kremlin and often served as a short cut between it and the foreign Embassies where he spent most of his time. Once, after Stalin had told one of our Ambassadors how much he liked Edgeworth pipe tobacco, it was Shteiger to whom I was told to deliver a can of Edgeworth once a month.

As the tempo of the purges increased, Shteiger seemed to grow more and more depressed. But he never failed to turn up at every diplomatic function. One evening after a cocktail party at the Embassy I was taking Shteiger home in my car. The newspapers that day had announced that several of our mutual friends had been executed by the usual Soviet method – shot through the back of the head.

As we drove through the cold snowy streets Shteiger was unusually silent. I tried to make conversation about the weather.

"Yes," he finally replied. "It is dangerous weather – very treacherous. In times like these one must be very careful to protect the back of one's head." He stroked his neck and smiled. Then he lapsed into silence.

The very next day Shteiger failed to turn up at an Embassy party. A few weeks later *Pravda* announced that Boris Sergeyevich Shteiger had been discovered to be a traitor and had been shot – through the back of the head.[12]

WHEN ORDERS CAME sending me to Berlin I lost little time in getting underway. After Moscow, Berlin at first seemed strangely free. There was little or no hesitation on the part of the Germans to go out with foreigners. Hitler's policy of "guns for butter" lent a peculiar charm for Germans to the butter-laden tables of foreigners.

By 1939, when Hitler was using his guns, and butter was not the only food missing from Berlin tables, the pressure on foreign households was considerable. At that time Alexander Kirk was in charge of our Berlin Embassy and George Kennan, my first boss in Moscow, was his Counselor. Kirk solved the entertainment problem by giving an enormous buffet lunch each Sunday. There were perhaps a hundred guests who had standing invitations and another hundred who were invited occasionally.

---

12. Boris Shteiger (1892-1937) worked at the Committee for Enlightenment and was the authorized contact for the diplomatic corps as well as an NKVD agent. He also was the model for Bulgakov's Baron Meigel in *Master and Margarita*.

One Saturday Kirk called Kennan into his office and told him he'd been ordered to Paris for consultation and wouldn't be able to give the usual Sunday lunch.

"Please take the necessary steps to call it off," he told Kennan.

A few days later he returned from Paris and called Kennan into his office.

"You did a pretty good job canceling the Sunday lunch," he told him. "There were only two people you forgot to tell."

"Who were they?" George asked.

"The chef and the Japanese Ambassador," Kirk replied.

EXCEPT FOR ITS outward and material pleasures Berlin was no real improvement over Moscow. It wasn't long before you became aware of the hand of the Gestapo. Stories of concentration camps, tortures and killings were as numerous as they later proved to be authentic. Besides the Government itself, the "leaders" hardly commanded your admiration or respect. In Moscow they were just as ruthless, cruel and treacherous, but things were done with a certain air of oriental dignity. In Berlin it was screaming speeches by Hitler in the Sport Palast, the flamboyant boasting of Goering, the blustering of Goebbels, and the beating and bullying of the police. It was the ostentatious brutality of the Nazis that literally added insult to injury.

Occasionally in Moscow we caught glimpses of trains of exiles leaving for Siberia. Often enough we got frantic calls at night about the arrest of some friends. But it took the Nazis to make a spectacle of their brutality. Shortly after the Munich Pact, Goebbels started a pogrom of Jews throughout Germany. It started one Tuesday in November, 1938, when truckloads of Nazi toughies set out to smash up Jewish shops and beat any Jews they found in the streets. Throughout Tuesday and Wednesday the pogrom continued, getting worse every hour. Tens of thousands of Jews who thought their last day had come crowded into the Consulate begging for visas. Someone – doubtless Goebbels himself – started the cruel rumor that President Roosevelt had sent the Jews of Berlin a present, consisting of thousands of "quota numbers" entitling them to immediate visas. Bellevuestrasse, where the Consulate was, became so crowded the staff had to get into the building by a fire escape in the rear garden. Telephone calls from Jews who couldn't get to the office themselves blocked the switchboard completely. An American staying at the Esplanade Hotel across the street was forced to send us a telegram to find out about getting a new passport.

Throughout Germany, but particularly in Berlin, gangs of hoodlums swarmed through the streets burning Jewish property and manhandling their families. Eyewitnesses told of children being thrown out of windows and beaten as they landed in the streets. The big Jewish department stores of Isaacs and Wertheims were wrecked. Grand pianos were pushed through the railings of the galleries and dashed to pieces seven or eight floors below. When everything had been destroyed, the mob set fire to the shambles that remained.

By Thursday the pogrom had reached such a pitch that even the Government was reported to be worried about the hysteria they themselves had started. That afternoon I gave a small birthday party for a Dutch friend. The Dutch Consul General showed up with one eye closed and his head gashed by a brick someone had thrown at him while he was defending a Dutch Jew's shop. A German acquaintance dropped in – in an SS uniform. But he was quickly ushered out by indignant guests. There were ten or fifteen other guests unseen by my Dutch friends or the SS men. They were Jews who had come looking for refuge and I had crowded them into my bedroom until the storm subsided.

It was late in the evening before the invited and the uninvited had gone. I called my police dog, Midget, and went for a walk through the streets to see what was going on. On each corner a pair of SS men were standing and as gently as possible trying to stop the few remaining mobs of boys who were still breaking windows and looting. By this time the mobs had already started to lose any pretense of merely demonstrating against Jews and were openly breaking into and looting any shops they could safely ravage. As I walked down one narrow street I passed a gang of about twenty boys probably between sixteen and twenty-two years old. They whistled at the dog and I spoke to her in Russian. When they heard the foreign language they crossed the street toward me and I edged myself up against a high iron paling fence.

"Are you a Russian?" the leader asked me.

I was just angry enough at the whole performance to say I was and what the hell were they going to do about it?

The mob crowded closer and I snapped my fingers at Midget who stood beside me. It was the signal for her to bark and she let out a low ugly growl. The crowd backed away.

"A Soviet Russian?" someone in the crowd asked. "Yes," I answered. "I'm a correspondent for *Pravda.*"

The boys in the back of the crowd began to push forward again. I snapped my finger again and Midget growled louder. For a moment I was sorry I'd not allowed the GPU dog trainers to teach Midget to attack humans. But the boys responded to her barking and stood back.

"A Communist?" someone else asked.

"Of course," I answered, "and damn proud of it."

I thought I had better get on the offensive. "I suppose you're all Nazis? A great Party that is! And this is certainly a fine performance you've been putting on the past three days! The proudest day in the history of German culture." Someone in the crowd started cursing and pushing toward me. Midget growled some more. Then suddenly the leader of the group turned to one of his neighbors:

"Take the gang away. I want to handle this fellow alone." He was a big husky fellow and I wasn't exactly happy at the prospect but I was glad to see the rest of the crowd obediently march off down the street.

When they had disappeared, the man in front of me suddenly seemed to relax his belligerency. "Are you really a member of the Communist Party?" he asked.

I figured I'd better keep up the pretense and swore mightily that I was. He seemed to believe me for he stuck out his hand and grabbed mine: "So am I."

For two hours we walked up and down the bank of the Kaiser Friedrich canal while he told me his story. He wasn't really an enrolled member of the Party, he explained, but he had been a Komsomol before Hitler came. And his brother was a high Party functionary who was hiding in Prague. I asked him why a Communist should be leading a gang of hoodlums in an anti-Semitic riot.

"Can't you see why?" he answered. "It's the only way to show these damn Prussian idiots what a mob can do if it wants to, even against the police. They're so full of 'Peace and Order' in Berlin they'll never have the nerve to seize power unless you can show them."

It was a novel approach and I wondered whether it had the approval of higher Communist Party authorities. I rather doubt it. But anyway my acquaintance and I soon became good friends and at least once a week we met by the canal or in a beer hall where he told me what the "underground" was doing in Berlin. It made good reading in reports to Washington but it never seemed to have much effect on Hitler. In fact I doubt if a single Communist Party has ever turned out to be as useless to the Kremlin as the one in Germany after 1933.

After the pogrom in November, 1938, the applicants for visas in the Consulate nearly swamped us. For weeks, long lines stretched far down the street all day long, and late in the evening when we couldn't hold a pencil any longer hundreds were still being turned away. For ten, twelve, and even fourteen hours a day, they came up to our desk, all with the same story, all with the same plea – a visa.

For me it was a new and bitter experience. There were only just so many visas we could issue under the law and they had all been spoken for, for the next ten years. It didn't matter how desperately they needed to get out, there was nothing we could do about it except listen patiently and answer firmly.

I'd been at it since eight o'clock one day. It was already long after the normal closing time and I was pretty well exhausted. Two young couples diffidently stood before my desk. They'd just arrived from Breslau, they explained. They had just been married.

"We're all partly Jewish and we decided to join forces and make one last try to get out of Germany before it's too late. We've tried everything we could. We've been to every consul. We tried the Czech border, but they caught us and sent us back. We've no friend or relations abroad, none who could vouch for us. You are our last chance. If you refuse there's only one way out." One of the boys made a motion across the arteries of his wrist.

He spread a map out on my desk. "Here," he continued, "look at this." It was a chart of the Pacific Ocean.

"Here," he went on, pointing. "Here's an island that belongs to the United States. Johnstone Island it's called. We've looked it up in a geography book. It is uninhabited but we might be able to get along. We wouldn't be bothering anyone. We wouldn't be competing with anyone for jobs. We wouldn't be 'public charges' as you call it. But maybe we could just live. That's all we want – just to live." His voice broke and he stopped.

"I'm very sorry," I broke in. "But those islands are closed to everybody. They're under the control of the Navy and we can't issue a visa to them. No one is allowed to go there. No one, Americans or anyone else."

"But maybe you could ask your Navy to let us go. There are four of us. You could send them a telegram. We'll pay for it." The boy dug into his pocket excitedly and produced a roll of Reichsmarks. "We've still got a little money."

I shook my head but he went right on: "Please! You know what's happening here. You know we young Jews can't survive in Germany. We have to go or else there's just one thing left. We're not going to let them murder us like animals."

I'd heard the same plea before, a dozen times a day. It was all perfectly true what they had said. There was just one thing about them I couldn't understand, but I hesitated to ask them. After all I was a foreign Vice Consul living in comparative safety and comfort.

Here were two strong young men driven to complete despair by their wretched "leaders" and all they could think of doing to protest was to kill themselves.

"Tell me," I said eventually. "If as you say there's only one way out, isn't there anyone you'd like to take along? One man or two or three? Perhaps it would make it pleasanter for those who stay behind."

For a long minute they stood and looked at me in horror. "You mean Hitler?" one of the girls whispered in terror. For a moment longer they stood and stared at me. Then they turned and walked limply out. I left my desk and went to the window and watched them. They turned down Bellevuestrasse and across the street into the Tiergarten. They were still walking slowly; their hands tightly clasped together.

I'm afraid I'd hardly thought of those two young couples again for nearly ten years. By that time Hitler had killed himself not two hundred yards from the old Consulate. The war was over. Berlin was a pile of rubble. The beautiful Tiergarten was a desert of tree stumps and hideous statuary. I was glad to be leaving after a short postwar visit . Ahead of me was Asia, paralyzed by civil war and hunger.

The big four-motor plane I was riding in glided down toward a tiny golden-white spot sparkling in the brilliant Pacific sun.

The flight clerk came out of the pilot's cabin:

"Fasten seat belts and put out your cigarettes. We'll be landing in five minutes. Johnstone Island."

I looked down again at the spot below us. I could make out a wooden control tower, a few Quonset huts, a water tower, and two long oily brown runways. Aside from that there was nothing but sand and coral. I recalled the two couples from Breslau. Looking at the desolation below I doubted whether they would have survived there, even if they hadn't slashed their wrists in the Tiergarten.

13

EAST MEETS WEST

One evening I was reading in the semi-subterranean apartment I had rented in Berlin after the Munich crisis. It was small, damp and dark, but it had what I thought was the advantage of being practically a cellar. Until I saw it after the war I was under the impression it would make a good air-raid shelter. It now looks like a brickyard.

I heard the doorbell ring and the maid went to answer. A moment later a cloud of little wicker baskets floated into the living room and dissolved in the middle of the floor. A small, round, yellow-brown Chinese emerged from the heap.[13]

"Me," said the Chinese pointing at his bulging stomach, "me, Yang."

"I'm Mr. Thayer," I replied.

"You, Master," Yang corrected.

A COUPLE OF months before I'd been at a New Year's party in Vienna. All Vienna parties are apt to be gay, but this one was particularly so. It was to be the last one before Hitler marched into Austria – and every Viennese knew it. We'd started by going to the

---

13. Some readers may find Thayer's tone and language describing Yang and other non-white persons in this and succeeding chapters to be politically incorrect. We have decided to keep these passages intact, if only because they are an accurate reflection of early twentieth century American attitudes toward race and non-white cultures.

traditional performance of *Die Fledermaus* at the Opera. Richard Tauber was singing. Since he was partly Jewish, this was to be his last performance – and the audience knew that too. Not until he had sung practically every one of his old Strauss favorites did the crowd permit him to leave the stage.

It was almost midnight when we arrived at the Consul General's house. Walter Duranty was there. Bill Shirer came in, looking exhausted after having produced a broadcast to America of Christmas carols sung by some Viennese children. Chip and Avis Bohlen were there on vacation from Moscow. There were a great many other people as there always are at the Wileys – Russians, French, Poles, Austrians and, finally, Fu, the Wileys' Chinese butler, very elegant in his white silk robe and a trayful of whiskeys and soda.[14]

It must have been about five in the morning when Fu came to me for the tenth time:

" 'Nother whiskey soda, maybe?"

I thanked him and said I'd had plenty already. "But what I really would like is a Chinese servant like you to take care of me in Berlin."

"Wanta Chinee boy? Okay, Fu fixee."

When Fu woke me the next morning I'd completely forgotten our conversation.

"Planee late, mister," he warned and added, "I fixee Chinee boy."

"What Chinee boy, Fu?"

"Last night you say you wanta Chinee boy. This morning I sendee telegram Harbin and tell my fren Yang he come Berlin."

As soon as I was dressed I went into a huddle with the Wileys.

"Now what? What can I, a poor Vice Consul, do with a Chinese servant?"

But the Wileys told me how good Chinese servants were and how useful it would be to have a permanent servant instead of having to train a new one at each post.

---

14. William Shirer (1904-1993) was a foreign correspondent in Berlin during the rise of the Nazis. He later became a historian, and authored the seminal work, The Rise and Fall of the Third Reich. Avis Bohlen was the married name of Avis Thayer – Charles Thayer's sister.

"And besides, you already have a household with that secret police dog of yours. One Chinese won't add very much to the crowd."

So I let things slide and waited to see what would happen. From time to time I'd receive little notes from Vienna which invariably ended with, "My best to you, from C. C. Fu." They kept me posted as to Yang's progress from Manchuria.

SO THE SURPRISE was not as great as it might have been when Yang appeared in the living room.

"Maybe I see Master's house?" Yang asked when he'd extricated himself from his baskets.

I showed him through the four-room apartment. When the tour ended in the kitchen he turned to me:

"How many coolie Master have?"

"Coolies? I don't have any coolies. Fu said you'd do everything."

"Me!" he replied incredulously. "Fu say me do everything? Yang cookee – no coolie."

A lengthy conversation followed with me trying to catch on to Yang's pidgin English and he obviously understanding little or nothing of what I was saying. At last I went to the telephone and called Vienna. Wiley answered the phone: "Yang has arrived," I told him. "But there seems to be a rather fundamental misunderstanding as to what he's supposed to do."

"Let Fu talk to him," John observed confidently. "He'll straighten him out."

I passed the phone to Yang and for a half hour a lively chat went on. Fu and Yang hadn't seen each other for ten years and I realized they had a lot to tell each other but as the conversation continued I wondered whether Yang understood how far he was from Vienna and what a long distance telephone call costs. Eventually, however, he stopped and handed me the phone. Wiley was on the other end:

"Fu says to give Yang cigarettes."

"Cigarettes? You mean that's all that's bothering him?"

"It seems," John answered, "Yang tried to buy some cigarettes on the Trans-Siberian for gold rubles and found them a little expensive. He thinks his salary won't cover his smoking bill."

A quick calculation of the cost of the telephone conversation compared with the current cost of tobacco prompted me to agree at once to supply Yang with all the cigarettes he could smoke. Besides I'd never had a servant who didn't help himself freely to my cigarettes. Yang was delighted, Fu was relieved, and John and I more than satisfied with the negotiations.

Although my knowledge of pidgin English was very imperfect, I soon began to catch on to Yang's chatter and he, too, began to pick up a smattering of German, but not without several difficult moments.

A FEW WEEKS after Yang arrived I attended a wedding in London. It seemed like a good opportunity to send Yang to Vienna to see his old friend Fu. I gave him a large piece of cardboard explaining who he was and where he was going, took him to the station and put him on the Vienna Express.

"The train gets to Vienna at eight and then you go see Mr. Wiley, the American Consul General," I explained. Yang said he understood and smiled gaily as the train pulled out of Berlin.

A few days later I returned to Berlin and found Yang waiting for me. "How was Vienna?" I asked him.

"Vienna plenty nice," he replied, "but plenty hard to get to."

I asked him what the trouble had been.

"Eight o'clock come. Train stop. Yang get off. Go see American Consul General. But he not Mr. Wiley," Yang answered.

"What do you mean. Of course the Consul General in Vienna is Mr. Wiley."

"Not Mr. Wiley," Yang insisted and began to fish in his pockets under his smock. He pulled out a visiting card. It was addressed to me and read:

"Glad to help your boy out of his linguistic and geographic difficulties."

It was the card of the Consul General in Munich. Only some time later did I learn that the train stopped in Munich at eight p.m. and Vienna at eight a.m. the following morning. My mistake.

BEFORE YANG AND his baskets of baggage arrived, I'd had a local German cook who spent most of her time complaining about the kitchen utensils. According to her all the pots acted like sieves and all the sieves acted like pots. The knives didn't cut. The meat chopper was "kaput." The coffee pot was a hunk of rusty metal. I took what she said at a fifty per cent discount and told her we'd have to get along on what we had till Yang arrived. Then he could choose for himself those things he needed. I figured Yang would be with me quite a while and a small investment in kitchen equipment wouldn't be wasted. Apparently Yang, too, expected to stay a while. A few days after he turned up he got chatty one evening and confided that he liked "Master." He said he hoped he was finally going to have a steady job because he liked steady jobs. The trouble with his old employers in Harbin had been that they were changing so often.

"I workee Mr. Page seven year. Then he go way. Workee Mr. Edwards six year. He go way. Workee Missee Williams ten year. She go way. No good like that. Yang like steady job – no changee all'a time."

So I gave Yang a Sears Roebuck catalogue full of handsomely colored illustrations of every sort of instrument a cook ever thought of. "Just pick out what you think you'll need and I'll send for it."

Two or three days passed and Yang said nothing about new pots. I reminded him that he had better order what he needed. Yang thought for a long minute. Then he spread his hands a good three feet apart:

"Maybe Master buy me big knife?"

I bought the nearest thing to a sword I could find in Berlin and Yang was delighted. The big knife followed us around the globe for the best part of ten years.

In spite of the cook's charges that the kitchen equipment was a mass of wreckage, Yang managed to turn out the best food I'd ever had in my own home. His big specialty was his curry, which came in several varieties. There was a "ten curry" which consisted of rice and curried chicken surrounded by ten different sorts of delicacies, from bamboo shoots to peanuts. There was a "fifteen curry" with fifteen little side dishes and finally there was the extra-special-super "twenty-five curry" with twenty-five sorts of roots, shoots, nuts and herbs, surrounding the chicken and rice.

Another dish Yang introduced me to was his "thousand year eggs" which he had brought me as a present from Harbin in one of his little wicker baskets. The eggs came in a thick casing of dried clay, in which they had reputedly been cooking for a thousand years. Once, when no guests were around, Yang admitted that maybe they hadn't been there a thousand years: "Maybe only two-three hundred year," he said with a wink. When the news got around Berlin about the thousand year eggs, there was a rush to my underground apartment. But Yang was pretty niggardly and only served the precious purple delicacies when I was alone. We made one exception when Prentiss Gilbert, the Counselor of the Embassy, begged me for just one taste:

"I've been describing how they taste to boring dinner partners for the past thirty years and I just want to see how close to the truth I've been." Actually, thousand year eggs taste just like hard-boiled one day eggs – except more so. Prentiss Gilbert had to admit his description was a little off.

But there was one cooking problem which stopped Yang cold. That was how to open a European oyster. He'd bought some for a dinner party one evening shortly after he arrived. I was in the living room having a German lesson from a formidable-looking bearded professor from the University of Berlin. Suddenly I heard a series of noises from the kitchen that sounded as though Yang were riding a motorcycle around the china closet. I tried to ignore it, but a few minutes later Yang came into the room, his brown face dripping with sweat.

"Master, oysters no open – velly solly."

"Don't be silly, Yang. Of course they'll open if you only know how. I'll show you."

I went into the kitchen, took a large knife and began to pry an oyster apart. The knife broke but the oyster stayed shut.

"Damn Nazi steel," I complained and went out to the car and fetched the tool kit.

I chose a sharp screwdriver and attacked the oyster again. The screwdriver slipped and tore a hole in my thumb. I grabbed the oyster with a pair of pliers and tried again.

As the number of tools grew, and the blood from my thumb spread over the kitchen, Yang stood by impassively, his arms folded across his fat stomach. But at last even his patience gave out and he went back into the living room:

Professor, maybe you can open oysters, yes?" That night we had consommé as a first course.

YANG HAD BEEN in Berlin about six months when I was ordered to Washington. One morning at breakfast I told him the news.

He was silent a moment, then said:

"Master, how we go to America?"

"We'll go on a ship, of course."

There was another pause.

"Big ship, Master, or little ship?"

"A big ship," I replied. "It'll only take about six days."

Again Yang thought for a long time, his face screwed up in a knot. Finally:

"Master, maybe you go on ship and send Yang on train. Maybe train to America cheaper."

I got out a pencil and a large piece of paper and tried to explain the geographic difficulties involved in his suggestion. He had obviously never seen a map, and equally obviously he didn't understand a word I was saying. But he realized that the train idea was out for some reason and reconciled himself rather sourly to the idea of the ship.

It wasn't until we'd been at sea for a day that I realized what was worrying him. He told me he'd once been on a ship in the Yellow Sea and hadn't enjoyed it much. Yang's cabin was in the depths of the hold and when he didn't turn up the first morning at sea I went down to see how he was getting along. Yang was lying on his bunk.

"Master, I wantcha go downstairs," he moaned. "Please, Master, let me go downstairs."

"But, Yang, you are as far downstairs in this ship as you can get. If you went any further you'd come out the bottom. Get up on deck and get some fresh air."

"No, Master. I wantcha go downstairs," he wailed.

Eventually I pulled him out of the bunk and helped him up toward the deck.

"Please, Master, let me go downstairs," he kept whimpering as he hobbled along.

Finally we reached the after deck and Yang looked around bewildered. He looked to the right across the sea and then to the left. Then he went to the rail and looked ahead and then down at the swirling sea below.

"Master" – he was almost in tears now – "Master, is there no place where I can go downstairs?"

At last I caught on to what he meant.

"Sorry, Yang, very sorry. The first place you can go downstairs off this ship is in New York in four days. Now lie down on the deck and get used to it." He lay down, but he never got used to it.

A few days later we arrived in Washington. As we drove off from the Union Station in a taxi Yang stared a little bewildered at all the unfamiliar sights. Suddenly he caught a glimpse of a colored man on the sidewalk:

"Look, Master, look!" he shouted excitedly. "Man all black!" By way of explanation he pointed to his own yellow cheeks.

YANG QUICKLY MADE friends with the white, colored and yellow faces in Washington and our kitchen soon became the social center of "Que" Street. One evening while I was reading I heard strange noises coming up from the basement kitchen. Two voices would occasionally explode with laughter and then subside into absolute silence until another guffaw from both roared up the kitchen stairs. The thing that puzzled me was that no words were being exchanged. I went downstairs to investigate and found Yang and another Chinese sitting at the kitchen table busily scribbling Chinese characters on scraps of paper. When I appeared in the doorway, Yang hastily explained:

"My friend, he Cantonese. Me, Manchulee. I no understandee what he speakee. He no understand me speakee. But writee understand easy." The advantages of character writing over phonetic alphabets was readily apparent.

We didn't stay long in Washington and we were soon off again on another big ship – this time bound for Hamburg.

IT WAS THE summer of 1939 and the annual war scare was building up to a climax – this time the real one. The Hamburg city authorities began installing emergency artesian wells. In the parks, workmen were digging shelter trenches. Householders started sandbagging their basement windows. Yang had been brought up on the guerrilla activities of the Manchurian warlords and he was frankly and openly contemptuous about all these elaborate precautions just because there was going to be another war. Besides, he had developed a lively dislike for the Germans. "Deutschee," he called them condescendingly. But then Yang disliked all "foreigners" which meant everyone except Manchurians, Americans and, for some reason, Russians.

"Deutschee," Yang said, "all flaid of war. Deutschee plentee bad to Yude [Jews]. Deutschee plentee laugh at Chinee. But all'a same, Deutschee flaid of war."

He stubbornly refused to help my landlord build the air-raid shelter in our apartment house. "Deutschee flaid of eggplant. Yang no flaid eggplant." But I told him that whether he was afraid of airplanes or not, the law said he had to help build the shelter. He gave in very ungraciously, muttering, "All'a same Deutschee plentee damn fool."

Eventually the war came and, shortly afterward, the first RAF leaflet raid on Hamburg. I was standing in my pajamas on the balcony of my apartment watching the spectacular, though singularly ineffective, efforts of the German flak to bring down the British. There was a patter of feet behind me and Yang appeared.

"Yang, I've told you ten times that if there's an air raid you have to go down to the shelter. Get going before you get arrested or get hurt!"

I could see Yang smile in the light of the tracer shells.

"Master no go shelter, Yang no go shelter," he answered stubbornly.

"I don't have to go to the shelter. Vice Consuls don't go to shelters. But you must. Besides, you might get hurt." But Yang didn't move.

"Yang no go downstairs. War all'a same to Yang. If Ingleesee [English] kill plentee Deutschee they can kill Yang, too."

Presently the British planes passed by and the firing stopped. Only then Yang agreed to slip back into his cubbyhole behind the kitchen. As he went he mumbled: "Deutschee plentee damn fool. No hittee nothing."

Only a day or two later I was finishing my breakfast on the balcony of my apartment when I caught sight of Yang in his blue smock bustling up the street at a very good clip. As a rule Yang was never in a hurry and I watched him curiously to find the reason for the haste. A few seconds later a half dozen hausfraus appeared around the corner, running after Yang as fast as their overweight bodies would let them. But Yang had a good lead and darted in the gate, up the steps, and through the front door before the leader of the posse had reached the house. She stared up the steps, muttering something to her companions and then turned and walked away.

I went into the kitchen and asked Yang what he'd been up to.

"Nothing, Master, nothing. Yang no do nothing," and he smiled a little sheepishly.

"Why were those hausfraus chasing you, Yang?"

"I don't know, Master. Hausfrau plentee fool maybe," and his face broke into an enormous grin. It was obvious I wasn't going to get anything out of him so I dropped the matter.

That evening, just as I finished dinner, six elderly Hamburg workmen, dressed in their Sunday best, their round heads closely shaven, called at the apartment to see the *Herr Vizekonsul*. Yang showed them in and stood back of my chair while they lined up in front of me and bowed respectfully. I asked them to sit down but their German training had taught them their position and they refused.

The spokesman of the group explained that they had come to ask the Herr Vizekonsul respectfully to punish his Chinese servant for an incident that happened this morning at the market. It seemed the wives of the six workmen were standing in line together with Herr Vizekonsul's cook and, quite naturally, they began to discuss the war situation and even had asked Herr Vizekonsul's cook for his views. The cook, however, had made a very insulting remark and when they protested, he ran away. They would appreciate it if Herr Vizekonsul would oblige his cook to apologize.

I looked at Yang. He was grinning from ear to ear but he said nothing. I could see at once that he wasn't going to say anything to help the situation. It was a question of either getting into a tangle with the local population or of trying to force Yang into a disastrous loss of face. So I turned to the six men.

I was not aware, I said, that it was forbidden to foreigners to express their views about the war situation or any other situation in Germany, particularly if asked. If there was such a prohibition, it was up to the city authorities to inform me and not a delegation of private citizens. If the gentlemen desired I advised them to carry their complaint through proper channels to the Stadthalter. If he saw fit he could take the matter up with me.

The men protested mildly, but they saw the logic in my bureaucratic approach and after a series of further bows departed.

When Yang had shown them to the door, I called for him. "Now, Yang, you tell me exactly what happened this morning at the market or there's going to be trouble."

"I no do nothing, Master, nothing," Yang answered, still grinning. "I just stand in line waiting to buy fish and old big fat hausfrau ask me how soon Deutschee win war. That's all!"

"And what did you say?"

"I no say nothing, Master. I just laugh and tell fat hausfrau, 'You think Deutschee win war maybe? Ha-ha!"

14

WAR

The outbreak of war in 1939 was one thing in the Hamburg fish market, but it was another thing entirely in the Consulate General. All summer long tourists from America had kept pouring into Europe to sightsee or visit relatives. As the summer wore on and the annual crisis got hotter, we got more and more outspoken in our arguments with the tourists, to go home before it was too late. In the closing days of August we met each shipload of tourists as they arrived in Hamburg Harbor and tried to persuade them of the dangers of going further. But in times of apparent peace Americans aren't very easily persuaded by their consuls.

"The war scare's an invention of Chamberlain," some of them said.

Others, less subtle in their political thinking, merely said, "Baloney."

But when the Polish war started on the first of September they quickly changed their tune. It wasn't necessary any longer to go down to the docks to find them. They came to the Consulate by the hundreds.

At first they merely asked advice – and got it, bluntly. "Go home and go quick," we said.

Even then some of them hesitated: "It's just a bluff by the darned European politicians. They're trying to scare us. The British won't fight. The war will be over in ten days."

But we had reason to think otherwise. The British Consul came around and told us London was going to ask us to take over his office as soon as England got into the war. Just to be on the safe side, he turned over to us his cash and accounts, his inventories and his keys, and went home to wait.

"But when will we be notified officially?" we asked before he left.

"When you get a telegram from the Foreign Office in London with just the word WARONE; that's it. You should acknowledge it with the code word WALLUP! From then on you're the British Consul too."

It sounded like a business-like and brief enough procedure which contrasted favorably with our own. Two years later, when Pearl Harbor was attacked, I was sitting in Kuibyshev with the Embassy. We got the news of the attack and the declaration of war by radio several hours later. Thirteen days afterward we got a three-page telegram from Washington repeating the Congressional resolution declaring war, word for word. Personally I thought the British had the better system.

For two days after the Polish campaign started nothing happened. Nothing, that is, in the way of telegrams from London. The Consulate in Hamburg, however, was as active as a beehive. Instead of the fifty or so visitors we normally had each day, they now came in thousands. Outside, air-raid precautions were being put into effect. German fighter planes started patrolling overhead. Whenever they became bored they'd nose-dive, aimed – so it seemed to me – at the back of my neck.

The captain of a small American freighter came up to the counter where Vice Consul Thayer was sitting perched on a high stool. What was he to do?

"Get your ship out of the Elbe, and quick."

An irate client with a thick accent stepped up: "The Consul in Breslau said there'd be a war in twenty-four hours and told me to leave. Nothing has happened in two days and I know there ain't going to be no war. I want the price of a return ticket to Breslau."

I told him, as politely as the circumstances permitted, to go to hell.

An old lady with a half dozen children was next in line: "My husband telegraphed from America to ask you what we should do."

"Join him," I told her.

A colleague handed me a thick sheaf of telegrams from Washington. "They're all asking after Aunt Fanny," he whispered...

Yang suddenly appeared in front of the counter with a tray of food. I'd been on the job nearly twenty hours without a break and it was welcome.

By that time all trains were overcrowded and uncertain. So we organized bus caravans to the Danish frontier to get all the Americans who were willing to leave out of the country.

The dive bombers overhead started screaming down on us again. I shivered...

The telephone operator called across the room: "The Consulate at Copenhagen wants to know how many Americans from Hamburg to expect tonight." I looked at the check list in front of me.

"One hundred twenty-seven in all, if that last bus ever gets through."

A belligerent little customer came up, swinging from the shoulder. I remembered him as one of those I had tried to dissuade from coming ashore a week before.

"It's a damned outrage," he started. "The Government can't leave us stranded like this! They've got to send us a battleship!" I suggested he go out and rent one from the Germans. Maybe they had some extras.

Another fellow came up with a long harangue about the iniquity of Chamberlain: "There ain't going to be no war, I tell you I know it. Chamberlain's just trying to scare us and you're in cahoots with him."

Over the heads of the crowd I spotted one of the British Vice Consuls. He was waving a telegram form at me.

"*WARONE*" it read.

Over the noise of the crowd in front and the dive bombers overhead
I shouted congratulations and asked a clerk to put a notice on the
bulletin board announcing war between England and Germany.

THE CROWD IN the Consulate had begun to thin out and it was
getting dark. We couldn't turn on the lights because we hadn't gotten
around to rigging up any blackout curtains. I went into the lavatory
(there were no windows there) and drafted the day's telegraphic
report to Washington.

The doorbell started ringing but I went on writing. When I'd
finished the cable, the doorbell was still ringing:

I went to the door and opened it impatiently.

A slightly disheveled young man was standing outside.

"Can I see the Consul General?" he asked meekly.

"Hell, no!" I answered. "Everyone has gone home but me and
anyway the Consulate is closed for business until tomorrow. Come
back then."

"But I was told to see the Consul General as soon as I arrived."

"I don't give a damn what they told you. Come back tomorrow.
And anyway who told you to see the Consul?"

"The Secretary of State, sir," the boy replied very diffidently. "I've
just come from Washington."

"What the hell does Washington think it is doing?" I exploded.
"We spend all our time trying to send everyone home and then the
State Department starts sending people over here. Who are you
anyway?"

''I'm sorry, sir, but I'm the new Vice Consul."

I groaned a bit ungraciously but let him in and told him to wait till
I'd finished coding.

I went to the safe to get out the codes. By this time another Vice
Consul had come back to the office to help me. He held a match
while I spun the dial on the safe:

"Right to twenty-five, left to thirty-three, right to eighteen," I murmured to myself and then tried the handle. The safe wouldn't open.

"You should start to the left," the other Consul suggested.

I tried it but the safe stayed shut.

I could hear the new Vice Consul giggling. We struck another match and tried again:

"Left!"

"No, right..."

The match box was practically empty by the time the safe door finally swung open. Half an hour later the telegram was coded and on its way.

I turned to the new Vice Consul: "Where are you staying? I hope not in the center of town. The British are sure to start bombing the railroad station any minute." (Little did we know that the British didn't have a bomber fit to use and wouldn't have for another couple of years.)

"I'm sorry but I'm staying at the Station Hotel. Maybe I should move."

I took him to the Station Hotel, picked up his bag, and brought him home to spend the night with me. He was still there when I was transferred the following year.

In the middle of the night the phone rang. It was the clerk at the telegraph office to say that all the telegrams we'd sent had been stopped by the censor. None of the telegrams had been especially important except a couple to Rotterdam and Copenhagen telling them to meet several hundred fleeing Americans and get them on some boats for home. I got the telephone operator and asked her to put me through to Copenhagen by phone. She tried and rang back: "Sorry, no phone calls are allowed to Copenhagen."

"Try Rotterdam."

"Sorry, no calls to Rotterdam."

Brussels, Amsterdam, the Hague – all the same reply. It was a nasty feeling being completely cut off from outside and I called the

Embassy in Berlin to tell them. The Charge d'Affaires, Alexander Kirk, answered the phone:

"Don't I know it!" he answered. "I've been trying to phone Washington for six hours."

A little while later the telegraph operator called back: "I thought you might like to know you could send telegrams to Rome."

That gave me an idea and I dialed the long distance telephone office.

A few minutes later I was talking to a very sleepy Secretary in the Rome Embassy. I asked him to telephone Rotterdam and Copenhagen and give them my message. Then I went back to sleep.

A few days later communications were restored but we had to talk in German. I was on the wire with the Consul in Copenhagen talking with his American secretary who knew about half the necessary German vocabulary. I, too, knew about half – but it was the other half. However, somehow we managed to make ourselves understood until I started making polite conversation while waiting for some information from the file room.

"Are the lobsters in Copenhagen as good as ever?" I asked.

"I'm not a lobster," the girl retorted angrily.

"I didn't say you were a lobster. I asked if they were good in Copenhagen."

"Of course I'm good. Just what are you driving at? I never heard a more impertinent remark."

"I asked if the lobsters were good, damn it. Next time I'm up there I'll take you out and we'll try them out."

"Try me out?..." A string of good old Yankee invective followed. I was about to try again when suddenly a third voice broke into the conversation speaking fluent English:

"For God's sake, speak English!"

It was the censor.

The moment the British declared war the British Consul and his Vice Consul and two secretaries were interned in the best hotel in town. And I was assigned the job of looking after them and their office.

One evening I had gone to the British Consulate to get some papers and as I left I started, as usual, to seal the Consulate with sealing wax. It was late in the day and it was already quite dark. I took out the sealing wax, a piece of ribbon, and our American seal and started to work. It wasn't long before I'd come to the conclusion that the ordinary two-armed man is not designed to fasten a ribbon on a vertical surface with hot sealing wax. I burned my fingers. I burned the ribbon. I covered the floor with melting wax. But the ribbon wouldn't stick.

Suddenly I felt a firm hand on my shoulder. I jumped and turned around. An enormous German policeman was standing in the gloom behind me.

"Come along quietly now and don't make a fuss. No monkey business."

"But I'm an American Vice Consul and I've a perfect right to be here. I was just trying to seal up this damn door."

The policeman was firm and eventually I agreed to come along:

"But first you've got to help me with this door. I can't leave it unsealed. Here, hold this ribbon flat while I heat the wax."

The policeman stooped down and put his thumb on the ribbon. I heated the wax with a match. The match went out and I couldn't see. I plunged the stick of wax where I thought the ribbon ought to be. The cop jumped and barely suppressed a curse. "That was my thumb," he said, a little plaintively.

"Sorry," I said and tried again.

Eventually we brought the door, the ribbon, and the wax and seal together and all was in "best butter," as the German expressed it.

"Now what?" I asked the policeman after I thanked him. "You had better come along to headquarters and tell your story to the Gestapo."

At Police Headquarters the Station Captain couldn't find the Gestapo's telephone number, which gave me a couple of good openings for comments about police who are so secret you couldn't find them. But eventually we got through and the Captain caught hell. Consular officers were not to be detained under any circumstance, he was told, and besides the American Consul General was already raising the devil about his missing Vice Consul.

I was about to leave when the air-raid siren went off for the first time since the war began.

The Captain officiously ordered everyone into the cellar.

"Not I," I said stubbornly.

The Captain looked at me perplexed:

"But, please, Herr Vizekonsul! Everyone must go into the cellar. Besides, we have a very nice cellar with a room for visitors and some excellent Mosel wine. And you know the law! Everyone must go."

"And you'll detain me again if I don't, I suppose? And you'll catch hell again for arresting an American consular officer?"

The Captain shrugged his shoulders in despair as I marched out onto the street. The last pedestrians were just running for cover. The siren was screaming wildly. A plane zoomed overhead at house-top level. I didn't dare look up, convinced that it was a British bomber and that at any moment I'd be blown to bits. I hurried on through the deserted streets. I tried not to run just in case someone recognized the American Vice Consul and saw how scared he was. A police car dashed past:

"Get into a cellar," they shouted and sped on.

At long last, out of breath and scared half out of my wits, I reached the Consulate. The Consul General was waiting for me at the door:

"Take it easy," he said. "The Air-Raid Center just phoned to say it's only a practice raid."

AT THE ATLANTIC Hotel, where our Consul General lived and where the British contingent was interned, life was a little dull. But each evening we foregathered in our Consul General's suite and listened to the BBC's account of how the phony war was doing. The Gestapo guards of our British friends were at first a little reluctant to ignore Dr. Goebbels' order not to listen to the BBC, but we easily convinced them that they shouldn't leave their British prisoners unattended during the newscasts.

Early one morning, two or three weeks after the war had started, a phone call came from Berlin to ask which of the British Consular staff had been arrested and put into jail. I replied that as of the night before no Britisher had gone to jail. But Alexander Kirk, who was on the phone, was insistent and finally said:

"Well, if they're not in jail now, they soon will be. The German Foreign Office has just told me they were going to hold two of them as hostages for the German Consul and his secretary whom the British arrested in Glasgow."

I hurried down to the hotel to find all four Britishers in the midst of a hearty English breakfast. My news worried them a bit and they began speculating as to which of them the Germans would choose. Aside from the two consuls there were two girl secretaries, one of them a tough thirty-year-old English woman and the other the eighteen-year-old daughter of a local British businessman, who had never been away from home for the night until the Germans interned her. A few minutes after my arrival a couple of detectives from the German police turned up with orders to take the junior Consul and the eighteen year old to the Hamburg prison. We wished them Godspeed and I promised to call on them during the course of the day.

It wasn't till late afternoon that I succeeded in getting to the prison. It wasn't exactly a homey place. While I waited in the visitors' room I could hear the clank of iron bars and the ringing of hobnailed boots on the steel floors in the corridors outside. After a few minutes they brought in the young girl. When she saw me she threw herself around my neck and burst into hysterical tears. I eventually got myself untangled and tried to comfort her as best I could. I gave her some pajamas and a package of odds and ends her worried mother had sent her and told her I'd be back to see her soon. As soon as she was led back to her cell I went and called the Chief of the Hamburg Police:

"You could have taken either of the two girls as hostages," I told him. "One of them is a big, husky woman who isn't going to mind a little jail life. The other is a poor little child who will probably never get over the effects of a night in prison. So you went and chose the young one."

The Chief of Police was very apologetic and said he understood and would see what he could do. I got back to the waiting room of the jail just as they led in the English Consul, flanked by two Gestapo guards. The Chief of the Jail, a retired Army Colonel, warned us to speak only in German. I told the Chief I'd arranged for meals for the two Britishers to be brought from the Atlantic Hotel. Also I'd brought a few small items the Consul might need. First I took from my briefcase a phial of sleeping tablets. Immediately the Chief objected.

"I'll take them and give the Consul one every evening."

The Consul flew into a rage:

"What do you damned Germans think we British are? Do you suppose that just because you can lock us in a stinking jail, we'll commit suicide? Before this war is over it will be you and not I who will try to kill himself."

The Chief was a little taken aback and finally agreed to let the Consul keep his pills.

I took advantage of this concession by the jailer to press forward.

"Now here I have a bottle of Scotch whiskey. Englishmen always have a Scotch and soda with a little ice in it at six o'clock in the evening. I'll have the ice and soda sent over from the hotel," I said to the Chief, "and I'm sure you'll be so kind to have it served in the Consul's cell promptly at six p.m."

The Chief looked slightly upset at my presumption but finally said he would see that the Englishman was served his Scotch and soda each evening.

This new concession began to make me wonder just how much we could get away with.

"Now there's one more thing," I went on. "A half hour before dinner, which will be served at eight in the evening, an Englishman always has cocktails – Martinis, usually. I've brought the shaker and the mixings and the hotel will send the ice." I reached into my briefcase and pulled out a bottle of gin and a bottle of Vermouth. I turned again to the Chief of the Jail:

"Now you take four parts gin and one part vermouth, put them in the shaker and..."

But I could see I'd reached the limit as the Chief exploded:

"God damn it! I'll let him have his sleeping pills and his whiskey and soda. He can even have the gin and vermouth, but I'll be damned if I'm going to mix cocktails for my prisoners."

A few days later London relented and released the German Consul at Glasgow and the British Consul and his secretary were returned triumphantly to the Atlantic Hotel.

15

RETURN ENGAGEMENT

After four years in Moscow and a year in Berlin, the State Department told me I need not return to the Soviet Union for ten years. Nine months later a curt telegram came to Hamburg, ordering me back to Moscow "as soon as possible." (The State Department invariably orders you to leave for a new post almost before the orders are issued, but I've yet to arrive at a new post where they aren't surprised to see me so soon. Perhaps I've taken the Department too seriously.)

However, I was determined to take one last look at the West before the war reduced it to ashes. So I headed for London via then-neutral Brussels for a ten-day vacation. I got to the German frontier at Aix-la-Chappelle late one night. The frontier, I was informed, had been closed "for the night." The guards were stubborn and wouldn't let me through until I hinted I was carrying some important documents. Sumner Welles was at the moment conferring in Berlin on a possible peace effort. Not even Hitler's border guards wanted the war to go on if it could possibly be stopped. Although I hadn't specifically stated I was carrying peace proposals, they evidently thought my reluctance to admit it was due to secrecy or modesty. The fact was the only official document in my pocket was my passport. At any rate heaven and earth began to move to reopen the frontier to let the mysterious courier across. They looked for a car, then a carriage, and finally a bicycle to carry me the mile or two to the Belgian railhead. After I'd strapped my suitcase to the back of the bicycle and was about to push off into the night, the head of the guards warned me that the final outpost was not reachable by phone and so had not been warned of my approach. It was just possible he might shoot at me. The guard presumed I was quite willing to take the risk. But the thought of being shot dead for the sake of an extra day's holiday didn't appeal to me at all and, besides, the international situation was tense enough without American Vice Consuls getting shot up in the dark. I told him politely that I most certainly did object to proceeding at my own risk. I unstrapped my suitcase and went to the Station Hotel where I was soon installed in a comfortable room. I'd hardly gotten to sleep, however, when the head of the Border Police appeared.

Would I mind crossing the frontier on a railroad engine which they'd managed to scare up for me?

I agreed that a steam engine ought to be safe enough and within an hour I was riding across the frontier in the cab of my private train. That evening I was being entertained in the best restaurants of London as the "latest arrival" from Germany.

For three days I was wined and dined all over town. But then someone else turned up from Germany and I was a has-been. And something else happened which prompted me to speed my departure for Moscow. I had brought with me from Hamburg some samples of the leaflets the RAF had been dropping. Few of the leaflets had actually ever reached Hamburg, due apparently to a certain confusion as to just where Hamburg was. But about twenty miles north of the city was a large forest where I frequently went shooting over weekends and it was swamped with the leaflets. Judging from the present state of Hamburg, the RAF eventually corrected whatever navigational error brought about this slight mistake.

For some reason, possibly modesty on the part of the Ministry of Information, but more likely an understandable anxiety to avoid public criticism (not entirely undeserved) as to the quality of the leaflets, they were considered "secret" and the British newspapers were unable to get copies of them. On my first evening in London, unaware of the Information Ministry's reticence I had given sample leaflets to several American journalists. The next morning a photostatic reprint of one appeared on the front page of a London newspaper. Immediately questions were asked in the House of Commons and it was decided to investigate the source of the leak.

I left for Moscow the next day.

MOSCOW HADN'T CHANGED too much in the two years I'd been away. There were some new faces among the diplomats and a rather larger contingent of Germans than in the past. Politically there'd been a few zigs and zags in the Party line which resulted in the Germans being very good friends and the Americans very evil enemies. But this meant the German diplomatic contingent had to be excessively polite to Soviet officials. No longer was it possible for them to drive through a red light or tell a Soviet policeman to go to the devil, or make rude comments about the Five-Year-Plan. As one German diplomat, Gebhart von Walther said wistfully:

"Oh, for the good old days of bad relations!"

Our relations with the Russian population were probably more restricted than ever before and even travel began to get impossibly difficult. After I'd settled back into the familiar groove, I made one attempt to get out into the countryside. First, I asked Intourist to get me a reservation on one of the Volga River excursion boats, but Intourist replied regretfully that the boats were all being repaired. Then I asked to visit a horse-breeding farm near Moscow. That, too, they explained was closed for repairs. When I asked how you close a breeding farm for repairs, they said they weren't experts in such matters. Eventually, however, they said I could take an airplane to Rostov on the Don and visit some farms down there. The airplane flight was a little hectic, as the plane was badly in need of repair, but after a few unscheduled stops in beet fields and prairies, we finally arrived in Rostov, where I was met with great cordiality by half the city hierarchy.

I asked them to arrange a visit to a collective farm the next day. They looked at each other a little embarrassed and then one of them replied regretfully that there weren't any collective farms in the Rostov area but there was a splendid champagne factory right in town. I said I didn't want to see any champagne factories and that I was surprised they didn't want to show me a collective farm. They said it was a very special champagne factory and that every cultured person ought to see it as it was very scientific and the champagne was very good. Besides, the only collective farms worth seeing were several hundred miles away. I said I was sure the champagne was very good but I still wasn't interested in tasting it and that I was surprised there were no collective farms in Rostov Oblast. I added that I thought my American newspaper friends in Moscow would be interested to know that contrary to the impression they'd gathered from the Soviet press Rostov Oblast had not been collectivized 99.9 per cent. Under the circumstances I thought I should send them a telegram to correct this rather serious mistake. Could I have a telegraph blank so that I could telegraph the Moscow correspondent of *The New York Times?* The city officials looked even more perturbed and asked if I wouldn't like to go up to my room and have a bath. I said I thought we ought first to fix the itinerary for the following day. Otherwise they might be seriously inconvenienced in the morning. They suggested that perhaps there was one small collective farm about twenty miles away which I might go to after I'd visited the champagne factory. I said I would agree to that provided the car that took me to the champagne factory remained at my disposal and wouldn't have to go away for repairs as soon as it had deposited me at the factory. They saw the logic of the request and promised that I could keep the Intourist car all day.

The next day an Intourist Ford drove me to the champagne factory. I went through it so fast that when I came out the other end the conducting party was still a hundred yards behind. When I got to the yard I discovered the Intourist Ford had disappeared. While I was blowing my top the factory Director caught up with me and explained that we were expected in his office for a wine-tasting ceremony. I told him I never drank wine before noon and besides I wasn't going to stop yelling until a car was produced for me at once to take me to the collective farm. At that moment the President of the City Soviet, the Mayor, appeared and promised to let me have his car if only I would come to the wine tasting. He explained that the entire local bureaucracy, including the President of the Oblast Soviet (the Governor) and the whole City Council had been counting on the wine-tasting party ever since they'd been told by Moscow that I was coming. They would be very disappointed if their American friend let them down at the last moment. Besides, it was eleven o'clock already and they felt sure I could stretch a point about drinking before noon for the sake of Russian-American relations. But I was still skeptical about the car and it was eventually agreed I could take the key of the Mayor 's Lincoln with me upstairs so that no one would take the car away. So I put the key in my pocket and joined the elite of Rostov in the wine-tasting room.

The affair started off with the usual number of toasts: to Stalin, to Roosevelt, to Hull, to Molotov, to Mikoyan, the head of the Food Commissary... Who was the head of the American Food Commissary? I considered appointing Mr. Private Initiative to the post but thought better of it.

Then the Director of the factory praised Soviet Industry in a long speech and explained how Stalin wanted to make everyone happier by giving them plenty of champagne. Then the Technical Director, an old Frenchman who had been stranded in Russia after the Revolution, arose and made a long plea that the wine growers of France should follow the example of the progressive wine growers of Soviet Russia and learn how to make good champagne in six months rather than wait several years to make the filthy old bourgeois stuff they turned out nowadays. As the old Frenchman sat down he turned to me and whispered:

"Have you ever heard such horse manure?"

By that time I'd had enough and announced I had to go to see the collective farm. A cry of protest went up. They hadn't even started to show me their new *red* champagne they'd just invented thanks to the leadership of Stalin and Mikoyan. I said I'd tasted red champagne in France and besides my doctor had forbidden me to drink any. But what about the sixty-year-old Napoleon brandy they had just succeeded in producing in three months, thanks to progressive Soviet science? I regretted exceedingly that sixty-year-old liquor always made me sick. But wouldn't I taste their non-alcoholic champagne? I made such a face at the suggestion that they thought I was going to be sick right there. Eventually they gave up and followed me down to the waiting car. Not until I was comfortably settled beside the driver did I pass him the key and tell him to start off. The Mayor and a little man in the familiar blue suit of the GPU, who was introduced as an agronomist, got in behind.

There was a good deal of whispering between the Mayor, the "agronomist" and the chauffeur before we drove off. At the first intersection the chauffeur turned in the direction of the center of the town. I pointed out to him as firmly as possible that I'd been in Rostov before, that he was heading not out of town but into town, that I knew there were no collective farms in the City Hall and please would he immediately tum around and go in the opposite direction. He must have been impressed because with a shrug of his shoulders he wheeled around and started for the countryside.

We'd been driving about ten minutes when the "agronomist " leaned forward and whispered anxiously to the chauffeur. A moment later I was not surprised to see him pull the choke lever practically out of the dashboard. The engine coughed and died. The chauffeur looked pleased and said:

"Sorry, the engine is *kaput*. We must go home."

I leaned forward, pushed in the choke, suggested he step on the starter and get going. I was no progressive Soviet chauffeur, I admitted, but I did know something about bourgeois American cars.

The chauffeur once more shrugged his shoulders, started the motor and off we went.

Another five minutes elapsed and again the "agronomist" started whispering to the chauffeur. A moment later the driver switched off the engine, leaped out of the car, lifted the hood and began to attack it with a wrench. It was obvious, given half a chance, he would take the motor apart. I slid over into the driver's seat, started the engine and called to the driver that if he wanted to come along he could jump in behind. With that I set off at a fairly good clip down the road toward open country.

Immediately an indignation meeting started in the back seat. I had no right to drive a State automobile. I told them the Mayor himself had loaned it to me and it wasn't my fault if the chauffeur was either an incompetent or a saboteur. The Mayor thereupon subsided but the "agronomist" grew more vehement. I had no right to drive a car without a license. I pulled out my driver's license and passed it back to him for inspection.

I was violating the traffic law and should be arrested, he said.

I passed back my diplomatic card which said I couldn't be arrested.

I was kidnapping the Mayor and they would ask Moscow to have me recalled when we got back.

I stopped the car and invited the Mayor to get out if he wanted to. He didn't, so I drove on.

By this time we were well out in the country and the flat plains of the Don Valley stretched out on either side. A mile or so further the road passed by the barns and huts of what was obviously a collective farm so I pulled up and got out. Five minutes later the proud President of the collective farm was showing his American visitor around the plant while the "agronomist" and the Mayor walked dejectedly behind. The President of the farm told me they'd had a bumper crop, that as I could see from his barns and the newly cut fields their harvesting losses had been negligible. The cattle in the barns looked sleek and fat. It was certainly one of the most prosperous collectives I'd seen in all the years I'd spent in Russia. "You should be proud of it," I said rather pointedly to the "agronomist," but he just looked sour and didn't say anything.

When I got ready to go back to town I offered to drive, but the driver said with a slight twinkle in his eye that he thought he could nurse the car into town. A half hour later the Mayor and I were sitting in my hotel room drinking a glass of whiskey. The "agronomist" had disappeared – doubtless to report the outrageous behavior of the American. I turned to the Mayor:

"It just doesn't make sense to me that you should want to prevent an American from seeing your farms. They're in better shape than they've been for years. You ought to be proud to let us see what you've done."

The Mayor looked helpless and raised his hands in the air: "My orders were that you weren't to leave town."

Two days later when I returned to Moscow I told a Foreign Commissariat official of my adventures.

"But don't blame the Mayor," I added. "He did his damnedest."

Except for my trip to Rostov and one or two courier runs to Persia, we were pretty well confined to Moscow and its small pleasures. One of these was Sir Stafford Cripps' Rolls-Royce. It had belonged to a British subject who had died in Leningrad and, in order to get her estate settled, Sir Stafford Cripps, then the British Ambassador, had put it up for sale. The chief American mechanic in the Embassy, a yeoman in the Navy, Stannard, took a look at it and reported it had possibilities. Together we arranged the purchase for fifty dollars and one rather badly damaged typewriter. Sir Stafford seemed satisfied with the deal and we were delighted.

The Rolls was about twenty-five years old. It was a limousine and the crate-like body sat high above the chassis so that it towered over any other car on the road. It must have been thirty feet long from bumper to bumper. But Stannard insisted it had an engine you could do things with. Whatever the things were, Stannard did them. And then one evening he and I took a spin together on the one good road in Russia – the Mozhaisky Chaussée which led to my dacha and, incidentally, to Stalin's too.   .

The old-fashioned crate immediately attracted the attention of other motorists and we were soon the butt of any number of not very funny jokes about capitalist backwardness. Eventually we got a little fed up with progressive Soviet wit and the next joker to come along was challenged to a "little race." We suggested for the starting point of the race a point about one kilometer ahead and the finishing point one kilometer beyond that – a good half mile before a sharp turn where the chaussée went through a dangerous underpass. The Russians accepted the challenge and agreed to a stake of twenty rubles. They started off in leisurely fashion toward the starting point. Their car was a Soviet Ford which was quite good and had a top speed of sixty-five miles an hour.

As soon as they'd gone on Stannard and I got to work. I took the wheel. It was the simplest job, Stannard explained. He took over the controls. He twisted valves, he pumped pumps, he adjusted levers. The Rolls began to pick up speed. Stannard pumped harder and we nosed the car into a higher gear. The speedometer didn't work but I could see we weren't doing so badly as we reached the starting line. The Russian Ford was waiting but with its quick pick up was off ahead of us.

By this time Stannard was sweating and pumping and turning levers and switching switches. Then he slipped into a super-high speed gear. I hung on for dear life to the enormous steering wheel trying to keep the top-heavy crate on an even keel. A few moments later we were roaring down the chaussée at a good seventy-five miles an hour. We passed the Russian Ford in a burst of speed and crossed the finish line with a hundred yards lead.

But then came the job of slowing down. I slammed on the foot brake for all it was worth. Stannard manned the hand brake at the same time as he unwound the valves and gears. Very gradually the huge box responded and in a minute or two we pulled up by the side of the road just short of the underpass. We were limp with exhaustion when the Russians shamefacedly pulled alongside and passed us their twenty rubles. I was just able to make a few comparisons between progressive Soviet engineering and old-fashioned British techniques before they drove off.

Although a little wearing on the nerves and muscles, we found the sport good fun and took a spin on the chaussée several more times to turn a few honest rubles. But then our Embassy Counselor, Walter Thurston, saw us performing one evening and called me in the next day to say he thought it was just a little undignified for diplomatic secretaries to be racing Rolls-Royces on Stalin's favorite highway. Besides, he said, it didn't look particularly safe.

The old Rolls had rather a sad end. When war broke out with Germany, we kept her in running form in case it was necessary to abandon Moscow in a hurry. We figured we could put a couple of large drums of gasoline in the back seat and drive her with the caravan of Embassy cars until she broke down. At least she could serve as a tank car for as long as she kept going. But we left Moscow by train and the Rolls sat unused in the backyard of the Embassy until one of the first German incendiary raids. A small bomb went through the roof and the back seat. Fortunately it didn't explode. But it did succeed in putting the Rolls permanently out of action. I am told that someone later sold the nickel in the radiator to the Soviet Scrap Metal Trust for seventy-five dollars – not a bad bargain considering we'd bought it for fifty dollars from the future Chancellor of the British Exchequer.

Even then the Rolls didn't cease being useful. When the going got rough in Moscow after the bulk of the diplomatic and Government staffs had evacuated to Kuibyshev, the Americans all collected in the Ambassador's residence at Spaso House, thus putting a considerable strain on the available plumbing facilities. So our Embassy carpenter, Leino, a very intelligent and resourceful American-Finn dug a pit under the differential and with a few modifications of the bombed-out back seat turned the car into what was probably the first Rolls-Royce water closet in the history of plumbing.

16

SIDE DOOR TO RUSSIA

Before World War II, the most popular visitor at the American Embassy in Moscow was the diplomatic courier from Washington. He didn't travel in a reindeer sleigh and he didn't wear a white beard, but he made up for it by turning up every other Thursday instead of just on Christmas. He brought us not only super-secret instructions from the Secretary of State and mail from home, but also everything the Soviets had left out of the Five-Year-Plans – from Band-Aids to outboard motors.

When the war broke out, the courier was one of its first victims. The Nord Express from Paris to the Soviet frontier stopped running even before the war started. First the courier was shunted around through Scandinavia or Switzerland; but then as the war developed he was diverted further south, until eventually he had to go by way of Central Africa and thence north to Iran. At Teheran, one of us from the Embassy usually met him and carried the pouches up to Moscow. It was on one of these trips to Teheran that I found Djulfa – the side door to Russia.

Before the war, the usual way of getting from Teheran to Moscow was to take a car to Kazvin and then cut north through the Elbrus Mountains to the port of Pahlevi, at the southern end of the Caspian Sea. There you could catch a little Soviet steamer called the Warrior that once a week, weather permitting, would take you to Baku.

From Baku you could get a Russian "Express" to Moscow. (Russian "Expresses" are a somewhat unique institution. It once took me five days to go six hundred miles in one. That's an average of five miles an hour if your arithmetic is the same as mine.)

But there was another road from Teheran to Moscow, although hardly anyone had ever even heard of it. In fact, I'd only found out about it from an old German globetrotter who had crossed there before the Russian Revolution. It went through the Southern Caucasus and avoided the Caspian Sea altogether.

Provided your visa authorized your crossing the frontier that way, you passed Kazvin and kept going west to Tabriz, the capital of Kurdistan. From Tabriz a little used road led north to the village of Djulfa, on the Persian side of the Caucasus Mountains.

There are really two halves to Djulfa – the Persian half and the Russian half. Dividing them is a fierce little mountain river called the Araxas. A rusty old iron bridge provides a slightly rickety link between them. It was built in the days of the Czars when a railroad line – long since abandoned – connected Tabriz with Tiflis in Russian Georgia. At least that was the way things were back in 1940. Later, when Persia became a supply route for Russia, it may all have changed. But I haven't been back since then – and for reasons you'll soon understand, I have no immediate plans for doing so.

The Djulfa route had officially been closed for many years and I'd always before traveled by way of Pahlevi and Baku, and each time I'd promised myself never to do it again. For one thing, the Caspian has been getting shallower for the last few thousand years, and nowadays it only takes the backwash of a couple of Persian mosquitoes to stir up a first-class storm. Besides, the *Warrior* is anything but a luxury liner. It has the seaworthiness of a canoe and is the natural habitat of cockroaches and bedbugs. To cross the mountains from Kazvin to Pahlevi is about as nerve-shaking an experience as I know. The road, a very narrow one, winds precariously along the edges of cliffs and mountain rivers. A steady stream of overloaded, swaying trucks driven by opium-dazed drivers roars along at breakneck speed all day and all night. I'd once had to spend two days at the top of the pass trying to extricate an American diplomatic courier – he was an ex-FBI agent, at that – from a combination of acute dysentery and a broken rear axle. But that's another story.

So, when the courier had arrived and turned over his pouches to me, I asked the Soviet Consul at Teheran for a visa to go by way of Djulfa. He first told me very emphatically that the border was closed. But I pleaded with him, reminding him of the *Warrior* and the mountain road. I described my allergy to bedbugs and heights. He was obviously one of the more human specimens of bureaucracy, for he listened sympathetically and eventually gave me the visa for Djulfa.

Before he could change his mind I hired a car and took off for Tabriz. My Moslem driver saw fit to bring along one of his wives and a year-old child. "They'll so enjoy the ride," he said. I don't know how the wife liked it, but from the time we left Teheran till we drove into Tabriz late that night the child maintained a noise-level roughly equal to that of a fire siren.

From Teheran to Kazvin, where the main road turns north to Pahlevi, a continuous convoy of trucks kept the dust high about us so that we could scarcely see the edge of the road. At Kazvin we left the main highway and struck out for Kurdistan. The traffic dwindled noticeably and only infrequently did we meet a truck or passenger car. Persians evidently don't often find it necessary to go up into the wild highland country of the Kurds.

Tabriz was once the southern terminal of the railroad from Tiflis and its stone buildings still give a strange, musty, European atmosphere to an otherwise eastern town. I spent the night in an old dilapidated inn and set out early the next morning, with the driver but minus mother and child, for the border directly to the north. The road from Tabriz was little more than a track through the barren, rocky country. There was no traffic except for an occasional camel or donkey train or a solitary tribesman. By noon we had reached the foothills of the Southern Caucasus and, after a few more miles of winding through the sparsely settled, parched hills, we pulled into the half-deserted border town of Djulfa. Once, I imagine, when the railroad was operating, Djulfa may have been a fairly active little way station. But today it is not even the end of the line. The western-style stone station house is deserted, its windows boarded up. Around it, sprawl the mud brick, flat-roofed houses typical of the East. As we drove through the bazaar half the little booth-like shops which lined the road on either side were closed. In only one or two were the shutters propped open to provide shade for their sleeping owners. In the dim light behind them you could just make out a few bottles of saffron or curry, an old tire or two, and perhaps a few broken kerosene lamps. In the middle of the village we stopped at a rundown teahouse to ask for the Customs Officer. The shop owner admitted there was such an official, but added that since the border had been closed for so long, he had no idea where to find him. I sat down at a dusty little table in the shade of a big plantain tree and sent the driver to rout out the missing official.

They evidently did not have much trade in the shop, for it took upward of half an hour to stoke up an old copper samovar and produce a cup of very mild tea.

I'd hardly finished the tea when the driver returned with a sleepy-eyed, gray-bearded old gentleman in a peaked cap. He saluted me solemnly, bowed, and announced that, despite the inconvenience of the hour – his siesta time no doubt – he was at my service. I told him I wanted to cross the border to Russia. He blinked a moment and asked me to repeat. I said I wanted to go across the bridge to Soviet Djulfa.

"Cross the border? Over the bridge? Soviet Djulfa? But no one ever does that, not in twenty years has anyone crossed this frontier. Besides, the Russians won't let you."

I showed him my passport and he examined the Soviet visa.

"It may say so in your passport – but those Consuls down in Teheran don't understand. And why do you want to go to Soviet Djulfa? Do you know what it's like?"

I explained I only wanted to pass through Djulfa, that my destination was really Moscow.

"Moscow! May Allah save you! Djulfa is bad – but Moscow!" He shook his head in sympathy for the benighted foreigner. "An American," he muttered to himself, "and he wants to go to Soviet Djulfa and Moscow." It was obvious he considered the Araxas the edge of the habitable world. Beyond it lay the mysterious other world of Russia. Eventually I persuaded him that, mad or not, I was going to cross the frontier.

"*Enshallah* – Allah wills it!" he said at last. "If you must, I'll let you – but remember – it's your own responsibility."

We climbed back into the car and headed north again for a mile or two along the railroad track till we came to the Araxas River, where a rusty old trestle bridge carries the tracks across into the Soviet Union. At the southern end of the bridge a tiny wooden shack was labeled in faded paint: "Frontier Station." Inside, a Persian soldier was dozing on the floor, his rifle across his stomach. The Customs Officer produced some rubber stamps with which he adorned my passport, borrowed my fountain pen to add a few more illegible hieroglyphics, and officially declared me checked out of the Shah's Empire. The soldier took my bags and diplomatic pouches and deposited them in the center of the trestle. The official gravely shook my hand and climbed wearily into the car as though he'd seldom had such a hard day's work.

He looked at me a moment and then rolled down the car window so that he could talk to me:

"Friend, are you sure you know what you're doing?" he asked paternally. I nodded that I was. He shook his head in commiseration and the car started off. In a few minutes he, the driver, and the car were a tiny dust cloud in the desert to the south.

It was already dusk when I finally marched onto the bridge. A slight wind had blown up and above my head the rusty iron rods and beams rattled and clanked. As I stepped from sleeper to sleeper my boots sank into the rotten wood. Between the sleepers I caught glimpses of the swirling river forty feet below. The span was hardly more than a hundred feet long, but it seemed endless. As I finally approached the far end, I made out a ragged, dirty, yellow sheepskin coat leaning against a post. A pair of black eyes peered at me from behind the long, oily wisps of wool. As I came abreast of the post the coat sprang to life and a rifle, complete with bayonet, poked into my stomach.

"*Stoi!*"

I'd had some experience with Soviet border guards before and I thought I knew most of the tricks of dealing with them. Approach Number One was a hearty smile and a lusty "Greetings, Comrade." I explained to the good man that his Government had given me a visa – a written permit to cross the bridge. The guard didn't budge – neither did the bayonet. I pulled out my passport and thrust it toward him over the rifle. He struck my hand away with the flat of his bayonet and growled, "No one gave me any orders about you; go back where the hell you came from."

Approach Number Two was the sterner approach: "Soldier: Call the Commander of the Guard and behave yourself in front of an official."

The bayonet dug deeper into my overcoat and the guard growled: "Go to hell."

"Soldier, I've permission from Stalin to cross this post? and in writing!"

"Comrade Stalin hasn't told me about it and until he does you're not crossing any post I'm on. Go back where you came from."

By this time it was getting dark and my bag of frontier-crossing tricks was running low, so I walked back to the wooden shanty on the Persian side of the river and asked the sleepy guard for a telephone to call the Russian Command Post. There wasn't any telephone, he told me, except in the village two miles back.

"Then I'll have to go back there and call the Russians," I said, and moved off toward the town. The Persian jumped in front of me. A Persian rifle began to dally with my coat button. "Oh, no you won't –

you've been checked out of Persia and you can't come back till you've a new entry visa."

"But look here, friend, the Russians won't let me off the other end of the bridge, you won't let me off this end – what do you want me to do, jump into the river?"

The guard smiled. "*Enshallah*," he remarked with some finality. He dozed off to sleep, his rifle still pointed at my stomach.

I walked back to the middle of the bridge and sat down on my pile of suitcases and diplomatic pouches. The wind had grown stronger, and the old trestle began to creak and shake. In the gorge below the Araxas swirled and hissed over the rocks in its shallow bed. All in all the situation was not very good. There had been times before when border guards and policemen had made my road a blind alley, but this was the first time I'd been in an alley that was blind at both ends. I tried to think of some new approach to the guards. The courteous old Persian was the result of an ancient and apparently easygoing civilization. The sheepskinned Soviet on the other hand was the result of the world's youngest and brashest system. Nevertheless, in their different ways each was as effective as the other – and as unapproachable. There seemed to be no way out but to wait. If there was anything to oriental fatalism something was bound to happen.

Another hour must have passed before a light showed in the door of the Russian guardhouse and the change of guard came out. I jumped up and hurried toward the ceremonious little group. They were probably swapping passwords when I shouted: "Hey! I've a visa to cross here – for God's sake let me in!"

Three rifle bolts clicked simultaneously and a particularly sour voice – obviously at least a sergeant's –growled: "Citizen, go back where you came from."

There was nothing for it but to crawl forlornly back to my pouches and try to barricade myself from the wind, which by this time was neither light nor warm.

As the bridge rocked and groaned I thought of the *Warrior*. Was it really so bad? At least it had cabins to shield you from the wind – and a little bar where you could get a glass of vodka. It did have bedbugs and cockroaches – but at least they provided company and kept you busy. Here on the bridge, alone, cold, hungry – completely cut off from life – I regarded the *Warrior* with something akin to affection. I thought of the pass across the mountains, the dizzy precipices – but they were no worse than the grim sight which greeted me every time I looked down at the river below. I was still huddled there an hour or so later when a friendly voice startled me: "Comrade, you haven't got an extra cigarette, have you?" It was the new Soviet guard. As I lit his smoke, his young and not-entirely-unkind face showed up for a second. Then he started back to the bridgehead.

Such a contact could not be allowed to lapse.

I called: "Listen friend, I've a package of twenty cigarettes – American. If you'll call the officer in charge..."

He stopped, hesitated a moment and muttered he couldn't leave his post. "I'll see what I can do when I'm relieved," he added.

I wasn't particularly optimistic about the future. I snuggled back between the pouches and tried to shut out the wind. The bridge still shook and groaned and creaked. The river hissed and snarled down below. The moon came up over Mount Ararat and I wondered what Noah would have done if he had been stuck without a visa after the Flood. I don't know how long I lay there shivering. At last someone called to me: "Comrade!" (That was encouraging, it's always "Citizen" in Russia when trouble lies ahead.) I got up and walked gingerly toward Russia again. A flashlight popped on and blinded me. "Your passport, please." I dug the little book out of my pocket and held it in front of me. A hand darted out and snatched it. "Thanks." I decided quickly I'd better make the most of all these politenesses and started forward – but the same voice turned to stone: "Halt, go back where you came from."

I growled back that he damn-well wasn't going to swipe my passport and leave me to die unidentified on a railroad trestle. "Wait till I tell Washington about this!" I added. It was a little too obvious that Washington was going to know little and care less for some time

– not till some mail clerk counted his pouches or a personnel chief checked on the number of Vice Consuls in circulation. I'd heard of cases when it had taken years to discover a pouch was missing, and as for Vice Consuls...

So I crawled back to my cave of pouches and tried to reconcile myself to the worst. I snapped the handcuff of the "secret" pouch to my wrist. It would look better when they dredged me up from the river.

I curled up again among the pouches, and time dragged along. I was very cold and much hungrier when I heard footsteps on the bridge. I scrambled to my feet just as a squad of Russian soldiers came to a smart halt in front of me. Four soldiers seized my bags, two more ranged themselves beside me and a young officer politely told me to follow him. In a few minutes I was on a truck between two shiny bayonets, bouncing over the road to Soviet Djulfa, the other Djulfa – or, rather, the other half of Djulfa. I thought of my courteous old friend the Customs Officer. It seemed days ago and thousands of miles away that I'd said goodbye. And yet, all I'd really done was to get to the other side of town.

It was well after midnight when we drove up to a neat little building in the center of town. "The Hotel," the Lieutenant explained affably, but there was something in the way he said it and in the way the soldiers stared that set me to thinking. "You can spend a night here and go on by the morning train to Yerevan and Tiflis. I have a couple of soldiers going that way and they'll be glad to go with you."

He ushered me into a very small, but clean room with a cot, table and chair, but no window. I remonstrated that I couldn't possibly sleep without some ventilation. After some shuffling about I was politely ushered into a second room similarly furnished, but with a tiny round window, heavily barred. I pointed to the bars and asked: "Against burglars?" The Lieutenant grinned and left me.

I unrolled my sleeping bag on the cot, pulled out my toilet kit, and started out the door. A soldier jumped in front of me, his gun at the port, and told me very firmly to stay in my room.

"Look friend, I only want to go to the bathroom. I've been traveling all day. I'm dirty and..."

The Lieutenant appeared and I repeated my modest request. Gallantly he waved aside the guard and escorted me into a small and rather smelly courtyard. Behind us came the guard, his rifle at a smart shoulder-arms. I looked inquiringly for some plumbing but the Lieutenant just waved majestically.

"Anywhere at all," he said.

Back in my room I called pompously for the maitre d'hotel. The guard looked puzzled. The Lieutenant too looked perplexed, but after five or ten minutes he returned with a third character carefully decked out in a starched white coat, a clean white towel around his waist .

"I'll have dinner in the main dining room," I said. "Just something simple – an omelet perhaps and a bottle of red wine. I'll wash up and be ready in ten minutes."

The "maitre d'hotel" gaped. He began to shuffle and squirm.

I repeated: "I'll be ready in the main dining room in ten minutes. That is all."

He started toward the door – under his white towel I could see the striped trousers of the NKVD border police.

At the door he stopped and turned to me: "Where the devil do you think you are?" His voice was polite – just very bewildered.

"In the Djulfa Hotel, of course."

"Hotel, hell! This is the jail."

But the NKVD is always resourceful – even in Djulfa. Eventually an excellent omelet and an even better bottle of wine were served in my room. The next morning my hospitable Lieutenant escorted me to the station. His two soldiers and I had a very pleasant journey through the Southern Caucasus. As we passed Mount Ararat I asked them what they would do if Noah were to alight from his Ark without a visa. They didn't know.

By mid-afternoon I was strolling through the pleasant streets of Yerevan, unaccompanied except for the inevitable little man in the black leather cap and the double-breasted blue suit-badge of the ubiquitous Secret Police.

17

THE TARTARS PAY UP

The German attack on Russia in 1941 was probably one of the best-telegraphed punches in military history. For months the cables between Moscow and the western capitals burned with guesses as to when it was coming off: May 1, May 15, May 23, June 15. Yet, twenty-four hours before the attack on June 22 the American Embassy still had its full contingent of peacetime Vice Consuls, visa officers, and wives. It had always been a source of worry to those of us who had charge of the Embassy's larder. Every extra mouth made us a little less mobile – a characteristic we believed would be invaluable in the event of a war.

After a hard guerrilla war between the feminine element of the Embassy and the bachelors, the latter managed to get the ladies into airplanes bound for Sweden and Persia, and by the evening of June 21 they were well out of the country. At that point we cracked a bottle of champagne, went to bed, and woke up to find Russia at war. It was not a happy situation, but at least we were on a streamlined wartime footing.

But even this didn't solve our problems. In the first place, it was all very well to have been forehanded enough to have a large supply of food and drink in the cellar in Moscow. But suppose Moscow should fall and we would have to take off into the steppes? Just how were we going to lug along several tons of canned food? Besides, we'd reckoned without the Pentagon. As soon as the war started, a stream of officers from Washington began to descend on us. They were sent to observe the Red Cavalry in action, the Red Artillery in action, the Red Air Force in action, and even the Red Fleet in action. Four years later, when the smoke cleared away on VE Day, some of them had visited a quiet sector or two of the front. Others had watched the front coming at them, but the large majority, to their fury, had seen less of the war than the average Russian *muzhik*. But they were all of them good company and if they were frustrated it was through no fault of their own. And besides they had to eat, smoke and, occasionally, drink. All of which emphasized the importance of keeping close to our supplies.

There was one further difficulty. Even the most undiplomatic official could hardly go to the Russians and say: "Look here, we've got some rations in Moscow and we want to move them to a safe place in the east because we think Moscow may fall and you fellows may forget to provide us with food or transportation at the last minute." In the first place, the chances were the Russians didn't want to face the possibility of Moscow being evacuated. In the second place, it wouldn't be too tactful to tell them they were going to forget us and our food. And in the third place, if we all left together and they didn't have any food they would probably not be too concerned whether we had any or not.

As usual, Ambassador Steinhardt had a bright idea to get us out of our predicament. The food was to be labeled "Archives." He explained to the Soviets they were secret documents which it was dangerous to leave in the front zone. "Wouldn't it be wise," he asked the Foreign Commissariat, "to move these secret documents into the zone of the interior, to Kazan on the Volga for instance?" The Foreign Commissariat agreed and a small staff consisting of the First Secretary, Charlie Dickerson; the Assistant Military Attaché, Mike Michela; and varied assistants, including Yang, Midget and myself was soon on its way to Kazan accompanied by a boxcar full of "Archives."

All went well until a case of the "Archives" was dropped on the station platform in Moscow and a thin stream of brown liquid smelling peculiarly like brandy trickled across the ground. We looked a little embarrassed, the porters looked a little amused, and the baggage master made some cryptic remark about the strange form our archives took. I attempted a feeble explanation about American archives being different and needing a preservative but the explanation fell as flat as the case of brandy.

After some thirty hours we arrived in Kazan and were met by a bustling shirt-sleeved comrade who immediately took charge of us and our cargo. We were all used to being taken in hand by Intourist agents wherever we went, so we shook hands affably and, like Stanley in Africa, murmured: "Intourist, we presume." But our shirt-sleeved guide replied, "No, I'm the President of Tartary." Before we left his bailiwick, we were going to have many dealings with him, including one kidnapping and some near riots, but we never quite got over the conviction that he was more like a Cook's Tour man than the president of one of the Constituent Republics of Russia.

He was kind enough and provided us with a large wooden house in the Street of the Wolves where we spent several lazy weeks guarding the "Archives." Kazan was a pleasant enough little provincial town on the Volga, and many of its inhabitants still remembered the American Relief Agency under Herbert Hoover, which had taken the edge off the famine after World War I. But Kazan soon began to fill with refugees from western Russia and its quota of food had to be spread thinner and thinner over the growing population. While we relied largely on our own supplies, we did get some provisions from the local Kremlin and we soon began to share the natives' resentment of all outsiders. Once or twice a rock bounced against the shatterproof glass of our station wagon, and occasionally we were told in no uncertain terms where the Tartars would prefer to see us – and it wasn't in Kazan.

We didn't have much to do. Our communications with Moscow over one slender telephone line were very precarious. Our only source of news by radio was all too frequently interrupted by local electric power failures. Before long the morale in the house on the Street of the Wolves began to waiver.

And then Midget, my police dog, came in heat.

We'd been sitting about, one evening after dinner, playing chess and discussing the gloomy news from the front and speculating on our chances of getting out of Russia alive if Moscow were to fall. The prospects didn't seem too good. For one thing, the only two routes out of Kazan, besides the railroad back to Moscow, were the southern branch of the Trans-Siberian and the Volga River to the Caspian Sea. Neither was particularly inviting and as we went to bed we agreed the future was not very rosy.

I'd hardly gotten to sleep that evening when I was awakened by a bloodcurdling shriek from Charlie Dickerson who was sleeping in an alcove off the corridor next to me. When I reached his bedside he was mumbling incoherently about being attacked by wolves so I figured he'd just had a nightmare and suggested he take a glass of water. The next day the news from Moscow was no better. When we heard the evening broadcast on the BBC our spirits were even lower than on the night before. The capital had been badly bombed. The Germans were only a hundred kilometers away and the prospects looked generally bad. We went to bed in a thoroughly depressed state of mind.

Just as I was dozing off that evening another scream came from Charlie Dickerson next door. This time he was out of bed and thrashing around his alcove before I could get to him.

"It's wolves, I tell you. I know damn well it's wolves. They came right into the room and were sniffing around the bed before I even got to sleep." Mike Michela and I did our best to soothe him. Eventually we got him back into bed.

But when he repeated the performance on the third night there was no holding him. "I stayed awake on purpose," he said, "and kept a flashlight in my hand. Just as they started for my bed I turned it on. There were three of them and they were making straight for the bed."

Mike and I looked at each other and shook our heads. Poor Charlie, he was a very level-headed fellow and it wasn't like him to crack up so easily.

Charlie snorted angrily, "Don't stand there looking at me as though I was crazy. I tell you there were three of them as big as a good-sized police dog – bigger than Midget anyway."

At the sound of Midget's name there was a whimper from under Charlie's bed and Midget, who had had every dog in the neighborhood chasing her for days, crawled gingerly into the lamplight.

After that we locked Midget in a closet off my room and Charlie was no longer bothered by wolves.

NOT LONG AFTER the battle of the wolves we got news by radio that the Lend-Lease Mission under Lord Beaverbrook and Averell Harriman was coming to Moscow. The following day several of us were ordered back to Moscow to help the Mission. I arrived to find myself the local secretary of the American Mission, which meant being local interpreter, travel agent and general messenger. It kept me busy almost twenty-four hours a day without much let-up for a week or so. Only once was there a moment of relaxation, when I took a group from Washington around Moscow to look at the "bomb damage." Moscow had not really been badly hit by bombs, but the generally run-down condition of most of the buildings occasionally misled our visitors. Several times I was forced to admit that the cracked walls, broken cornices and torn-up streets were probably caused more by the way the buildings were built than by outside influences. When we came to one building, near the Borodino Bridge, which was completely flat, I had to explain that one of the two wings had collapsed shortly before the war began. The other, I was glad to say, was due exclusively to the predatory Germans. It was hard to tell, I explained, where Socialist construction left off and German bombing began.

But eventually the negotiations were finished and the Mission left again for home via Archangel. I accompanied them on a little destroyer, the *Harrier*, as far as their battle cruiser, the *London*, which was waiting for them in the White Sea. It was a bitterly cold, jet-black night and the sea was tossing the *Harrier* around like a cork. Three times we tried to make fast to the cruiser and each time the hawsers snapped. At last, by some mysterious feat of British seamanship, we managed to get our passengers across to the cruiser, but only after Beaverbrook had angrily refused to be moved on a baggage tray. "I won't be carried around like a damn whiskey and soda," he protested.

When the last passenger had been moved across, the big ship's propellers started up at full speed and she slipped swiftly off through the giant waves toward the north. We on the *Harrier* heaved a sigh of relief and were about to go below to the warmth of the captain's cabin when the loudspeaker from the *London* suddenly boomed across the waters: "*London* calling *Harrier*. *London* calling *Harrier*. Well done, *Harrier*! Well done!"

It was one of those times when British understatement comes into its own. The poor *Harrier* had not accomplished its mission without paying for it. As we turned back to Russia, the captain announced that we had bashed a good-sized hole in the hull just at the watermark. However, we managed to reach a small emergency port, the name of which I have forgotten, and there we were picked up by the yacht of the Admiral of the White Sea Fleet and brought to Archangel. The next day we were back in Moscow.

But we were not to remain very long. The German advance showed no signs of slowing down, and each day the operations chart in the Military Attaché's office showed them closer to Moscow. Outwardly the population of Moscow was calm, but close below the surface it wasn't hard to detect the mixture of bewilderment and anxiety which dominated everyone. Little by little one organization after another was transferred to the east. One day I received a call from some friends in the ballet:

"We're not supposed to tell you, but we're leaving tonight on a special train for Kuibyshev. The grand opera and the whole ballet corps and orchestra are in one train and there doesn't seem to be any arrangement for feeding us. Could you give us some food?"

I told them I couldn't give them anything from the Embassy but I had a few cans of leftovers in my apartment they could have.

Two days later Ambassador Steinhardt called a meeting of his Military, Naval and Political staffs.

"How long can Moscow hold out?" he asked us. The argument was still going hot and heavy an hour later when his Secretary put his nose through the door: "Molotov wants to see you in twenty minutes at the Kremlin, Mr. Ambassador."

"Well, I guess that's our traveling orders," Steinhardt said. "I just wonder where they're going to send us."

I recalled my conversation with my friends in the ballet: "Kuibyshev, most likely," I suggested.

An hour later Steinhardt was back. "We've got just six hours before we leave for Kuibyshev." He turned to me: "How the hell did you know?"

The next six hours were on the hectic side. We'd been getting ready for a possible move for weeks, but even so, getting the Embassy staff notified, packed and assembled was no easy job. We'd been wise enough to evacuate the Embassy wives before the war started, but when the time came to move the rest of us, there were several indispensable Russian women secretaries, several small children and, last but not least burdensome, the woman correspondent, Alice-Leone Moats.[15]

By evening we were all assembled in the ballroom of Spaso House where the Embassy staff had first foregathered with Ambassador Bullitt one spring morning eight years before. It was a gloomy evening. Outside it was half-raining, half-snowing. The slush-

---

15. Alice-Leone Moats (1908-1989) – an American journalist and author, born in Mexico to wealthy and socially prominent American parents. Later in life she became a conservative columnist.

covered streets were practically deserted. Most remarkable of all, you couldn't find a policeman anywhere – the one and only time that had happened since the Revolution in 1917. (Later we found they'd all been shipped off to the front to plug a gap in the front lines northwest of the city. They did their job well and the German divisions were stopped a few miles from the outskirts.) Overhead we could hear the drone of planes and the banging of the anti-aircraft artillery.

Inside, in the ballroom, seventy-five men, women, and children stood around or sat on the floor waiting for the final word to move. Each time a gun roared outside, Ivan Yeaton, our Military Attaché, shook his head gloomily and announced that it was the sound of German field guns.

"It's no use even trying, Charlie," Ivan shouted at me. "They must have surrounded the city by now. We'll never get out of Moscow with the Russians." But I was busy collecting extra blankets and electric heaters, or having hurried last-minute conferences with the small staff under Tommy Thompson and Freddy Reinhardt, who were to remain behind.

At last word came that the evacuation train was waiting for us in the Kazan Station. A few minutes later, a long caravan of cars, followed by two trucks loaded with extra supplies, wound out of the Spaso House gate and through the deserted city. At the station confusion reigned supreme. No one knew where the train was, except that it wasn't at the platform where it was supposed to be. No one knew how many passengers it could carry, or what provisions for feeding us had been arranged.

"There'll certainly be a dining car," Molochkov, Chief of Protocol, kept repeating, but he didn't sound very convincing. It was Molochkov's job to act as nursemaid and chaperone to the Moscow Diplomatic Corps. An air raid was in progress outside. A part of the station had been hit the night before. Finally, someone found the train – without a dining car, but with a large boxcar behind the engine. No one knew what the boxcar was for, but the American contingent didn't wait to find out. As soon as the station master's back was turned we drove our trucks of supplies up the platform and in a few seconds had stowed their load into the car. On top of them we shoved one of the Embassy messengers with instructions to bolt the door from the inside and not let anyone in until he heard my voice telling him to.

A few minutes later the train pulled slowly out of the station. On board were the British, Polish, Yugoslav and American Embassies. Another section of the train with the rest of the Diplomatic Corps followed a few minutes later. I stared gloomily out of the window at the faint outlines of the buildings as we passed. It was not exactly the way I would have planned to say goodbye to Moscow. But I was soon torn away from my sad thoughts by the announcement that Ambassador Steinhardt had lost his umbrella in the rush. I tried to tell the Ambassador that where we were going there'd be a lot more snow than rain for the foreseeable future. But Steinhardt was stubborn. So we searched the train and eventually found the umbrella in Sir Stafford Cripps' compartment, where some porter had, naturally enough, thought it belonged. Cripps, who had never had much love for his late Prime Minister, the umbrella-carrying Chamberlain, was glad to be rid of it.

It is just five hundred miles from Moscow to Kuibyshev, about as far as from Detroit to Washington. Even by Russian railroad standards, we thought, it wouldn't take us much more than eighteen hours. So we were a little disappointed when we woke the next morning to find we were only twenty miles from the Kremlin. It turned out that the Germans had made a desperate attempt to surround the city from the south. Fortunately, a Russian counter-attack with a cavalry corps had turned them back just before they reached the rail line leading east. Shell fire had torn up the tracks for a few hundred yards but after several hours' delay they had been repaired and we were off again. Thereafter a series of unexplained stops slowed us down so that by noon we had hardly gone ten miles more. By that time the Moscow Diplomatic Corps was getting hungry and they told the harassed Chief of Protocol so. The latter smiled affably and said he'd do something about it. At the next halt I went up to the boxcar and got a few cans of tuna fish and a can of Saltines. Ambassador Steinhardt produced a Sterno can and an old pewter bowl. The Saltine can was converted into a coffee pot and before long we'd managed to feed at least the American contingent – with one extra cup of coffee for Ambassador Cripps.

But the roaring appetite of a couple of hundred British, Polish and Yugoslav diplomats was still the dominant note of the train. We Americans had enough food for ourselves, but we figured it wouldn't last very long if we fed the whole gang. Night came and still no food was produced by Molochkov, the Chief of Protocol. By the second morning the half-starved Diplomatic Corps was in an ugly temper and in no mood to hear the unfortunate Molochkov repeat that he was about to do something about it. Eventually he pacified his charges by promising to call up from the next station and order a meal at the first big town ahead. But we didn't stop at the next station. Instead, when the train halted we were in the middle of the half-deserted steppe. The only sign of life was a small collective farm a quarter mile across the fields from the train.

Diplomats are generally accused of being rather pampered, impractical types, but when they've been without food for thirty-six hours, you'd be surprised how they can improvise. The train had hardly come to a stop before a mad horde streamed from the doors toward the farm. It looked like a football crowd storming the goal posts at the close of a game. In a few seconds a couple of dozen chickens, geese and ducks had been flushed from the farmyard and were being pursued by posses of diplomatic Counselors and First Secretaries across the fields. A Pole and an English Colonel, "Pop" Hill, found the chicken coop simultaneously, just as one of the farmhands was coming out with the day's take of eggs. The farmer took one look at his attackers, dropped his basket of eggs, and set off toward the horizon as fast as he could run. Pop and the Pole each seized a handle of the basket and started to pull. For a second it looked as though there was going to be a serious falling out between allies but calmer councils prevailed and they eventually agreed to go fifty-fifty.

A little while later, when the engineer blew his whistle to reassemble his passengers, a wild-eyed crowd of disheveled raiders clambered back on board carrying their loot. It included a fair number of chickens, geese and ducks, a couple of dozen potatoes, and even some bread. Last to climb aboard was the Yugoslav Secretary, Bogich. Bogich weighed easily three hundred pounds and his appetite was fabulous. I had often seen him tuck away a whole roast when we served together in Hamburg. But this time his hands were empty, his coat a mass of mud, his trousers ripped and covered with thorns and burrs. I asked him what luck he had had and he growled something about the relative speed of a chicken and an overweight Serb. For a moment I thought he was going to break down completely as he looked at the food his colleagues had collected. But he gathered himself together long enough for me to duck into my compartment and grab a can of tuna fish which I surreptitiously slipped into his pocket. Immediately his usual grin came back and he hurried off to his bunk for a feast.

The collective farm took the edge off the diplomatic appetite for the day and the following afternoon – the third since we'd left Moscow – Molochkov managed to establish contact with a station up the line. When we reached it, an enormous meal of hot soup was waiting for us.

That was the last food, except for the fast dwindling reserve of tuna fish we Americans had, until we reached Kuibyshev five days out of Moscow on our five-hundred-mile journey at five miles an hour.

In Kuibyshev our luck changed, at least temporarily. Molochkov announced there would be a luncheon at the Grand Hotel within an hour. It was a banquet: beef, ham, cheese, fruits, vodka and even caviar. We gorged until we couldn't swallow another sturgeon egg. As we left the table, I turned to Molochkov and asked what time supper would be.

"Supper? You want supper too?"

I explained a little apologetically that we capitalists still had the silly habit of eating three times a day. Molochkov called the hotel manager:

"When will supper be ready?" he asked sternly.

The hotel manager gaped.

"Supper! Good Lord, you've eaten all the rations I'm entitled to for the next two weeks!"

But we managed somehow. For a few days we subsisted on black bread, sugar and coffee, and the few potatoes we managed to buy in exchange for dollars at the market.

Then one day a Volga River barge with the supplies we had cached in Kazan tied up at the dock in Kuibyshev. The barge captain sent word that we had just two hours to unload it. The ice flow from the north was only a few miles upstream, he explained, and he would have to get started ahead of it if he was going to reach the Caspian Sea before the Volga froze. There were no stevedores in those days in Kuibyshev – at least for private hire. So we mobilized the Embassy and just before the two hours were up we'd landed the last case of "Archives." It was a strange crowd of workers. It included one Ambassador, a couple of Generals, an Admiral, and an assorted crew of Colonels, Navy Captains, Secretaries of the Embassy, and journalists. From then on our menu developed a little variety. By the time our own supplies began to give out, the Russians had organized a special store where we were able to buy practically everything we needed to keep alive.

18

FISTICUFFS WITH VISHINSKY

Soon after our arrival in Kuibyshev, Ambassador Steinhardt went to call on the Acting Foreign Minister, Andrei Vishinsky. Before we left Moscow, Molotov had told Steinhardt that he and Stalin would fly to meet us in Kuibyshev. But when we arrived Vishinsky was holding the fort alone.

I went along with Steinhardt as interpreter and found Vishinsky holed up in a little hotel room. As yet the Foreign Commissariat had not gotten around to opening an office. Vishinsky gave the only chair in the room to Steinhardt, and he and I sat on the bed while we discussed business. Vishinsky told us of the defeat of the Germans on the outskirts of Moscow and explained that due to it, the rest of the Government had decided to stay in the Kremlin for the time being. But on other fronts things were not going so well and Vishinsky seemed very depressed.

As we rose to go, Vishinsky turned to the Ambassador:

"I'm afraid I've one more bit of bad news," he said.

Steinhardt stopped with his hand on the door knob. Vishinsky continued in a low, serious tone of voice:

"Yes, we must confess that we have made a serious strategic blunder in this whole business. We hope it will not prove too costly."

"But what is it?" Steinhardt broke in impatiently.

"Well, you see," Vishinsky went on, looking at me, "through some gross blunder we have evacuated the ballet and the American bachelors to the same town."

As things turned out, the ballet was our lifesaver during the cold, gloomy months that followed. Every other evening they performed *Swan Lake*, while on alternate evenings the opera did *Onegin*. Since there was nothing else to do, the ballet fans got to know the choreography of the swans pretty well.

The tiresome monotony of Kuibyshev came to a sudden halt on December 7, 1941. When the radio operators tuned in their receivers that Sunday morning, it didn't take them long to spread the word through the crowded little building that housed the Embassy. I dare say the reaction among the Americans on the banks of the Volga didn't differ very much from that on the Mississippi. At first we were a little dazed, then relieved that at last we were in it for fair. By nightfall, the Army officers among us were composing cables to the War Department requesting reassignment to troop duty while the rest of us were drafting urgent requests for permission to enlist. I doubt if any of those messages was ever read at home. At any rate there were no replies.

A few days later, on December 20, 1941, to be exact, the telegraph office nonchalantly brought around a radiogram it had received a couple of days before. Just what they'd been doing with it in the meantime, they couldn't say. I still have the original text. I quote exactly. It begins:

YOU ARI ANSTRUCTED TO NOTIFY IMMEDIATELY
THE GOVERNMENT TO WHICH YOU ARE
ACCREDITED THAT THE CONDGES OF THE
UNITED STATES ON DECEMBER 11 DECLARED
THAT A STATE OF WWR EXISTS DETWEEN THE
UNITED STATES AND GERMANY...

It was signed by Cordell Hull. Despite the quaint spelling, we didn't have much trouble figuring out what he was trying to tell us about Pearl Harbor. When we sent the word along to the Foreign Commissariat, Vishinsky complained that we were a little slow informing him of something he'd heard on the radio nine days before. We explained that it was hardly our fault if it took the telegraph office seven days to receive the radio message and another two days to bring it down the street to us.

The news was so good from the Russian point of view that even Vishinsky didn't argue the point. In fact, the Russian population, including the ballerinas, was in such a state of joy at the prospect of having us as allies at last that they forgot for a while that we were really only capitalist beasts at heart. Besides, the few luxuries we'd managed to bring down from Moscow with us proved to be almost irresistible temptations to our old friends. The ballet corps, the grand opera and its orchestra were all housed together in a large schoolhouse on the outskirts of town. They had no furniture, no beds, and not too much to eat. An invitation to dinner at the American "Embassy," an equally barren schoolhouse but where there was a certain amount of food and drink, was not to be ignored.

Furthermore, the Secret Police, who usually warded off any contacts we Americans might have with the Russians, had apparently been more than a little disorganized on the way from Moscow. At any rate, for several months they were still trying to get acclimatized and didn't seem to worry too much about the extracurricular activities of allied diplomats. In fact, in their anxiety to find food and blankets they were only too glad to share such tips as we could give them as to where to find a store of coal or a supply of bedding. Before long, the head of the Moscow contingent of the GPU in Kuibyshev became quite a buddy of ours. He was a very young and very large fellow whose name I think was Major Smirnov. We often met in the cafe of the Grand Hotel, and exchanged tidbits of housekeeping information over a glass of vodka. When at last his organization got squared away and settled down again to the old routine of following us about, I used to complain to him of the zealousness of his employees, but he always excused himself on the ground that it wasn't his boys but some zealots from the local Kuibyshev Secret Police who were responsible. I never quite believed him and often threatened to break off friendly relations if he didn't stop trailing our young attachés, whose friendship with the ballet was essential to morale. But it didn't do much good.

Then one evening, it was New Year's Eve, I went to a party at the Grand Hotel to celebrate the arrival of 1942. When I'd celebrated as much as I thought was good for me, I started home, but made the mistake of stopping by the main dining room to see what was going on. Most of the Diplomatic Corps and the foreign correspondents were busy forgetting the frustration of Kuibyshev over bottles of Russian vodka which the Soviet Government had provided for the occasion. In a far corner I saw Major Smirnov and a couple of his henchmen celebrating like everyone else. Smirnov caught my eye and signaled me to join him, but I shook my head and started out the front door. He chased after me and insisted I join him for a drink.

"I've had all the drink that's good for me already," I said. "And, besides, I never associate with the GPU after midnight."

This seemed to hurt his sensitive feelings for the next thing I knew I'd been lifted off the ground by a couple of his plug-uglies and was being gently carried to his table. When I'd been deposited in a chair beside him, Smirnov ordered a carafe of vodka for himself and another for me.

"When you've finished the carafe," he announced, "you can go home."

There was nothing for it but to go ahead and drink. Smirnov's companions had obviously already put away plenty and were feeling little pain. Beside me one of them was dozing quietly, his head bobbing up and down like the Dormouse at Alice's tea party.

I was about halfway through my carafe when I remembered that I had some business with Smirnov.

"It's bad enough having all the young attachés scared out of their wits by your flatfeet," I told him, "but now they've even started on me. As the oldest resident American diplomat in Russia I resent that. After all, we're allies now and I've even shaken hands with Stalin."

"So have I," Smirnov retorted. "And besides, you're not being followed. I looked into it myself the last time you complained and it's just not true. I went through the entire list and you're not on it. I resent being accused of having one of my best friends followed."

He seemed to protest too much so I went on. "Well, then, just tell me what the car with license number 67-879 was doing the day before yesterday?"

The Dormouse beside me suddenly woke up and looked at me:

"What was that number again?" he asked drowsily.

I repeated it and he pulled a little notebook from his pocket and looked at it for a second.

"You've a hell of a good memory," he murmured and went back to sleep.

Smirnov blustered: "He's drunk. He doesn't know what he's saying. Besides, I'll give him hell tomorrow. " But he knew his game was up and soon stopped his protesting. Two minutes later I had gulped the last drop of vodka from my carafe, wished the GPU a Very Happy New Year, and was on my unsteady way home.

LIFE IN KUIBYSHEV was not always as dull and gloomy as one would have expected in a small, overcrowded, provincial city where the temperature seldom climbed above zero Fahrenheit and the wind seldom slowed to less than twenty miles an hour. For one thing, the news from the front began to change for the better. When we left Moscow, the German armies were streaming across the steppes as fast as their motorized divisions could travel through the Russian mud. But then they were slowed down in South Russia and stopped dead at Moscow. In December came the Russian counter-offensive on the Don.

I had been traveling through Central Asia on a special train
carrying the Polish Prime Minister Sikorski and Andrei Vishinsky
on an inspection tour of the new Polish Army then being organized
in Russia. It was not a very cheerful tour. The new Polish divisions
fell into two categories: those with shovels and those without. The
divisions with shovels were able to dig underground shelters to
protect themselves from the bitter winds which swept the Central
Asian plains. Those without shovels were forced to freeze above the
surface.

At each camp we visited, huge quantities of food were unloaded
from our train and a great banquet was arranged. The Polish officers
were more than pleased with the banquets but they were very worried
lest we think we were sampling their usual fare. We told them not to
worry on that account. For one thing, every banquet from silverware
to waiters was so like the last one that it was obvious it all came out of
the same place – in this case the baggage car of our train.

Each banquet, too, was the occasion for a great deal of toast –
drinking and speech-making *a la* Slav. Russians and Poles haven't
gotten together much throughout their history, but whenever they
do, it's likely to be tough on the non-Slavs who happen to be around.
The main theme of the toasts and the speeches was the coming
defeat of the Germans. And the Poles, despite their lack of clothes,
food, shelter or even guns, had only one request that they repeated
monotonously: couldn't they be sent to the front to join the fight?
Each time Vishinsky answered their pleas with a promise that as soon
as they were properly equipped, they would be given a chance to
show their stuff. But that hardly satisfied the Poles. They said they
were ready to fight with what they already had. They even got down
on their knees in front of Vishinsky and implored him to let them
go at once. But Vishinsky was stubborn and insisted they couldn't be
sent into battle the way they were armed.

I couldn't help recalling these frequent scenes some months later.
There had been a falling out between Sikorski's Government and
the Kremlin and the latter had decided to disband the Polish units in

Russia. By way of explanation, Vishinsky held a press conference in Moscow in which he told the world that the Polish troops were being released because they refused to fight the Germans.

The inspection tour with Sikorski and Vishinsky ended at Saratov, a provincial city about two hundred miles south of Kuibyshev. From Saratov Sikorski took an airplane to Teheran and thence to London. The rest of us were headed back to Kuibyshev but just how we were supposed to get there no one seemed to know. We found out that Vishinsky had an airplane at the Saratov airport so I went out to thumb a ride with him. But Vishinsky said his plane was full. I was supposed to go back with the special train on which we'd come. I pointed out to him that it would take at least five days by train and that I had orders to return to Kuibyshev at once. But again Vishinsky got stubborn.

While I stood at the foot of the ladder leading up into the cabin of the plane, Vishinsky stood at the top of the steps, beaming down on me charmingly, saying "no." Vishinsky's "noes" later got to be famous at the U.N., but that one was the most impressive he ever gave me. The wind was whistling across the airfield, the thermometer stood somewhere around twenty below, Fahrenheit, and the prospect of being left stranded in Saratov was more than I could stand.

I can't claim to be as eloquent as some of our negotiators at Flushing Meadows, but after I had shivered and pleaded with Vishinsky for a quarter of an hour on the Saratov plain, he suddenly relented and with a graceful gesture told me to get in. He even asked me to sit beside him on the hard metal bench in the cabin.

The plane was a C-47 type troop carrier and in the cabin roof was a turret for a machine gun. Only there wasn't any machine gun. Nor was there the usual plastic dome – just a big open hole through which the wind roared as we gained speed and took off.

I don't know how cold it got in that cabin. But I do know that despite double-lined fur boots, several pairs of fur gloves, and two fur coats I was half frozen fifteen minutes after we'd started. Apparently I wasn't the only one for soon Vishinsky began rummaging around in his briefcase and pulled out a large bottle of Soviet brandy which he uncorked and handed to me. I took a large swig. He followed suit and handed the bottle on to the rest of the company which included a couple of American officers, Vishinsky's bodyguard, and a Soviet newspaper photographer. After a couple of rounds, the bottle was empty and we all settled down again to grit our teeth against the cold. Another quarter of an hour passed. I was shaking from head to foot, but I noticed that my neighbor Commissar Vishinsky wasn't doing much better. Suddenly, with a gasp of exasperation, he reached into his briefcase again and produced another bottle of brandy. We finished it off even more quickly than the first one and relapsed into frozen silence. At that altitude the alcohol didn't take long to go to our heads but our other extremities were soon as cold as ever.

I was hunched up in my furs staring at the floor and wondering how long I could take it when Vishinsky abruptly got up from his seat.

"There's no more brandy," he said, "and if we don't do something we'll freeze. Let's box." Without any further preliminaries he swung a haymaker at my stomach. Vishinsky never was one for telegraphing his punches and the next thing I knew he'd landed a fast right on my middle. But the furs deadened the blow and I quickly replied with what I thought was a knock-out punch in Vishinsky's ribs. In a moment the rest of the passengers had followed our example and a general free-for-all was under way.

A boxing match in fur coats at several thousand feet is apt to be a little strenuous and before long all of us were out of breath and swaying unsteadily as the plane lurched through the bumpy air. A left from Vishinsky caught me off balance and I collapsed on the floor. But Vishinsky wasn't doing much better and, as he landed his punch, he lost his balance and fell on top of me. By that time, the rest of the passengers were also exhausted and decided I made a pretty good mattress.

That is, all but the Soviet photographer who knew a good picture when he saw one. Like a flash, he was up on a crate with his camera snapping a cozy little group, centered around the Deputy Foreign Commissar Vishinsky. The only passenger not visible was myself, buried under the coats and boots of the others.

But eventually we got back to Kuibyshev and about a week later I was wrestling with a gale down the main street of town when I ran into my friend the photographer, who didn't seem to be enjoying the weather any more than I was. So I invited him into the Grand Hotel bar for a drink and in a few minutes we were relaxing over a carafe of vodka. As gently as possible I brought the conversation around to our trip from Saratov and to the boxing match. After about the third round of vodka I asked casually whether the photo of the fight had come out. With a sly grin the photographer reached into his pocket and pulled out a snapshot. A split second later it was in my pocket and the photographer was yelling bloody murder:

"You can't take that! That's State property! I'll call the police!"

I hurriedly explained that the photo would be much safer in my pocket than in his and that if the police were called the fellow who took a picture of Vishinsky drunk on the floor of an airplane was going to be the one in trouble. The poor man saw the logic of my argument and subsided.

The photograph of the aerial boxing match was promptly stored away among my papers. Only after Vishinsky began to cut up in the U.N. did I take it out and frame it.[16] It is now hanging on the wall of my office.

EVEN IN THE Foreign Service, assignments to places like Kuibyshev aren't permanent. Eventually I got orders to move on: to Kabul, the capital of Afghanistan, where, the State Department told me, I was to open a new diplomatic mission. Just why the Department chose someone who had been camping on the steppes of Russia to

---

16. Andrei Vyshinsky (1883-1954) rose to prominence as a state prosecutor of Joseph Stalin's Moscow show trials and, later, in the Nuremberg trials. He served as Soviet Foreign Minister from 1949 to 1953, after which he became the Soviet Union's representative to the UN.

set up shop in the middle of the Hindu Kush Mountains I couldn't understand. Perhaps, I thought, they figured I was acclimatized to outdoor life. But later I learned there was another reason. Seven years before, when the Afghans tried to persuade the Americans through Ambassador Bullitt to open a legation in Afghanistan, I had listened to the Afghan Ambassador's eloquent description of life in his country and had casually commented to Bullitt that it might be an amusing assignment. Eight years later, when the Department decided to accede to the request, the only person on record who had ever suggested going there was myself. I must, in all fairness to the Department, add that it was one assignment I never regretted.

It didn't take me long to leave Kuibyshev. But before I left I gave myself a farewell party. I had a slight suspicion that after more than seven years in Russia even the State Department would hardly be sending me back very soon. A celebration was clearly in order.

To vary the diet of canned frankfurters and black bread, I sent the Embassy messenger, armed with a case of vodka, some gold coins, and several sacks of sugar, out into the country to buy a pig. He got the pig all right. It was only a few months old and wasn't much more than a foot long but when he reckoned the cost in sugar, vodka and gold it came to about two hundred dollars.

The party was gay, as parties in Russia always were, and lasted for several days. Eventually, however, I got rid of my guests and went to the airport with Midget to catch the plane to Teheran.

The airport manager insisted that dogs weren't allowed on airplanes. Fortunately someone had brought some vodka along to keep us warm while we waited for the usual delays common to all airports. So I gave the bottle to the airport manager and by the time the plane was loaded he wouldn't have cared if I'd taken a herd of cows aboard.

19

BUS TO KABUL

A favorite opening gambit for frustrated Third Secretaries is: "Now when I was Chargé d'Affaires to Poland..." (A Chargé is a diplomat temporarily in charge of an Embassy.) The story usually goes on to describe some hair-raising diplomatic crisis about how the Third Secretary courageously delivered a twelve-hour ultimatum to the King. If you look into the matter further, you are likely to find that the reason the Third Secretary was Chargé d'Affaires was that the Ambassador had resigned from boredom, the Counselor was down with the mumps, the First Secretary had eloped with the office stenographer, and the Second Secretary had gone fishing for the afternoon.

Now when I was Chargé d'Affaires to Afghanistan, the Afghans wouldn't even let me into their country. Third Secretaries, they complained with a good deal of reason, were not the proper people to establish diplomatic relations between sovereign states. I argued without much conviction that I was a very special sort of Third Secretary and that anyway it was wartime and eventually my country would get around to appointing a real Minister. The Afghans said such being the case they might eventually get around to giving me a visa. So for nearly six months I sat about Teheran waiting for my visa until at last President Roosevelt named Cornelius Van H. Engert to be Minister. Then the Afghans said I could come to Kabul.

There were plenty of odd jobs to be done in Teheran in those hectic days of 1942, and it wasn't hard to keep busy while I waited for my visa. For one thing, there were the Poles whom Stalin had finally agreed to let out of the Soviet Union. They had originally been "transported," as the Russians euphemistically call it, from their homes in Poland when the Red Army shared the Fourth Partition of Poland with the Nazis. Presumably they were the Poles least likely to succeed under a Soviet regime and the Kremlin thought they'd be better off in Siberia. Then when the Nazis decided to start partitioning Russia, the Kremlin came to the conclusion that they'd made a slight error and they'd better let the Poles get out of Siberia before they started some more trouble. The only practical way to get them out was through Persia. The British and ourselves had agreed to take them over from there and take care of them until Poland was liberated.

After months of delay, the Kremlin sent word to Teheran that the first transport of a mere six thousand women and children would arrive in Persia within twenty-four hours. The British had planned to send a staff of experts to take care of them, but the notice from the Kremlin was so short that no staff was on hand when the trucks began to pour into Teheran. So an American Red Cross man, a local American doctor, an Indian Army surgeon and I formed a committee of four to handle the emergency. The Iranian Government rose to the occasion magnificently and allocated a primitive but nonetheless adequate camp on the outskirts of town for the Poles.

Typhus was raging among the refugees when they arrived in Persia and our greatest concern was to prevent its spreading among the Persian population. We had enough vaccine to immunize the Poles as they arrived, but if the epidemic once started among the Persians there would have been no stopping it. Our great difficulty was that the Persians, no less than their Government, insisted upon giving a proper welcome to their unfortunate fellowmen from Poland. They came out to the camp in droves, bringing gifts of flowers and fruits and sweets.

We threw a guard of Persian police around the camp with orders to keep everyone out. But the Persian guards had never had typhus and couldn't see much sense in preventing their countrymen from giving bouquets of roses to the miserable refugees. We cajoled, we argued, we explained, and the police promised to obey, but the moment our backs were turned, into the camp would come a swarm of Persians bearing gifts.

Finally I hid behind a tree near the main gate, waiting for the guard to relax. In a few minutes a large car drove up and a distinguished-looking gentleman got out and walked through the gate. The guard not only didn't stop him but even saluted. I sprang forward and began giving the guard the best tongue lashing my primitive Persian permitted.

I didn't spare the visitor either. The latter looked a little startled at first but eventually bowed low and introduced himself as the Prime Minister of Persia. I hastily changed the tune of my song but not the words and after an exchange of diplomatic courtesies the Prime Minister acknowledged the reasonableness of my position, delivered the roses he was carrying into my hands and retired to his limousine.

A few days later the British staff turned up and took over the camp and I reported back to our Minister, Louis Dreyfus, for another job.

Eventually my visa to Afghanistan came through and I started to make preparations for the journey to Kabul. The capital of Afghanistan is about fourteen hundred miles due east of Teheran. It is not a particularly easy fourteen hundred miles. The first two or three hundred miles cross the "Lut," the great Eastern Desert, between Kabul and Meshed in the northeastern corner of Persia. From there you cross the frontier to Herat. Between Herat and Kabul lie the westernmost ranges of the Central Asian massif, which stretch from the Himalayas on the east to the Hindu Kush in the west. There is a road through the Hindu Kush from Herat to Kabul, but in 1942 it was impassable even for a jeep. So you had to detour around the south of the mountains to Kandahar and then north again to Kabul. Between Herat and Kandahar there are three large rivers which start high up in the Hindu Kush and flow down into the Persian desert, where they disappear in the sands. There have been bridges across each of them at various times in history, but usually the spring freshets carry away a span or two.

So I wired Washington for permission to take an Army bomber, of which there were half a dozen in Teheran, to fly me to Kabul. The U.S. Air Force said they could take me to Kabul in a matter of four hours. But Washington didn't seem to think much of the idea because it never even answered my cable. So I decided to risk the overland route and wired the State Department for permission to borrow a military reconnaissance car the Army authorities in Persia said was superfluous. But that didn't seem to strike a responsive chord because I didn't receive a reply to that telegram either. Finally I wired Washington that unless I heard to the contrary I was hiring a thirty-passenger Chevrolet bus and was starting in two days' time. The cost, I pointed out, was almost as much as the bomber and three times as much as the reconnaissance car. There was still no reply.

In Teheran I'd had the very good luck to find a young American, Bob Allen, who spoke fluent Persian and knew something about State Department work. He agreed to come along with me as Legation Secretary. Bob had been brought up in Persia, the son of a missionary, and he not only knew the language but the people as well. Besides, he had a sense of humor essential for an assignment like ours. In addition to Allen, my staff included Yang, my Chinese cook who had already traveled halfway around the globe and back with me, and Midget, the police dog who had been with me for eight years.

Washington had promised to send all the equipment, forms, typewriters and other paraphernalia you need to open a Legation, but by the time I was ready to start only a suitcase of secret codes had arrived in Teheran. However, Dreyfus, our Minister, was kind-hearted and permitted me to rifle his own shop for the bare essentials – all except typewriters, which were at a premium all over the world just then.

We took all the benches out of the Chevrolet and bought a couple of second-hand overstuffed chairs which were strapped to the floor, for Allen and myself. We piled the baggage and equipment into the back of the bus, loaded the top with several hundred gallons of gasoline, and were ready to start.

Just about that time a jeep rolled into Teheran from India with Major Gordon Enders, who announced he was the new Military Attaché for the Kabul Legation. He also told me all the bridges between Kabul and Teheran were down and that the tribes in eastern Persia were on the rampage. But, he added, he had a machine gun, and he would be only too glad to escort me on the journey. Gordon had spent most of his life in impossible adventures, beginning with the Lafayette Esquadrille in World War I. Later he was pilot to Chiang Kai-shek, took part in a few expeditions to Tibet and, finally, radio-commentated at Purdue University. Furthermore, he had a wild-eyed Pathan tribesman as an orderly who, Gordon said, would help Yang keep us comfortable on the trip.

Gordon and his Pathan were all we needed to make the trip a success and the next day we started off. The start was delayed a bit by the fact that the Polish colony whom I'd helped when they first arrived in Teheran insisted on providing me with a "stirrup cup" before the take-off. It consisted of several cases of champagne, much toasting and well-wishing. But our high-noon departure eventually became a reality around five p.m. when we roared out of town toward the desert.

From the first, Gordon and his jeep developed a tendency to reconnoiter about ten miles out in front which, it seemed to me, minimized the usefulness of his machine gun. We were hardly seventy miles from Teheran when a couple of boulders in the middle of the road forced the driver of my bus to slow down and detour around them. As we did so, the nasty whine of a rifle bullet indicated to us that night traveling wasn't the healthiest pastime in wartime Persia. When we caught up with Gordon in the next village, we discovered that the bullet had punched two nice holes in the gas tank. However, the chauffeur, a slightly nervous Persian, managed to plug the holes with something that looked like chewing gum while we bedded down for the night in a local Chai-khana, or teashop.

For two days we ground our way slowly across the Eastern Desert and eventually we arrived in Meshed, where we were put up at the local American mission. I paid a call on the Soviet and British Consuls, visited the tomb of the ninth Imam, and off we set again for the frontier. After the rifle-bullet episode, we had confined our traveling to daylight hours, but my social calls in Meshed had put us behind schedule, so we decided to push on across the frontier to Herat despite the darkness.

It was about eleven at night when the bus reached the final Persian outpost. By that time Gordon Enders, his machine gun, and jeep had long since passed the frontier. The Lieutenant in charge of the outpost told us a little acidly that the tribesmen were in a particularly restless mood, which we gathered meant they were more than usually trigger-happy. Their favorite hunting ground, the Lieutenant went on, was the nine-mile stretch between his outpost and the first Afghan garrison across the frontier. It would be foolhardy, in his opinion, to attempt to cross the border that night. I agreed with him and said we would gladly accept his kind invitation to put up with him till morning. He replied with full oriental courtesy that he hadn't invited us to spend the night, that the tribes doubtless knew a busload of rich Americans was in the area, that he only had six soldiers and had no intention of spending the night fending off half a hundred restless tribesmen. In that case, I suggested, perhaps we'd better go back to the nearest garrison town. That, he explained, was a silly thing to do as it was thirty-five miles away and we could be sure we'd be attacked before we got halfway.

I pointed out he wasn't being particularly helpful. In front the tribes were milling about, in back they were just as dangerous, and we couldn't stay where we were. Did he have any constructive suggestions? All the Lieutenant could suggest was that we take what he called "the necessary precautions" and get away from his outpost as quickly as possible before we attracted the attention of the local tribes. In the absence of Gordon and his machine gun, the "necessary precautions" were a little scarce, but we did the best we could with the revolver which I loaded and gave to Bob Allen with instructions to sit beside the driver and be prepared to club him if he stopped. I loaded my shotgun and gave it to Yang and told him not to shoot unless I told him to. For myself I got out my hunting rifle. Between my feet I put the suitcase of codes together with a small bottle of gasoline and a box of matches. The least I could do, I decided, was to burn them if we got into trouble. Then we dimmed the lights and started out for the Afghan border.

The road across the frontier quickly dwindled to a track and before long there was no sign of even that except for a series of cairns at irregular intervals. For nearly an hour we bumped over the rocky desert in low gear. Frequently we thought we heard shouting in the desert around us and once or twice lights seemed to appear in the distance. Yang knelt by an open window of the bus, sighting down the barrel of his shotgun into the darkness. Every now and then he began to whisper excitedly:

"Look, Master, look! Lobbers are coming, lobbers!"

But nothing concrete had showed up by the time we reached the boundary between Persia and Afghanistan. We stopped just long enough to read the inscription on the big stone column marking the frontier and then pushed on. It was still four or five miles to the first Afghan outpost and we figured we'd covered about half of that when there was a whoop and a yell and a troop of wild horsemen galloped out of the darkness. As they flashed by the dimmed headlights of the car we could make out their fierce, bearded faces peering from under tightly wrapped turbans. Embroidered cloaks trailed out over the backs of their little ponies. Tucked under their arms the short barrels of their Cavalry carbines pointed rather menacingly at us. Yang began to twitch nervously and look anxiously at me: "Shootee, Master? Shall I shootee?"

But there was something about the troop which puzzled me. Their capes and turbans and those ugly carbines all looked a little too much alike to belong to a disorganized band of tribal marauders. I asked Allen what they were shouting.

"They want us to stop," he replied rather unhelpfully.

I decided to take a chance and try to deal with them. I asked Allen to tell the driver to stop. But the driver would have nothing of it. He remembered my orders to Allen to slug him if he stopped and so far as he was concerned those orders still held. Besides, he didn't share my confidence in the charging band of horsemen outside.

One of the latter trotted alongside my window. His carbine protruded through the opening and practically touched my ribs.

I yelled at the top of my voice at Allen to stop the bus or else. Eventually he shoved the driver from his seat and put on the brakes himself.

When we had stopped, we shouted for one of the horsemen to come to the bus door. Yang's shotgun, Allen's revolver, and my rifle covered the door as one bandit swung off his horse and came toward the bus. He climbed through the door and harangued us for a moment. Allen turned to me and translated:

"He says, 'Welcome to Afghanistan!' He's the Captain of the Guard of Honor sent by the Garrison Commander to meet you."

Two minutes later we were seated in a circle around a bonfire with our new friends. A bubble-bubble pipe was produced and made the round of the party. It was my first and last experience with a water pipe, but I survived. Then we climbed back into the bus. The horsemen formed up in front and trotted solemnly ahead of us till we entered the fortress courtyard.

Enders was waiting for us in the Commander's quarters. He explained he'd arrived several hours before and told them of our approach. Thereupon they'd organized the Guard of Honor.

That night I surreptitiously removed the shells from Yang's shotgun just in case any more Guards of Honor appeared unexpectedly. But it didn't bother Yang, and for the rest of the journey to Kabul he knelt by his open window, the empty shotgun trained on the desert. Each time there was a movement among the rocks and dunes Yang would shout: "Look, Master, lobbers, lobbers!" But he never tried to shoot.

The first river we came to was the Farahrud. Contrary to reports, the bridge was still standing, although one section had recently been washed out and replaced by a rather rickety wooden span. We unloaded the bus and after a few tense moments the driver managed to get across without breaking through.

But the next bridge we came to, a day or so later, was thoroughly demolished and we pitched camp by the bank while we and the local authorities tried to figure out some way of getting across. The spring freshets had not yet subsided and the river, the Chashrud, was in flood. Eventually we managed to find a couple of good-sized barges which were lashed together, the front wheels of the bus on one and the rear wheels on the other. But then came the question of how to navigate the river. Finally a young tribesman appeared on a horse and offered to swim across with a tow rope. Once it was anchored on the other side we could swing across pendulum-fashion. It sounded a little precarious but there was no alternative, aside from waiting a few weeks for the river to subside. So off he went into the river with his horse and after a few exciting minutes succeeded in climbing out on the other side several hundred yards below us but with the end of the rope still tied to his horse's saddle. A couple of hours later we were all safely across the Chashrud.

The last bridge across the Helmand River just before we reached Kandahar looked easy enough when we first caught sight of it, but as we got closer we found the approaches had been washed away and that only a narrow S-shaped causeway led up to the bridge itself, at an angle of about forty-five degrees.

In charge of the bridge we found an old Hungarian engineer. It was difficult, he said, to get the local natives to work in straight lines, and hence the S-shape on the approach. Besides, the causeway had been washed out recently and they hadn't had time to build it up to a more reasonable angle. We might, nevertheless, take a try at it.

So once again we unloaded the bus and the unfortunate driver was ordered to make a run for it. The top of the causeway was a good thirty feet above the bank and if he should slip off the shoulder it was going to be a long drop to the bottom. But with a certain amount of browbeating the driver took his seat in the bus, backed well away from the bridge, and took a flying run onto the causeway. As he reached the incline the old bus shuddered and roared but its momentum got him well above the first curve before the wheels began to slip. A moment later he was halfway round the final curve, heading for the top. But then he lost his traction and the wheels began to spin wildly. The truck slid gently backward toward the edge of the causeway. At that point I turned my back and took a long walk into the desert. But the shattering crash I expected to hear as truck and driver hit the rocky bank below never came. When at last I came back, the bus was perched halfway up the incline, its hind wheels spinning in space, the chassis resting on the sandy causeway.

I looked at the Hungarian engineer: "Now what?"

"Oh, that's nothing. We'll lash the bus where it is and in the morning I'll get the local boys to pull it out. You can stay with me. I'm a pretty good cook and I've even got a shower bath in my garden. Besides, I haven't seen any Europeans for six months, and to be perfectly honest I rather hoped the driver wouldn't make it."

We spent a very pleasant evening with our Hungarian friend, who told us a long story of his escape from the Germans, the Russians, the Italians and various other nationalities. His story may well have been true, but I couldn't help feeling that it was something more like murder than burning nationalism which started him off on his trek to the Helmand River Valley.

When I woke the next morning, the bus was already safely across the bridge. I asked our Hungarian host how he'd managed it.

"Oh, it was simple," he replied. "I just called the local tribe and had them carry it across."

The rest of the journey was fairly smooth going. After Kandahar we turned northward again, up along the road Lord Roberts had marched down on his celebrated relief of Kandahar in 1880. Our last stop before Kabul was the walled city of Mukur. I was enjoying an excellent dinner in the local guest house when a servant appeared and told me I was wanted on the telephone. After a two-week trek across deserts and mountains, the last thing I expected was a phone call. It developed that there was a telephone line running all the way around Afghanistan. Each of the major towns had a party line – probably the longest party line in modern telephony.

The Afghan Chief of Protocol was calling me from Kabul about arrangements for my reception the next day. He explained that due to the absence of a railroad in Afghanistan, it would be impossible to meet me on the station platform as was the custom in most countries. Hence, in Afghanistan, they usually set up a reception tent about five miles from town, where he would greet me the following day. The uniform, he added casually, was formal dress: cutaway, striped trousers, and top hat.

I tried not to sound surprised and answered in my best French that my cutaway was buried in a trunk at the bottom of the bus, that it was undoubtedly very dirty and wrinkled from the journey and that anyway I had two hundred miles to travel across the desert the next day and thought little of the idea of doing it in a suffocating cutaway and silk hat.

The Chief of Protocol suggested that I follow the example of the British Ministers who usually stopped under a palm tree ten miles from town and changed there. I replied I thought less than nothing of that suggestion and proposed that since it was wartime I skip the glad rags and be met just as I was, in a cork helmet, khaki shirt and pants. I would be delighted if they were equally informally dressed. The Chief of Protocol, in flawless French, replied that there was no war in Afghanistan. His country was neutral and wasn't going to be forced out of its routine just because other countries couldn't get along peacefully. When the connection finally was cut off there had been no meeting of the minds. I tried to call back, but without any luck. (I was told later the Prime Minister had wanted to talk to his brother-in-law in Herat.)

The next afternoon, five miles from Kabul, our bus was flagged down at an enormous marquee that had been pitched by the roadside. Still in my khaki and cork helmet I was ushered into the tent and introduced to the Assistant Chief of Protocol dressed in full formal uniform. (Later, the Chief of Protocol, who became one of my best friends, told me he had deliberately stayed away, as he was afraid I would ignore his advice.)

We were offered some excellent melon and some fruit juices (Afghanistan is strictly non-alcoholic) and were then escorted to the Government Guest Villa, where we were to put up until we could find suitable quarters.

As the Assistant Chief of Protocol left me, he explained that the Foreign Minister would receive me as soon as he had time and in the meantime I would, of course, abide by diplomatic rules and refrain from establishing any contact with other foreigners. He added ominously that the Foreign Minister was very busy and it might be some time before I could be received.

At the end of a week of sitting with nothing to do in the Guest House, I was finally received very cordially by the Foreign Minister and told I could get on with my job. The Afghans figured, I guess, that by then I'd learned not to flout the rules of etiquette of any country no matter how far away it might be.

They were right.

20

BEHIND THE KHYBER PASS

According to the Afghans, the tribes which finally inhabited Europe started out from Afghanistan. Just how they started out is not clear, but some non-Afghan archeologists suggest they came from further east and merely stopped off for a rest in Afghanistan. If they did, they showed excellent judgment. As a vacation resort it backs Switzerland off the map, and even California and Florida would have difficulty competing. Not that it has any first-class hotels or ski-lifts, or even a railroad. But it has the lakes, the mountains, the deserts, the sun, the snow, the fish, the game, and above all the Afghans themselves.

Although Afghanistan is as big as France, its population is estimated roughly at about fourteen million. The estimate is rough because no one has ever really tried to take a census, for the very simple reason the tribesmen consider it bad manners to count their families. And if an Afghan tribesman considers something bad manners, it would be very, very silly indeed for anyone to contradict.

The country itself lies around the southwest shoulder of the great central mountain massif that includes the Himalayas, the Pamirs and the Hindu Kush, the latter being the name of the Afghan share of the top of the world. On the north, the Hindu Kush runs out into the great northern plains where the wheat and the karakul lambs grow. The Oxus River cuts the plain and forms the boundary with the Soviet Union.

On the west and south, the mountains drop away into the deserts of eastern Persia and Baluchistan. The eastern frontier is the notorious Northwest Frontier of India, where the road from Kabul cuts through the Khyber Pass to the railhead at Peshawar in India. Kabul, the capital, is nearly in the middle of the country, seven thousand feet above sea level.

About a third of the population live in the plains to the north and south of the mountains and raise the grain and the sheep from which Afghanistan makes her living. Another two million are the so-called nomads who spend the winter along the Indus River in India. When spring comes, they follow the warm weather up the mountain slopes like a tide, plowing and planting the land as they go. Then in the autumn, when the snows begin to fall on the upper slopes of the mountains, they start back again, harvesting the fields they planted in the spring. By October, the valleys of the Northwest Frontier are dotted with their black tents and the passes are choked with their endless camel trains. At Christmas they are safely back in the warm plains of India whence they had started ten months before.

But by far the most lively part of the population are the tribesmen who live in the mountainous area between Kabul and the Indian frontier. Tall, well over six feet, blue-eyed, dark-skinned, thick black hair reaching to the shoulders, an ancient rifle slung over the shoulder, they are every bit as formidable as Kipling described them. When times are good, they can be persuaded to live quite peacefully in their wretched mountain villages, but when things go wrong nothing can stop them swarming down into the plains to loot, kidnap and raise general hell among the plainsmen.

Even in the best of times the Kabul Government frowns on expeditions into the tribal areas. Often, when I asked permission to go shooting in this or that range east of Kabul, my friends in the Government would shake their heads and say: "No, you can't go there. It is just a little too tribal."

The great national hero of modern times was the great
Abdurrahman Khan, who united the country in the middle of the last
century and ruled until about 1901. Abdurrahman came out of exile
in Russian Central Asia to defeat the current king in Kabul and unite
the tribes under his own rule. He carried on a series of wars with the
British, all of which he won up to the last battle which, as usual, went
to the English. Abdurrahman also had the distinction of being the
author of one of the liveliest autobiographies ever written, in which
he not only described his achievements but laid down a series of rules
for his successors to follow to keep his unruly countrymen in order.
He also had some advice for his British and Russian neighbors, the
gist of which was that they'd better be friendly to Afghanistan, or
else. Specifically, he told the British that if they'd keep the Russians
in order in Europe, he'd take care of them in Asia. But that was long
before Lenin, Stalin or even Mao Tse-Tung were even thought of.

Abdurrahman was at his best when describing his own tribesmen.
He was especially fond of one particular tribe which lived on the
Kashmir frontier. They were very brave men, he writes, and usually
loyal to the Crown, but once in a while they began killing one another.

"Now when people get into the habit of killing one another,"
Abdurrahman wrote, "it invariably leads to trouble." So he took a
few regiments of his troops and went up into their valley and cleaned
them up.

Human nature never changes quickly and to this day the tribes
lapse into killing spells. During World War II the Germans used to
take special delight in sending agents into the tribal territories to
stir up trouble for the British. During my stay in Kabul the town
was periodically buzzing with stories about secret meetings between
German emissaries and such strange-sounding local troublemakers
as the Faqir of Ipi and the Mad Mullah. The tribes never actually
rose, but I got the impression that the Faqir and the Mullah turned a
pretty penny at German expense.

Not all of the tribal areas were closed to foreigners, and
occasionally when work was slack I'd go up into the mountains and

spend a few days with one of the chiefs and try my luck at shooting ibex or wild boar.

Not long after my arrival in Kabul I visited the province of Badakhshan on the northern slopes of the Hindu Kush. I had come well supplied with a case of Army rations, but my host, the Governor of the Province, insisted I stay with him in his compound and eat from his kitchen. I had with me several companions, including an ex-champion prizefighter from Czechoslovakia, whose appetite corresponded to his two hundred and fifty pounds, but the table, or rather the floor, from which we ate was never short of food.

The Governor put us up in Durbar Hall, in the outer court of his compound. The inner court was reserved for his womenfolk and was strictly out of bounds for us foreigners. The hall itself had no furniture in it aside from thick rugs and innumerable pillows and mattresses. When mealtime came around, an oil cloth was spread on the floor in the middle of the room and a huge bowl of chicken kebab put in the center of it. The diners squatted in a circle around the bowl and helped themselves from it with their fingers. At first the problem of eating rice with my fingers caused me some trouble, but eventually I learned the trick of rolling the rice into a little ball and flipping it into my mouth with my thumb.

After my first hard day's hunting, I was ready to turn in, but my hosts had other ideas. The Governor had two sons about ten and twelve years old. The younger one suffered from cataract and was totally blind in one eye and almost blind in the other. Consequently he couldn't join in the great Afghan pastime of shooting. But, he said, there was one thing he could do and that was play chess.

When I first had joined the Foreign Service as a junior officer I was given one piece of good advice which I actually followed: young diplomats shouldn't play bridge, poker, or any other parlor game. As far as senior diplomats and their wives are concerned, there is a permanent open season on young bachelors who play bridge. And there is only one acceptable defense against an invitation to make up a fourth: I don't know how to play.

But there was one exception – chess. Apparently you are not apt to be asked by the Ruthenian Minister's wife to pop over for a game of chess. So for a while I tried to concentrate on pawns and kings and queens and the various directions they move in. But I can't say I ever had any success. In fact, up till the time I got to Afghanistan I had yet to win a single chess game and, quite frankly, I was getting a little discouraged.

So when young Abdul Azziz said he could play chess I saw my chance. It might seem like taking unfair advantage of a poor, sickly, young Afghan child, but with my batting average still standing at .ooo anything, I figured, was fair. So the chessboard and the chessmen were trotted out and we settled ourselves among piles of cushions on the floor of the Durbar Hall while the Governor and his henchmen gathered around us. It was still dusk when we started to play and it was well after midnight when we finally quit.

I haven't played chess since and my batting average is still .000.

But my luck was better in the shooting line and within three days I had shot four or five ibex – none of them very spectacular as trophies, but in a small way a tribute to my rifle power. When finally I was packing to go, I pointed out the case of Army rations I had in the car and asked the Governor if for once I couldn't furnish the final meal. At first the Governor refused on the ground that being a Moslem he could only eat meat with no pork in it. But I assured him that there were so many Moslems in the American Army that our rations took care of any objections on that score. So he finally agreed to "taste" one can of stew, explaining that his palate was accustomed only to kebab and, he felt sure, American stew was an acquired taste. Whatever the state of his palate, the Governor and his followers showed a remarkable speed in the acquisition of new tastes, for before I left Badakhshan two hours later, five of them had finished what the Army considers sixty man-meals.

The local officials were not always as cooperative as my friend the Badakhshan Governor. Not long after my visit to him, I made another visit into the Bamian Valley, where I pitched a camp on the banks of a small tributary known as the Kaloo River. When I sent word to the nearest village that I would like to hire some local guides to take me into the mountains, word came back that I would first have to talk to the Provincial Governor in the town of Bamian itself. So I went to Bamian, installed myself in the teahouse, and sent word that I'd be glad to call on the Governor if he would set an hour. The reply came back that the Governor was at a wedding and wouldn't be able to receive me for several days. I replied that I was telephoning the Prime Minister's Office in Kabul to ask if the Bamian Governor had authority to countermand the Prime Minister's permit to hunt in the Kaloo Valley. Before the telephone call came through, a courier arrived from the Governor's Palace with the word that he was prepared to negotiate the matter in the Governor's absence if I would only cancel the phone call to the Prime Minister. I agreed and we set about bargaining. The Governor's representative explained that the Governor's only objection to my hunting was that he was personally responsible for my safety and that the mountains around Kaloo were filled with mortal perils, making them far too dangerous for valuable foreigners like myself.

I thanked the gentleman for the Governor's solicitude and asked just what the dangers were. Had the Governor ever been hunting himself?

I was told that, although the Governor didn't hunt, he knew that the mountains were infested with wolves, bears and snakes which attacked on sight. I tried to argue that I'd never seen a wolf attack anyone, that I would give anything to have a bear come within gunshot, and that it was well known to Afghan experts with whom I had talked that there was not a single poisonous snake in the Hindu Kush. But my friend was not so easily squelched and replied politely that I had obviously been talking with the wrong people. After all, the Governor of Bamian ought to know what was in Bamian.

Eventually we came to a compromise which was duly committed to writing in English and Persian. I don't remember exactly how it read but it was something like this:

"On condition that His Excellency the Governor of Bamian removes the ban on my hunting in his province I hereby solemnly absolve him from all responsibility from any injuries I may receive by reason of: 1.) Wolves, 2.) Bears, and 3.) Snakes. (*Signed*) CWT."

The Governor accepted the compromise and within an hour of my return to camp the place was swarming with hunters and guides offering to show me the finest ibex hunting in Afghanistan. For almost two weeks I spent every other day perilously scrambling up and down precipices and the alternate days, with a trout rod along the Kaloo River, resting from my efforts. I never shot an ibex the whole time I was there, but neither did I fall down any cliffs. I often wondered what form the Governor's responsibility would take if I had broken my neck on one of those thousand-foot drops. After all, they hadn't been listed on my waiver.

When I returned to Kabul, I told my Afghan friends of the Governor's worries and they assured me that my contract with him would be placed in the permanent archives. In fact they were so amused with the incident that King Zahir sent me word that the valley of Kaloo would henceforward be removed from the Governor's jurisdiction and permanently turned over to me. It will be a nice place to go come the Atomic War.

But it wasn't often possible to take a two weeks' vacation in the mountains and most of my extracurricular activities had to be confined to Kabul and its immediate surroundings. Kabul itself has a restaurant which is opened for the duration of the national holiday, a festival which lasts for several days. There is also a movie house but I was never very much for movies, especially Indian movies. Social life was restricted largely to the Diplomatic Corps, since Afghan women are not permitted to appear before foreigners and it is generally agreed that stag parties are not very good as a steady diet. The result was that I spent most of my free time walking in the surrounding mountains or duck shooting in the valley. I was once even invited by the King to go duck shooting on an elephant. The elephant, the last of forty given by Queen Victoria to the King's great-grandfather,

Abdurrahman, of autobiographical fame, took sick before the duck shoot and I have never since had an invitation to shoot a duck from an elephant's back, though I daresay it might be fairly good fun.

But you can't shoot ducks all the year round, even in Afghanistan, and mountain climbing eventually can get tiresome. To keep myself amused I acquired a horse and later a falcon, with mixed results.

21

NUR JEHAN – LIGHT OF THE WORLD

The trouble with horses is that you should never talk about them at dinner – especially at diplomatic dinners.

I had tried it once in Moscow and ended up in a one-man effort to teach the Red Army how to play polo. I tried it once again in Afghanistan with more painful results.

It was at the British Legation. I was sitting beside the British Minister, Sir Francis Wylie, an official of the Indian Civil Service. The conversation was anything but lively.

"I thought I'd buy a horse," I said casually, a remark which under normal circumstances would pass as innocent enough.

"Not an Afghan horse, I hope," said Wylie. "They're too small. A little infra dig for an American official."

"What else is there? I can't send for an Irish hunter in wartime."

"But in India we've some fine animals – I'll get one for you."

At that moment the Persian Ambassador's wife on my left asked me peremptorily what the word for "butter knife" was in American, and the matter of the horse lapsed. Affairs lapse easily in Central Asia.

Two weeks later the British Minister called me on the phone:

"About that horse. General Whiteside of the Northwest Frontier Force is sending you a fine young mare. Just had a wire – left Peshawar today with her *sice* – good chap."

"Who's a good chap?" I asked, "General Whiteside?"

"No, my dear fellow – that is, he is a good chap too, but the *sice*."

"What's a *sice*?"

"*Sice*, my dear fellow – he's the groom. Good man, Whiteside says – reliable chap. He's agreed to stay on here permanently with you."

"Damn nice of the *sice*," I remarked a little dubiously.

"It's all quite cheap – that is for you Americans – about eight hundred dollars and a few more per month for the *sice*."

General Whiteside proved to be a good judge of horseflesh. The mare he sent me would have been a prize in anyone's eyes. Her name was Nur Jehan, or "Light of the World."

I took her out for her first gallop after a day's rest. She pranced and reared and kicked like a two-year-old – not meanly or nervously, but out of sheer good spirits. As we trotted out of town she tossed her head contemptuously as she passed the little Afghan ponies which pulled the Kabul cabs. Once in the fields, her hooves scarcely touched the ground. There was nothing "ornery" about her – she was just having a hell of a good time.

Back at the house, she turned as gentle as an old lady. Yang passed me a lump of sugar and I held it under her nose a moment, and then started up the steps of the terrace toward the living room door. Without hesitating a second she followed after me, daintily taking the stone steps like a ballerina. As I gave her the sugar, the *sice*, who had been with her since she was foaled, whistled gently. She turned and clambered down the steps toward the stable.

The *sice* was a big, tall, Pathan – that Northwest tribe which has kept things hot for several centuries along the Indian-Afghan frontier. He couldn't have been much over twenty years old, but he carried himself like an old tribal chief.

Every morning for several months, I rode Nur Jehan. Rain or shine, Yang would drag me from my bed, push me into a pair of jodhpurs, and help me into the saddle while the *sice* held Nur Jehan. Then with a half dozen assorted dogs – and occasionally a falcon on my wrist – we'd lunge out the gate and into the fields that surround Kabul.

It was an ideal country for riding and falconing – flat, with an occasional irrigation ditch to jump, plenty of pastures and a network of paths which in spring were lined with wild rose bushes.

At first Nur Jehan seemed to enjoy these rides as much as I. She'd prance and rear as I mounted, and plunge off out of the gate with heels in air. But after several weeks she suddenly became meek, stopped dancing and kicking, and within a day or so was restlessly thrashing about her stall. Obviously Nur Jehan was sick.

The servants were in an uproar. Yang accused the *sice* of putting mice in the oats. The *sice* accused the gardener of putting a hex on the mare. The cook complained the stove didn't work. I complained the food was no good. Even the dogs grew restless. The whole household seemed to get sick along with Nur Jehan.

Finally I called a veterinary, a foreigner in Kabul. He looked gloomily at the horse – and announced she must be bled.

When Yang heard the vet's prescription he flew into a tantrum. "Master, you no let doctor take blood from horse. Blood make man live. No blood, no live. Doctor, he damn-fool."

I was inclined to agree with Yang, from a purely practical point of view, but since I was not a vet I hardly dared refuse professional advice. I had always associated bloodletting with Dickens and Scott, but then who was I to judge. In the valleys of the Hindu Kush I had seen local medicine men prescribing remedies from the medical books left behind by Alexander the Great. The hillsmen seemed to be getting along all right.

So I told the vet to go ahead and see what happened. The results were not encouraging. The mare grew visibly weaker. She began to sway unsteadily from one side to the other. Then she tried to lie down – a fatal move for a sick horse. While the *sice* prodded her to keep her on her feet, we rigged a sling from the rafters of the stable and passed it under her belly. This seemed to support her for a time, but soon she was sagging helplessly in the ropes.

As Nur Jehan weakened, the gloom around the house grew heavier, for the mare was the favorite of them all – Chinese, Afghan, Hindu and Pathan. Then, to make matters worse, a series of catastrophes were visited upon the household by God, Allah, or Mithraz.

First it was Midget, who had been married with considerable éclat to King Zahir's favorite police dog. She was just about to whelp. She went swimming in an irrigation ditch and tore one of her breasts to shreds on a broken bottle. By the time I got her home from the veterinary, the puppies were already on their way. Two hours later she had produced a litter of seven – two of them dead.

Out in the stable, Nur Jehan grew still weaker. By this time the veterinary had given her up for lost and suggested I shoot her. But Yang and the rest of the household utterly rejected the suggestion.

"He no doctor," Yang repeated. "He Goddamned fool. He no make people well. He kill people. Maybe he come round here again maybe we shoot him." Yang shook his fist at the door through which the vet had disappeared.

And then came the earthquake.

I was sitting by the fire in my living room, entertaining a correspondent from *The New York Times*. Correspondents used to get to Kabul about once every other leap year in those days and when one showed up it was an unusual treat. He'd already been there several days and had asked all the usual questions about the political, military, moral, economic and nightclub conditions of Afghanistan. He'd even touched on earthquakes. I'd explained to him that earthquakes in Afghanistan were rarely dangerous. Single tremors were mere trifles. Double tremors were very rare and could be ignored. Triple tremors happened so seldom that no one knew whether they were dangerous or not.

Suddenly the room began to rock and the pictures on the wall slid lazily to one side.

"Don't give it a thought," I said. "Just a slight tremor."

The correspondent looked relieved.

Abruptly another tremor shook the room.

"That's unusual," I commented and the correspondent shifted uneasily.

A third shock opened a crack in the ceiling, and a shower of plaster sprinkled down on us.

This time I was a little short of comment and so said nothing. The correspondent and I just sat rigidly in our chairs and stared at each other silently.

Suddenly the chimney of the fireplace seemed to leave the wall as a violent convulsion hit the house.

It's hard to say how long it took us, but it couldn't have been more than a few tenths of a second before both of us were out the door and in the garden.

The quake died away as quickly as it had arisen and we strolled as nonchalantly as we could back toward the house.

"Remind me to make a note of that in the morning," the correspondent muttered. "Earthquakes aren't dangerous in Afghanistan."

Aside from the ceiling and the crack in the chimney, the earthquake left no visible damages – but it left its mark on the household morale.

Then one day Yang came to me in consternation.

"Master, I know what's wrong – it's that falcon you have. Bird in house always bad luck. Send bird away please."

I laughed and told him not to believe a lot of old Chinese wives' tales.

"But, Master," he persisted, "see what happen. Horse sick, dog, puppy die. Then earthquake and now look what happen to me!"

He lowered his head and showed me a great gash across his scalp.

"But, Yang, the falcon didn't claw your head, did she?" "No, I hit head on window, but it's falcon's fault."

The falcon was Yang's special hate. I think he detested her even more than the vet. It may have been because Confucius or some other Chinese philosopher disapproved of birds in the house. But I'm inclined to think it was because the falcon was anything but housebroken and used to leave her calling card on every piece of furniture within reach – and a falcon's reach is very long indeed.

The household by now was close to mutiny. Nur Jehan's illness had reduced morale to the vanishing point, and I was losing my grip on the crew of cook, houseboy, waiter, groom, stableboy, gardener and kennelman.

Then I thought of the Veterinary School of the University of Pennsylvania. At home it had always been considered the tops in horse sickness. So I wrote a cable to the school, describing as best I could all the symptoms Nur Jehan had developed, and urgently asked them to reply by cable telling me what to do. In those days cables from Kabul had to pass through half a dozen communications systems, each with its own fat tolls, and the rate to Philadelphia was something over a dollar a word. I can't recall exactly what it cost me but it was a little less than the price of the mare.

While we waited for the reply, the cook, a devout Moslem named Saadi, took the initiative.

I was sitting in the living room one evening, my falcon on my wrist – a necessary ritual in training a young bird. The Afghan hounds were lying on their respective cushions before the fire. The police dogs were in their baskets by the door. Yang came in and announced that the servants wanted to see me. I told him to bring them in.

Solemnly they filed into the room, the cook in front. The gardener, the *sice*, the yardboy, the houseboy, and the rest followed behind. They stood silently in their long pajama-like white uniforms, their turbans neatly wrapped about their heads, their black hair reaching below their shoulders, their feet bare. (In Afghanistan, it is considered disrespectful to wear shoes in the presence of your superiors.)

A long silence was broken by the cook:

"Master, horse very very sick. Only one thing can save him."

"What's that?" I asked.

"Only Allah – only God save horse," he replied. "Master, let me bring Mullah – the priest – from the Mosque. Maybe he can pray and save Nur Jehan!"

Afghans are fanatical Moslems and it doesn't pay to toy with their religion. My own experience with Mullahs was nil, but I knew them to be very powerful men indeed.

"But, Saadi," I replied, "Allah won't save my horse. I'm an infidel."

"Maybe you infidel," he answered, "but we Moslem and Nur Jehan is our horse too!"

"But the Mullah won't come to my house," I protested. "No Mullah will come to pray where an infidel lives."

"Maybe Master will go away while I fetch the Mullah," Saadi persisted.

I hesitated still, while the white-clad Afghans stared at me from the dark corner of the room. They began to murmur among themselves.

Yang looked at their tense faces and turned to me: "Please, Master."

"All right," I said. "I'll go for one hour, but no longer."

I went out through the garden and onto the street. I wandered through the ill-lit lanes of Kabul, the falcon on my wrist, with Midget beside me. It was a gloomy walk, for I was no less fond of Nur Jehan than the servants, but somewhat more skeptical of the Mullah's powers.

Eventually I came home and wandered into the stables, where the lamp was still burning. By the horse's head squatted the *sice*, his face wet with tears. Around Nur Jehan's neck was a chain of blue beads and to it was attached a locket. Inside the locket, I knew, was an inscription left by the Mullah. I didn't dare open it to see whether it said, as I suspected, "Death to horses of all infidels," or, as Saadi believed, some more charitable appeal to Allah.

Nur Jehan was no better next morning, when I glanced into the stable on my way to the office.

In the evening I walked home with forebodings. As I reached the gate, I noticed in the gravel the trace of something heavy having been dragged down the drive. I followed the track with my eyes and saw that it led to the stable door. The law of the Koran had been observed: the dead of today must be buried before nightfall.

A week or two later a cable came from the University of Pennsylvania.

"Your horse has incurable meningitis," it read.

22

THE FALCON

In the library of the British Legation in Kabul there's a book on the training of falcons, written about a century ago. It says that a properly brought up falcon develops a fawning affection for her master.

Perhaps mine was an exceptionally independent bird – or perhaps times have changed and falcons aren't what they used to be. At any rate, to the bitter, bitter end our relations were cold and professional, tempered, perhaps, with just a touch of admiration which, I like to imagine, was mutual. I would probably never have gotten mixed up in the sad business if it hadn't been for the gas rationing in Hamburg at the beginning of the war in 1939. Not even the *Obergruppen* fuehrer of the German Falconry Association could get gas to take his birds for an airing. But American Vice Consuls could get all they wanted. So when I learned of the *Obergruppenfuehrer's* predicament, it was perhaps inevitable that the rest of my weekends should be devoted to the falcons. The winter of 1939-1940 was probably one of the most miserable that Hamburg had experienced. The cold was intense, and the coal strictly limited. But for the Falconry Gruppe it was ideal. Norway's wild geese, reacting to the unusually low temperatures in the North, had come down to the comparatively mild climate of Schleswig-Holstein and hung about in huge cackling flocks.

I can't say we decimated those flocks. I often thought we could have done better with bows and arrows or slingshots. But once we brought down a big goose and the sensation was duly reported in the German papers as another triumph of the Teutonic race. The papers never gave much credit to the falcon from Greenland or the car from Detroit. But I dare say that, if put to it, Goebbels' Propaganda Ministry could have traced the Aryan descent of both without much trouble.

Months later, when the phony war ended and Goering's bombers met the RAF fighters over London and Coventry, I recalled those Sundays in Schleswig-Holstein when we sent up our Greenland fighters against the great Norwegian goose squadrons. I'm sure the RAF's mechanics thought they had trouble enough to keep a Spitfire in order, what with the motors and controls and machine guns. But to the laymen, the number of things that can go wrong with a falcon are incredible.

An overenthusiastic wag of a tail or stretch of a wing can shake loose a key feather, and back to the perch goes the falcon till a new one grows in or is spliced on. A sip too much of water, a thimbleful extra of beef, a slight draft and the whole power system is out for a week. A slight miscalculation as she stabs a goose and a claw breaks – another month in the hospital. But on those rare occasions when the controls stay together, the motor hums, and the machine guns don't jam, it is a sight worth several frozen hands and feet to watch.

The first time it happened – it was a very cold day, I remember, and my camera froze – we'd been tramping over frozen, snow-covered fields for hours when a shout from one of the beaters, or *jaegers*, as the Germans call them, warned us that a flight of geese was coming our way. By the time they appeared over the trees, the hood was off the falcon. As she pranced out on her master's arm her head jerked from side to side, peering excitedly about, looking for her prey. In another second she had spotted the geese and with the swing of a discus-thrower, the falconer launched her into the air. A moment later the formation caught sight of her and burst into a frenzy of chattering and cackling. The falcon, however, seemed to ignore the formation entirely. Her only interest was altitude. She climbed in

Thayer's Afghan Entourage. From left: Thayer's Afghan cook, Abdullah the falconer, and his longtime servant Yang.

tight spirals with quick, powerful strokes, until she was well above the flock. By this time the geese had already passed overhead and were well beyond us. As we watched from the ground through field glasses, the falcon leveled off and streaked with incredible speed past the tail of the formation, making for the leader. The cackling now reached a crescendo. The geese were putting their last ounce of energy into a frantic effort to escape. But their power was no match for the falcon's. She pulled even with the head of the formation. For a moment she hovered. Then, folding her wings back, she dove straight at the leader.

Through the field glasses we watched her "stoop," saw her turn on her side as she struck, driving her sharp talons under one wing of her victim. Then there was only a confused ball of feathers plummeting toward the frozen earth. A few feet above the ground the falcon shot out her wings, jerked her claws from the goose and let her stunned victim crash to the ground while she parachuted gently onto the goose's downy back. A few swift coups de grace from her hatchet beak put the goose out of further misery.

The event was duly celebrated in wartime watered beer by *Reichsjaegergruppe fuer Falkenrei* (Hamburg Division). I attended the celebration, thereby, no doubt, creating a dossier in the de-Nazification courts. But at the same time I became a devoted falconer.

I began to learn the falconer's language – a series of inconsistencies highly regarded by the profession. I've forgotten most of them now, but if I'm not mistaken they called a falcon's feet her hands, and a falconer's hand a fist-provided it has a falcon on it. Then there were jesses – straps to hold the falcon's hands by, and *federspiels* – literally feather games, or "lures" – which consisted of rather gamey crow's wings which were whirled around one's head on a piece of string to lure the falcon back at critical moments – such as when she started flying in the wrong direction. Then there was the "mews," where the falcons lived. A "cadge" was a sort of frame on which falcons were carried from the mews to the fields, unless you had a Chevrolet. The frame was carried like a litter on the shoulders of two men known as "cadgers" – or "caddies," an expression recently cadged by a more plebian sport several centuries younger than falconry. "Slicing" was the falconer's expression for being unhousebroken. As far as I know there's no such thing as a housebroken falcon. The product of a "slice" was a "mute." If you should walk too near the cadge, a falcon might slice and leave a mute on your best tweed coat. In Germany a mute was regarded as a badge of honor, coming from the king of birds, and it was considered very bad form to wipe it off. In the Orient they were less snobbish and more sanitary. When a falcon "stooped" she dived several hundred feet and ended by driving her claws into her prey.

MY FIRST WEEKS in Kabul were full of top-hatted calls, leases, contractors and plumbing systems. These essentials of diplomacy were eventually disposed of and a little spare time for serious relaxation developed. Investigations revealed a falconer to the Royal Court who looked after the King's falcons. The present generation of the Royal Family, however, was more interested in tennis and skiing than in fourteenth century sports. Abdullah, the falconer, was rapidly developing the fear psychosis of any Government servant whose job is done. So when I appeared there was joy in the Royal Afghan Mews. Having already acquired a horse from India and dogs from everywhere, it was easy enough to borrow a falcon from my friend Abdullah for an early morning outing.

There are no geese in the valleys of the Hindu Kush, but there are plenty of quail. The ordinary falcon in Afghanistan is smaller than his Greenland cousin and he rides on the right wrist instead of the left as in Europe. This difference, Abdullah explained, was because the so-called civilized Westerner had to keep his right hand free for his sword or pistol – even when hunting. In the East, where business and pleasure are still strictly separated, such precautions are unnecessary. In sport – as in war, Abdullah said – you put your best fist forward in Afghanistan.

I soon discovered other differences too, between occidental and oriental birds – or else I had forgotten what I'd learned in Hamburg. At all events, I returned from my morning rides, more of ten than not, with a bare right fist – to the chagrin of Abdullah, who obviously disliked spending his days retrieving the birds I lost.

It may have been the frequency of my empty-handed returns which eventually led him to propose I train my own falcon. "Begin at the beginning," Abdullah said. "It's not difficult – we train a bird in a mere six weeks." I was a little skeptical at first, but Abdullah was eloquent: "No one knows the real pleasure of falconry until he flies a bird he has trained himself. Besides, no European has ever trained a falcon here in Afghanistan. You'll be the very first." That should have been warning enough to lay off. But he continued to lure me on.

I consulted Yang, who used to smile superciliously at the meagerness of the bag I brought home to Hamburg years before.

"Any birdee no good luck," Yang said. "These birdee very bad luck."

Then my hand was forced by my Persian teacher, who was trying to make me write Persian in the right direction. Doubtless he thought an Afghan falcon would contribute to my reform. Several times I caught him in secret consultation with Abdullah. Then one bright morning he appeared with a young falcon on his wrist: "He's just been hooded for the first time and hasn't been trained at all – Abdullah will show you how to go on from here."

From that day on my entire life was changed. Abdullah first explained that the way to teach a falcon was to keep it on your wrist the entire day and to give it lessons each morning and evening for half an hour. I told him that modern diplomatic practice frowned upon the introduction of falcons into Foreign Offices and Legation Chanceries, so that I and my bird would have to be separated during working hours. "Then you keep him on your wrist all night," Abdullah snorted.

Falcon training in the East consists of a well-defined series of lessons, each intimately connected with feeding. The first thing is to persuade the bird to eat a piece of beef from your hand. The last is to lure her into letting you take from her the quail she has just brought down. In between there are hundreds of carefully defined gradations each of which must be perfected before you go on to the next. But there is one little catch to the process which Abdullah didn't explain until I was thoroughly involved in the business. If the loving falcon has completed say, Lesson Three, (flying across the room onto your fist), and by some ill chance makes a bad landing which invariably upsets her delicately balanced equanimity, you go back, not to Lesson Two, but to Lesson One. That's not so discouraging until you've gotten to Lesson Forty or Fifty and find yourself sent home to Lesson One again. It becomes a kind of eternal game of backgammon with a falcon as the checker.

There was still another joker in the problem, which Abdullah had been careful to conceal till it was too late to turn back. Apparently no one in the East would dream of undertaking to train a falcon until he had first trained his own fingers. He has to learn to maneuver his fingers, encased in a thick leather gauntlet, with the agility of a card shark and the foreknowledge of a fortune-teller. The mere act of picking a bird from her perch requires considerable manipulation. If the bird reaches for one of your fingers, which isn't exactly where the falcon thinks it should be, down comes the falcon with a beating of feathers and a torrent of ornithological abuse – and back you go to Lesson One. Since I've never been able to shuffle even a deck of cards, this used to happen rather often.

Despite these handicaps, things gradually progressed, though somewhat behind schedule. The *bashi*, as the falcon was called in Kabul Persian, condescended after a few days to peck at a tender bit of quail's breast as I drew it over her talons. It seemed to me rather fortunate for her that she showed such confidence in me, because she was already getting very thin. In fact, any more diffidence and she would have starved to death. (Abdullah had explained that a falcon's heart is her weakest point. A little too much food, or a little too little, and she is apt to keel over.) In another few days she was affectionate enough (or merely hungry enough) to hop a foot from her perch to my gauntlet.

This maneuver brought a few catastrophic near misses which ended with her flapping angrily on the floor and called for a return to the perch and more courting with a breast of raw quail (Lesson One). After several weeks – and as many returns to Lesson One – I was able to entice her across the room with a series of chirps which Abdullah said was the bird equivalent of a hog call. To me it sounded strangely like a variation of the Bronx cheer.

Every evening, at Abdullah's insistence, I sat by the fire trying to concentrate on Gibbon's *Rome* or Frazer's *Golden Bough*, while the *bashi* clung precariously to my gauntlet or pecked at my arm with what I hoped was real affection. It felt more like an Army doctor taking a blood test. Occasionally one of the younger dogs – there were a dozen or so boarding with me at the time – would leap at the bird with genuine canine affection. The inevitable result was that the *bashi* would have to retire to her perch for two or three days to regain her dignity before starting in again at Lesson One.

By this time I'd canceled all evening engagements. My friends, apparently unamused by the *bashi*, ceased to call. Yang deeply resented this isolation, for his only pleasure was in cooking his "twenty-five curry."

Nevertheless I persisted, under the goading of Abdullah.

Six weeks had long since passed when Abdullah announced that training in the open air could now start. For this purpose I bought a long piece of string – the strongest Kabul's bazaar could produce in wartime. One end was tied to the falcon's leg; the other, to a stake. No sooner had I removed the bird's hood than she sighted a sparrow across the lawn and flew at it with the intensity of a G.I. at a steak. Although I was pleased at this demonstration of keenness, my enthusiasm died when the bird got its string caught in the telephone line and ended up indignantly suspended in mid-air by one leg. We eventually rescued her but her affections had markedly cooled and Abdullah prescribed three days in a dark room before we could begin again with Lesson One.

A few weeks later we had made up the lost ground and were back again on the lawn. Each day, with the falcon on my wrist, I would stand in one corner of the garden with a somewhat disdainful Yang opposite me, awkwardly holding a live quail (also attached to a string). At a given signal he tossed the quail in the air, while I as elegantly as possible unhooded the falcon in the prescribed oriental manner, by seizing the feathered plume of the hood in my teeth. Then I catapulted the bird into the air and held my breath. The first week or so of this regime produced one of two results: (a) either my catapulting would catch the bird by surprise and plunge her head first into the grass, or (b) ignoring the expensive quail, she would catch sight of a sparrow, and end up high in a tree hugging her unfortunate prey. Result (a) was easy to deal with, result (b) was usually more complicated. In that event, the quail, which cost two rupees in the bazaar, would first be redeposited in its cage for a further experiment. Retrieving operations would then be undertaken. Sometimes these would continue far into the night with fire ladders, flashlights and a swarm of assistant falconers from the Court Mews. But occasionally when Abdullah wasn't looking, a few hefty yanks on the string would force the angry bird to the ground. On the following day we would go back to Lesson One.

There was one other variant in my falcon's repertoire. It only happened once, but it was enough to convince me that my bird was not going to develop the affection described in the book. In fact, it came very close to killing my last lingering ambitions as a falconer.

It was a cool Kabul evening. Yang and I were tediously tossing quails at the falcon and vice versa. Presumably the bird's string was attached to the stake. Afterward I thought I had forgotten to tie it, or that, being wartime austerity string, it just plain broke. But now that I think it over I'm very much afraid that Yang, who detested the bird, deliberately untied it. At any rate, Yang had tossed his quail and I followed quickly with the falcon only to see her cast a contemptuous glance at the two-rupee quail and soar off over the garden wall. The string flowed behind her like one of Isadora Duncan's veils.

My first reaction was that it was all for the best. My patience was fast running out. I had wasted too much energy already on falconry. But then I realized the hours, the days, the weeks I had wasted, the friends I had lost. And again I pictured the final scene luring me on: that day when Yang would hoist me onto my rearing mare while the Indian *sice* held her down with two strong hands on her bridle. Abdullah would place the falcon, my falcon, on my wrist. The stableboy would loose the dogs from the kennel. The gardener would swing open the gates, and with a shower of gravel, feathers, horses and dogs I would burst out into the unsuspecting streets of Kabul on my way to the quail fields. It was a picture that always stood me in stead when the *bashi* broke the rules in the book. Now it was enough to stir the household into action. Police, scouts, messengers – I alerted everyone in town.

Within an hour a small boy appeared with the news that he'd found the *bashi*. But not till he'd received five rupees would he tell me where she was. As I tossed him the coin he grinned mischievously. "She's in the Japanese Legation garden." He laughed and ran off. I was prepared for almost anything but that. We'd been at war with Japan since before my arrival in Afghanistan. I had, therefore, carefully avoided the slightest contact with the little men. And now the falcon had flown deliberately into the enemy's camp at her very first moment of freedom. I could hardly reconcile this with the book's comments on fawning falcon love. For weeks, against accumulating evidence to the contrary, I'd been persuading myself that the *bashi*'s eyes were developing a softer, kinder, more affectionate gleam when she looked at me. But I could only conclude it had been a thoroughgoing hoax. It was obvious that since the day she'd entered my house, she had loathed and despised me.

I had no time to lose in sentimental recriminations. I called for the yardboy to fetch a ladder and jumped into my falconing clothes. Even the book at the British Legation admits that the most affectionate falcon won't recognize you unless you always wear the same suit in her presence. Mine consisted of a worn-out tweed coat, riding breeches and a hat. The coat and breeches were ordinary enough, but the hat – Abdullah had chosen it for me – was a little out of the ordinary. Generally speaking, my taste in hats is considered by my friends as Victorian, but this one was definitely Louis XIV. It was small, bright green and carried a feather from the tail of what must have been on outsized pheasant.

Impartial witnesses have since told me that it was a picturesque procession – my feather and me, my turbaned yardboy and the ladder, and prancing all about me, the combined boys' clubs of Kabul. At the Japanese Legation I climbed up the ladder and onto the fifteen-foot garden wall. There on the other side, surrounded by a group of giggling Japanese, I spotted the falcon, perched serenely in a small cherry tree.

The situation was an awkward one. I couldn't ask the Japanese please to give me back my runaway bird. Even if I could have, it's doubtful whether they would have understood me. I couldn't climb into their diplomatic sanctuary without getting arrested. There seemed nothing for it but to lure my disloyal trainee back to me with Abdullah's variation of the Bronx cheer. At the same time I was aware of my very conspicuous position on top of a fifteen-foot wall, surrounded by a crowd of curious Kabuli. Under such circumstances, it was important to maintain the dignity becoming a diplomatic representative of a great power. But the chances of accomplishing my mission and maintaining my dignity were very small. I stretched out my gauntleted hand with a red, raw piece of meat and chirped. The *bashi* cocked an eye at me and turned back to the Japanese. The Japanese giggled louder. The crowd on the other side of the wall shouted encouragement. Something much more explosive than a chirp escaped me. For half an hour I sat alternately chirping and cursing. The crowd shouted advice. The Japs giggled. The bird continued serene in the cherry tree.

I was about to give up in disgust when one of the Japanese decided to catch the falcon himself. He had gotten within three feet of her when she flicked her tail and "sliced," depositing a "mute" conspicuously on his lapel. The Jap looked down at his coat and up at me, and lunged ferociously at the falcon. It was obvious he had not been raised in the occidental tradition of reverence for "mutes." The falcon took one look at the angry Jap, hopped from her perch and with two strokes of her wings sailed gracefully onto my wrist.

The giggling in the Japanese garden stopped. On the other side of the wall a roar of applause went up. I grabbed the falcon's jesses firmly and clambered down the ladder. The Swiss Minister, who was passing by at the time, told me the next day that he thought the local boys' school was acting out the Pied Piper until he saw me in the leading role. Whatever it looked like, it was a very triumphant procession that escorted me home.

Not long after this episode Abdullah pronounced the bird trained. "Now all we must do is put her in hunting trim and out you go to hunt." Putting her in trim, I discovered, meant dieting her to the point where she would fly at anything. "Enseaming" is what the falconers call it. It's a rather tricky performance requiring expert care. Too little trim – and the bird ignores the game and flies back to the mountains from whence she came. Too much trim – and her delicate heart gives out. Each evening for a week Abdullah came and gently felt the bird's breastbone to measure its sharpness – the gauge of her fitness.

By now months, not weeks, had passed since I'd first begun Lesson One. Finally, Abdullah came to the garden one evening and after examining the falcon's figure smiled: "*Khub-Fardah*. Good – tomorrow you take the *bashi* to the fields."

THERE IS A short sequel to the story of how I trained my falcon – and it followed with brutal suddenness. There was only one other witness to the tragedy that evening, but he can confirm the story and anyone in Kabul can tell you where to find Abdullah, the Falconer.

I was still squatting beside the falcon's perch trying to grasp the meaning of Abdullah's words "*Khub-Fardah*." It meant the end of the school, and the beginning of my professional career as a full-fledged falconer. Between us the proud bird preened on her perch.

Suddenly she grew quiet and her bright yellow eyes seemed to get dim. I thought I heard Abdullah mutter the word "heart." But before we could exchange words, her powerful beak reached up toward the trees, uttered a piercing wail, and the falcon toppled from her perch – dead.

23

THE LAST TREK

One of the most common traits of Foreign Service officers is their ability to believe that the post they are in is the hub of the universe. Its problems are far more important than those of any other post, as long as they are there. In the State Department, this state of mind is called "localitis," and its victims are ordinarily treated with sympathetic kindness.

When I arrived in Kabul, the war was raging in Europe, Africa and Asia. El Alamein, Stalingrad, Casablanca and Teheran captured the headlines for brief moments during my tour of duty, but after I'd been there a month I fully appreciated that their few seconds of glory were only transitory and that, in the end, the future depended on what happened beyond the Khyber Pass and the Oxus.

Occasionally Kabul's problems didn't seem to be very important but that, I figured, was only illusory. Sometimes even the State Department didn't seem to appreciate the vital significance of Afghan internal politics or the critical importance of the Kabul Legation. This was particularly apparent when, after six months of cabling for a typewriter, the Department compromised by sending me a water-cooler. Apparently in the heat of Washington some Kipling – lover in the Supply Section got himself confused with Gunga Din. When a local cultural society approached me with the request that we furnish it with much-needed equipment to start a theater movement in Afghanistan, I worked hard preparing a list of their precise requirements. At first I had tried to get the society to do it themselves, but they appropriately remarked that I ought to know much better than they. We had theaters in America. They had never had one. The only items they were sure they would need were:

Wigs, assorted
Noises, assorted (but especially for thunderstorms and cannonfire)
Costumes, assorted (for the usual plays one would act)
Scenery, assorted

They admitted this last item might be bulky and, since shipping was then at a premium, perhaps it would be best if Washington just sent some directions for making scenery. I sent this list in to Washington with the strong recommendation that in the interest of helping undeveloped areas the request be filled on a priority basis. I never received a reply. The same thing happened when the radio station asked for a clock with chimes like Big Ben that would chime the hours according to sun time instead of mean time. This seemed to require a little explanation, so I appended to my request to the Department a brief historical footnote.

In ancient times, before the present regime of King Zahir Khan, the Mullahs had practically run the country – even to the point of telling the time of day. One of the relics of their rule was the fact that Afghanistan ran on sun time instead of mean time, even as late as my arrival. (You may not know the difference between sun and mean time, and it really doesn't amount to much in the long run unless you are trying to pick up the six o'clock shortwave newscast from New York. In such case you are likely to find your watch ten to twenty minutes off.)

In the old days, time in Kabul was determined by the noon gun fired from the fortress. It was the prerogative of the chief Mullah to say when noon had arrived and for this purpose he set up a sundial in the courtyard of the main mosque. As the sun swung across toward its zenith, one of the minor Mullahs would squat down before the dial and await developments. When the shadow crossed the high-noon mark, the minor Mullah rose from his heels, gathered his white robes around him and hurried to the telephone. It took only a moderate amount of cranking on the phone to rouse the operator, who through long practice was able to connect the mosque telephone with that of the city fortress with a minimum of delay.

Very often, when the Mullah rang up, the Officer of the Day was in the guard room where the phone was. If not, it was only a matter of minutes to rouse him from his quarters and get him to the phone. Thereupon the Mullah gave him the okay to go ahead with the noon gun. The fortress guard was under standing instructions to be in or around the gun emplacement whenever the sun got high, and as soon as the Officer of the Guard appeared they were ordered to load up the old howitzer with powder but no shot. Then, when all was ready, the Officer of the Guard gave the signal, a lighted match was applied to the powder train, the charge set off, and the inhabitants of Kabul hastily set their watches to precisely high noon. I never could find out what happened in cloudy weather.

But when we asked for a large supply of acetyl salicylic acid tablets, the Department reacted immediately, pointing out that we had asked for enough aspirin to keep the entire population of Afghanistan free of headaches for twenty-five years.

Between keeping Afghanistan in cultural, chronometrical, pharmaceutical and other supplies, there was still a little time to slip off for a few days shooting, fishing, or even falconing in my private valley of Kaloo or in the mountains around Kabul, provided the tribes were quiet. There was one particular mountain, though, that had always attracted my attention. It was very near the center of the Hindu Kush and, according to the map, its highest peak was somewhere around 23,000 feet. Several times I had tried to get up to it, but each time either the tribes were restless, or the snow too deep, or some other objection occurred to the Afghan powers-that-be. Finally, however, I managed to convince the Prime Minister's Office that conditions were okay and he gave me permission, provided I would take with me a platoon of soldiers and one of his own plainclothes men as a personal bodyguard. The soldiers were always a nuisance, because they had a habit of stealing all the chickens and ducks in every village at which we stopped, which in turn required me to pay large tips to repay the despoiled villagers before they would agree to guide me through their shooting country. However, the Prime Minister was very stubborn and it looked like my last chance to try for what I called "Dushmani Man" Mountain (which according to my version of Kabuli Persian meant "My Enemy"). So I set off in a military reconnaissance car followed by a truckload of soldiers.

On the way, we spent one day on a small mountain where there were said to be some fine ibex, but after twelve hours of exhausting climbing all we managed to flush was a herd of small mountain sheep not worth shooting at. So we climbed down the valley to the highway where we'd left the car, soldiers and bodyguard, and motored another ten or fifteen miles to the nearest approach to "Dushmani Man." We left the car by the road with most of the soldiers and started up to the highest village on the mountainside.

It was already dark when we finally came through the low mud gates. There we were met by the village elders. They had already heard of our approach and had fixed up a large room on top of one of their mud houses for us. A rickety ladder led to an upstairs verandah on to which our room opened. Inside there were a couple of rugs spread on the floor, and in the middle of the room a charcoal brazier in which not charcoal but some rather damp twigs were burning and producing a thick acrid smoke which hung in a cloud under the ceiling.

I had spread my sleeping bag in a corner, boiled some tea in a small field stove and prepared to turn in, when the elders called to pay their official respects. For half an hour in my very halting Persian I discussed their problems: the state of the local school, the various diseases that ravage the mountain tribes, the condition of the crops, and the efficiency of the local Governor. Then the elders rose, prayed to Allah my stay would be happy, and retired.

Hardly had they left when the village hunters whom I had summoned marched in and sat down along the wall opposite me. There were eleven of them and as fierce a looking crowd as ever I hope to meet. Their dark faces were covered with heavy, black beards leaving only a slit for their mouths and a patch on each cheek from above which their great blue eyes shone. Long, matted black hair reached to their shoulders. Each of them carried an ancient muzzle-loading rifle which he propped against the wall beside him as he sat down.

I told them I wanted to climb the great mountain the next morning in search of ibex. Eleven shaggy heads immediately shook an unmistakable "no." It was far too dangerous a mountain for valley dwellers, they explained. And besides, they said, pointing to my house slippers, I didn't have the right kind of shoes. I fumbled in my knapsack and produced a pair of climbing boots. These were passed around and carefully examined. Eventually it was agreed they were pretty good for climbing, but not of course as good as the sandals they wore.

Still, they said, it was out of the question for a Kabuli like me to go up on the mountain. It was very steep, and even if they wanted to, they wouldn't be able to carry me, and, of course, I wouldn't be strong enough to walk. I told them that was my business and that I'd been climbing a good many mountains and was in pretty fair training. After another thirty minutes of arguing, the hunters finally agreed they'd try it, but they doubted if I could reach the high plateau where the ibex grazed.

I asked them who was the senior hunter who would organize the party, choose the route and so forth. The eleven looked at one another and exchanged a few muttered words. Then one turned to me and explained that in their village everyone was equal. There were no bosses. I replied that I admired the democracy of their communal life but I found it a little difficult when it came to organizing a hunt.

So after some more chatter, I turned to one who looked a little more forceful than the rest and said that he was going to be boss for the trip whether he liked it or not. He refused at first, but the others seemed to agree with my selection and after a little cajoling he undertook the job. Ten minutes later all the arrangements had been made. One group of five, including myself, would go up the main valley and two other groups of four would climb along the adjoining valleys and ridges to drive the game toward us. We would set out promptly at three in the morning (it was already nine at night) and wait for the dawn at the treeline, where the going was too steep for night climbing.

The hunters got up, slung their rifles over their shoulders and once again joined in a prayer to Allah for a safe and successful expedition. As they filed out the door, the man I had selected as chief stopped them:

"Remember, brothers," he cautioned them: "It's going to be a tough job tomorrow. So keep out of the harem tonight." They growled assent as they turned and walked out.

When they had gone I set my alarm and crawled into my sleeping bag for a few hours' sleep.

WHEN THE ALARM rang I climbed into my boots, stirred up some coffee and gnawed a slab of flat, unleavened local bread. Beside me my "bodyguard" was still sleeping soundly. I shook him and told him to get going. He looked at me a little incredulously:

"Me? Go up into that mountain? Hell, no! I'll wait for you down here. But please be careful, because if anything happens to you the Prime Minister will have me blown from the mouth of a cannon." With his duty thus done, he rolled over and went back to sleep.

In the courtyard below, the hunters were assembling as I climbed down the ladder and a few minutes later we were trudging silently up the slope toward the great black mass which seemed to hang over us out of the starlit sky. It was nearly six o'clock when the column halted at the opening of a rocky gorge which led up abruptly to the peak above us. The hunters scurried about for a few minutes collecting brush and dried brambles. Before long a blazing fire was lighting up their scraggly black faces as they sat cross-legged in a circle around the fire.

"How long till dawn?" one of them asked me, knowing I was the only one with a watch.

"About ten minutes," I answered.

Five minutes went slowly by. You could hear only the crackling of the dried twigs and brambles.

Then my neighbor looked at me again: "You said ten minutes and thirty must have passed already. Does that watch work?"

I told him it was working well and that only five minutes had passed. But the tribesmen obviously didn't believe me and began to exchange strange glances. Sitting up there nearly fifteen thousand feet above the world, surrounded by eleven wild mountaineers, I confess I began to have a slightly uneasy feeling. But I comforted myself with the thought that at least they didn't covet my watch.

Then, at last, dawn broke and we slung our rifles and started off up the gorge. The sky at dawn was clear and it looked to me as though it was going to be an ideal day, but the tribesmen sniffed the air and shook their heads. "Snow," they muttered.

For two hours and more we scrambled over the loose stones and rocks. The going was slow but we didn't stop for rest and our progress was fairly good. Already the mouth of the gorge below us had disappeared and the 23,000-foot peak ahead seemed visibly nearer. Between it and ourselves were the flat plateaus. As we searched them with our field glasses we could make out a small herd of ibex moving slowly toward the neighboring gorge. Then, suddenly there was a loud clap of thunder and a moment later snow began to fall in thick heavy lumps. The leader of the hunters stopped and turned to me:

"Don't you want to go back? This snow is dangerous. Besides, you won 't be able to see any game."

But we'd gone so far already and the plateaus with their ibex seemed so near as I looked up at them that I didn't have the heart to turn back. So for another half hour we trudged through the growing drifts. By that time we were far enough up so that the lack of oxygen was making itself felt. A half dozen steps were all you could take before you had to stop for breath. As I stood panting, the leader turned to me again: "Give up? You'll never make it now."

I suggested we stop for a few minutes under an overhanging cliff and talk it over. Someone managed to find a bit of brush under the snow and we lit a tiny fire. The cliff gave us some protection but outside the gorge was a wild roaring cloud of snow. As we watched it, a low rumbling sound arose from the gorge below us. A moment later it grew to a thunderous roar. The hunters with me froze where they stood and looked at each other.

"Avalanche," one of them said and gingerly stepped from the mouth of the shelter into the swirling snow. A moment later he came back. "It's about five hundred yards below us," he announced, "and it has blocked the gorge completely."

I turned to the leader questioningly.

"All right," he said. "Now we don't need to decide. We'll have to keep going and cross the ridge above us into the next gorge. We can go down that way unless it gets blocked by an avalanche too."

Without wasting any more time we set out again. By that time the snow was up to our thighs and each time we took a step we paused a moment before we dragged the other foot ahead. I'd heard that avalanches were caused by noises and each time anyone opened his mouth I turned on him savagely.

Another hour of crawling brought us to the last ridge over which the ibex had disappeared. On the other side, the hunters told me, we could start downhill again. It wasn't a very big slope – perhaps two hundred yards, but it lay at a forty-five degree angle and the snow by then was over our belts. Each step meant a long pause to catch enough oxygen from the thin air.

Eventually we made it, and as we crawled toward the crest, the head hunter motioned me to get down low. "There'll be ibex on the other side," he said. So we crawled the last ten yards or more bent double. When we reached the top and slowly raised our heads to look down the other slope, it was as bare as old Mother Hubbard's cupboard.

Four or five hours later we were down near the foothill approaches. As the last traces of daylight disappeared we reached the village from which we'd started. The elders and most of the population were out to greet us. They were obviously disappointed that we brought no game, but just as obviously surprised to see us at all. They had heard the avalanche too, they said, and when we didn't show up in the afternoon they assumed we'd had it. But the happiest of them all was the Prime Minister's bodyguard. "It was the most horrible afternoon I've ever spent," he told me. I suggested he might have come along with us.

"DUSHMANI MAN" WAS my last anti-ibex operation. A few days after my return to Kabul a telegram from Washington ordered me to go to London with all possible speed to be Secretary to the Secretariat of the European Advisory Commission. It didn't sound like a very imposing job and London after the peace and quiet of Kabul didn't seem too attractive, but after eighteen months behind the mountains I was ready to get a little closer to the scene of action.

My first problem was to get myself a seat on an airplane. I wired to the priority board and sent them a paraphrased copy of my orders, which, like all telegraphic instructions from the State Department, was signed "Hull." I paraphrased the signature to read "Cordell." Whether or not the priority board thereupon assumed I was a close friend of the Secretary of State, I don't know, but I did get a Number One Air Priority from Karachi to London (which was the purpose of the operation).

My next problem was to get my household under way. It included Yang and a variety of dogs. Midget's puppies had always been a subject of controversy, but the Kabul litter was the most difficult of all. From the moment of her arrival in Kabul, Midget had been a center of attraction. The tricks she'd learned from the GPU were particularly intriguing. Everyone in the Royal Palace wanted a puppy from her, but as there were no male Belgian shepherd dogs around I was finally persuaded to marry her off to the next best thing, which was the King's prize German shepherd. The marriage was a great success. Midget's confinement was a little upset by the accident in the irrigation ditch, but a litter of five puppies survived.

Immediately the question of how to distribute them arose. It seemed as though every Prince of the Royal Family had been promised one, either by the King or by me. For some time the storm raged and eventually tempers got so hot that King Zahir appointed his uncle, the War Minister, now the Prime Minister, Shah Mahmud Khan, to settle the fight. For that purpose, I was invited to have tea in the Minister's great Durbar Hall and bring all the puppies with me.

An additional difficulty was that I had promised Yang that whichever dog was left for me was to go to him. Of the five puppies four were fine, black, husky dogs, but the fifth was a sorry little runt with a yellow back and a black belly, ears that flopped stupidly over his eyes, and a long, scraggly tail that seemed to have no relation to the rest of the body. The runt evidently realized his inferiority because he never played with the rest of the litter and slunk about by himself with his tail between his legs.

When the War Minister sent for me, I hurriedly bought five dog chains in the bazaar and piled all the puppies and Midget into the car together with Yang. Yang was very gloomy about the whole procedure and kept telling me that sure as fate I was going to get the runt for him. I told him not to worry, and that I was sure I could fix things to get him a better one. But Yang was unconvinced.

We arrived in the Palace grounds and the puppies piled out onto the driveway. Simultaneously, every one of the five new chains I'd just bought broke and five wild puppies lit out in every direction with half the Afghan Army in pursuit. Unfortunately, the Palace grounds were used as a sort of pet farm for the Royal Family. Prize peacocks, pheasants, and every other sort of fancy bird strolled leisurely around the park – until the puppies broke loose. By the time they were rounded up, at least one peacock had lost its life and several others their tails. A few mangled pheasants and swans were also strewn about the lawn and the lily pond.

With the help of the soldiery, we eventually managed to corral the puppies and usher them into the Durbar Hall. I had promised the War Minister they were all housebroken but after their escapade in the garden they had completely forgotten their manners. In a few minutes the fine old Bokhara carpets of the Palace were in urgent need of cleaning. But Shah Mahmud was a good sport and sipped a cup of tea unconcernedly as the puppies, chased by a half dozen lackeys armed with mops, performed around the room.

Just as things were settling down and Midget was calling her brood to order, the door opened and the King's champion German police dog, the father of the litter, pranced gaily into the room. One thing about canine fathers is their unpopularity with their lactating wives. King Zahir's dog was no exception. Midget flew at him like a tiger and within five seconds Durbar Hall was a whirling mass of dog flesh. But Shah Mahmud wasn't War Minister for nothing. A few claps of the hand, a few shouts, and once more the Kabul Garrison rushed to the rescue. It cost a bucket or two of water and a few badly chewed hands, but the two dogs were finally separated and peace restored to Durbar Hall.

By now the Persian carpets were beginning to show a certain amount of wear and tear and the War Minister decided to hasten the proceedings. He told me the King had commissioned him to divide the litter between the King, his cousins and myself. Before making his final judgment, he wanted to know which dog I thought was the best. I pointed to the yellow-backed runt and expressed the view that he had probably the greatest promise of all of them even though he didn't yet look very prepossessing. Considering what I really thought of the dog, I thought my speech was fairly convincing and I felt confident I had succeeded in palming him off on one of the Princes. But I had figured without my friend Shah Mahmud's

Afghan shrewdness. He examined the runt carefully and then the rest of the pack.

"I agree," he said at last. "The little fellow looks like a very promising animal and, therefore, I think you, as the owner of the bitch, should take him. In exchange for the others, we've decided to give you a pair of Afghan puppies."

When I left the Durbar Hall with the runt under my arms, Yang was waiting by the car. He took one look at the puppy and exploded.

"What did I tell you," he moaned and slouched gloomily back into the car. But the runt finally turned the tables and by the time we were ordered away had grown into a huge, intelligent and handsome dog.

A few months later, when I was ready to leave Kabul, it wasn't at all clear in my mind what I was going to do with my livestock. Death had deprived me of my falcon and my horse, but the kennel still had a dozen sheepdogs, mongrels and stray terriers which I'd acquired one way or another during my stay. I gave away all I could, willed the rest to my successor, and kept only Midget, her runt puppy, who had turned into a giant, and the two Afghans. I piled them all into a truck together with Yang and my baggage and sent them off across the Khyber Pass to Peshawar.

That evening, with a fine case of the flu and a fever of 103, I went to a farewell dinner given for me by the Minister of Court. Around midnight I was wrapped in a couple of sheepskin cloaks, strapped into Major Enders' jeep and off we set on the long ride across the mountains to India. I don't remember much about the ride, but I do recall that when I arrived in Peshawar I hadn't a trace of fever. Enders supplied the explanation when he announced we'd established a record covering the journey in something under six hours, as compared with the weeks it usually took the British Army whenever it got into an Afghan war. But then Enders had a jeep, not a train of camels.

At Peshawar, Yang, the fours dogs and I were piled into a couple of compartments on the Karachi express and after two miserable dusty days, one of them being Christmas, we pulled into Karachi.

Anyone who's been in Karachi knows it's a hot, bizarre sort of place any time of the year. But we'd just come from winter in the Hindu Kush and were dressed accordingly. When we assembled our forces outside the train, the local platform loungers had reason to stare. Yang led the procession dressed in a fur coat with a broad fur collar and a wide, crowned Cossack-like fur hat he had acquired in Russia. In his two hands he held the leashes of the four dogs who, after two days on the train, were straining ahead of him. Behind Yang came two large cartloads of baggage. I brought up the rear dressed, like Yang, in fur coat and large beaverskin cap. By the time we arrived at the Consulate, our little procession had collected quite a following, including at least three officials of the Indian Police who kept demanding to know just who we were and what we represented.

But at the Consulate we were met by an old friend, Ed Macy, the American Consul, who reassured the Police that we were not the advance guard of the Russian Army. Fortunately, Ed was a dog lover and promised to look after the canine part of the establishment until I could find some sort of transportation to the States for them. The next morning I took a plane to London and Yang followed shortly afterward on a boat.

The rest of the household had less luck. Midget's puppy got tick fever a few weeks after I left and died. The two Afghan hounds were shipped to a kennel up in the hills to wait till I could find some way of getting them home. They waited an entire year during which they ate a fairly large proportion of my salary in expensive Indian delicacies.

By then I was back in the Army, stationed at Belgrade with Tito. I had come to Bari for the Christmas holidays and was celebrating New Year's Day with the Fifteenth Air Force. It was a fairly gay affair, and, I thought, a good opportunity to broach the dog question to the Commanding General, General Anderson. So I told him I had a complicated logistical problem involving hares and hounds. That seemed to interest him, and I went on to explain that I was very fond of the old sport of coursing and that I had found a great many hares in Serbia but that my two Afghan hounds were in India. General

Anderson agreed that coursing was a very fine sport and strongly recommended that I bring the hares and hounds together. That, I told him, was my difficulty. I had made some careful calculations on the number of man-hours it would take to catch enough hares to make it worth while to ship them to India. I had also calculated how many man-hours I would need to get the hounds by plane to Belgrade. General Anderson examined my figures carefully and agreed they looked reasonably accurate. Obviously, he concluded, it was easier to move the hounds than the hares. Furthermore, he added, he had a great many planes flying material to Karachi for the Burma front which always flew back to Italy empty.

The solution was immediately obvious.

Within a few minutes, wires were dispatched to the kennels in India and the various other interested parties, and I went back to Belgrade. But I'd calculated without the Roosevelt family – Elliot Roosevelt in particular. A few days after my return to Belgrade a telegram arrived from the Fifteenth Air Force: "All bets off," it said. "You'll read the story of Elliot Roosevelt's dog Blaze in the *Stars and Stripes*."[17] I sent a wire to the kennel and told them to get rid of the Afghan hounds any way they saw fit.

But Midget was even less fortunate. I'd had her with me for nearly ten years. She had traveled with me through Europe, America and Asia in trains, ships, airplanes, Volga barges and autobuses. She was even more a part of the household than Yang, who'd been in the organization a mere seven years. So I told Ed Macy she had first choice on the first available space to America.

I'D BEEN IN the Embassy in London only a week or two when a telegram arrived through official channels and was routed to me and everyone else in the Embassy in the routine way. It read:

"Your black bitch sailed today."

---

17. Elliot Roosevelt, son of President Franklin D. Roosevelt, ended up in a scandal in 1945 when it was found his dog Blaze traveled by plane on emergency war priority.

On the margin was written in the Minister's handwriting: "I hope she wears a sarong."

But Midget's luck had run out. It was almost a year before I learned her ship had been torpedoed by the Japanese six hours out of Karachi.

But that was all in the future. My pets seemed safe enough when I took off from Karachi.

The journey to London was fairly mild compared to previous transfers. After all I had a Priority One ticket. There was a little trouble at Marrakesh, where the Air Force said they had "lost" my priority. So for three days I enjoyed myself seeing the sights and visiting the bazaar under the guidance of Josephine Baker. Each day I visited the airport to find out how the hunt for my priority was progressing.

I was returning one afternoon from the airport after an unsuccessful attempt to persuade the Air Force boys that my copy of my priority was as genuine as the one they had lost. A command car was about to leave for the hotel. In the back seat were a couple of youthful Air Force Lieutenant Colonels I recognized as unfortunate Plebes when I'd been a mighty Firstclassman at West Point. I started to climb in beside them, hoping they'd forgotten the number of times I'd made them shine my shoes or clean my rifle. I was halfway into the car when a fat Captain dashed out of the ATC office and tapped me on the shoulder.

"Son," he said, "I wouldn't crowd the Colonels."

I knew anything I might say would be the wrong thing, so I took a deep breath, counted ten, walked out into the desert, sat on a rock, and after a little quiet meditation came to the conclusion that I wasn't wearing the right kind of suit for the times.

In London I found out that the European Advisory Commission under Gil Winant, the Ambassador, was supposed to work out an agreement with the Russians about how to run Europe after the Allies had liberated it. I don't know how long it took Winant to calculate our chances of success, but after a month I was ready to admit a stalemate and retire to prepared positions.

The trouble was I had no prepared positions. For two years I'd been sending in my resignation to the State Department at regular intervals. But the Department always told me they knew better and that I was more useful in civvies than in khaki. Then one day in the bar of Claridges Hotel I met Brigadier Fitzroy MacLean,[18] a colleague of Moscow days, who was then heading an Anglo-American Mission to Tito. Fitzroy told me he was having enough trouble with the Anglo side of his Mission and wanted to split it into two. Why not join the new American Mission, provided he could persuade General Bill Donovan of OSS, Secretary of State Ed Stettinius and Ambassador Winant. He explained it would only be necessary for me to learn "a little parachuting."

There are a lot of things I've promised myself I'd never do. But the one I've been really sincere about is parachuting. I get dizzy when I climb onto a chair to change a light bulb. What would I feel like peering out of the door of an airplane a thousand feet in the air? Then I remembered the ATC Captain in Marrakesh. Was I to spend the rest of my career being told by fat Captains not to crowd the Colonels? So I told MacLean to go ahead and see if he couldn't persuade Donovan to take me, and Stettinius to let me go.

Stettinius agreed to give me military leave and Donovan agreed to look me over. The next thing I knew I was asked to report for a psychoanalysis. I'd heard that OSS had a better-than-average number of screwballs in it, but found it a little strange that they should consider it necessary to employ psychologists to find them. But I was told, a little sternly, that the psychoanalysis was to determine whether I was adaptable to conditions overseas. I explained I'd been getting along all right overseas for the past ten years. But they said no one could get into the OSS without a psychoanalysis. So I reported a little impatiently one day at what had once been a stately town house.

---

18. Sir Fitzroy MacLean (1911-1996) was a Scottish soldier, author and politician, reputedly one of Ian Fleming's models for James Bond. He was one of only two Brits who enlisted in World War II as a private and rose to the rank of Brigadier General. MacLean served in Moscow from 1937-39, one result of which was his superb memoir *Eastern Approaches*.

The first thing the doctors did was to tell me my name for the day was "Jim." I started protesting at once and pointed out that I'd always been known as "Charlie" by a very wide circle of acquaintances and saw no necessity for getting a new nickname. But the doctors made some excuse about security and the fact that no one was supposed to know who I was. Then they told me to go and join a table of fellow patients playing bridge. I said I didn't play bridge.

"All right. Go over to the other table and play some poker." (Evidently they figured I wasn't the highbrow type.) I told them very firmly I didn't play poker either. So they suggested chess and then checkers but I remained adamant.

"Okay," they ended wearily. "Just go and watch the others play." Kibitzing is the essence of diplomacy and I accepted the invitation enthusiastically.

After the bridge game they asked us a series of "intelligence" questions. The first was: "When did you last wet your bed?" I told them to go to hell and that I couldn't possibly remember. (Later a friend told me that's exactly the right answer.)

A number of equally incomprehensible tests took up the rest of the day until five o'clock, when the class was assembled in the ex-ballroom of the house. There on the parquet floor was a pile of planks, ropes, clamps and canvas which we were told was a pup tent.

"See how quickly you can pitch the tent without driving any nails into the floor," the doctor said.

In a second I'd stripped off my coat and was giving directions to my fellow psychoanalysis victims. "Here, grab this rope. Fasten those two planks. Straighten that pole." In less than two minutes the tent was pitched.

As we left the house that evening, the head psychologist asked me to step into his office:

"Jim," he started, but I interrupted and said my name was "Thayer" or "Charlie" if he insisted on being so familiar. The doctor looked slightly exasperated and started again: "Look here. You've been as uncooperative a patient as we've had all month. You wouldn't play bridge. You wouldn't play chess or poker or checkers. You wouldn't even give civil answers to civil questions. All right, that's your business. Perhaps for you this process seems a little superfluous. But what none of us understands is why when we asked you to pitch that silly pup tent in the middle of a ballroom you dash into action and pitch it in record time."

"Doctor," I replied, puffing out my chest, "you forget that I was Eastern-United-States-Boy-Scout-Pup-Tent-Pitching-Champion in 1923. My performance here was nothing to what I did at Swarthmore twenty years ago."

I never found out what sort of a grade I got at the psycho-analysis test but I can imagine. Nevertheless Bill Donovan must have overlooked it, because a few days later I was provided with a uniform, a pair of major's leaves and a new nickname and told to report to parachute school. There I was soon jumping out of second-story windows, rolling in sandpits, listening to interminable lectures on how to bury a parachute behind enemy lines.

And then one night I was sitting hunched up on the floor of a converted British bomber somewhere over northern England. All my fellow students had already disappeared through a hole in the bomber's floor. The plane was circling for the last run. I'd already done my preliminary daylight jumps and this was to be my final nighttime test. Each previous jump had strengthened my low opinion of parachuting and my morale was rapidly ebbing away.

Beside me in the darkened gloomy fuselage the dispatcher snapped the static line to my chute and showed it to me.

"Running in," he said in an irritating Cockney accent.

I eased over to the edge of the hole, taking care not to look down so I wouldn't get dizzy.

The dispatcher murmured some meaningless motherly words. "Take a look," he suggested. "'Tain't far down."

I would gladly have grabbed him by the neck and thrown him out the hole if I hadn't been so damn busy holding on to my own emotions.

"Action stations," the Cockney ordered.

I swung my legs down into the pit and worked myself forward to the edge of the hole.

A red light flashed on the wall beside me.

An interval elapsed which I would roughly judge to have been about three days. At all events, it gave me time for a fairly comprehensive survey of my past. Fifteen years before, the Government had undertaken to educate me. For four years I'd struggled with the military arts. For eleven more years I'd been taught visas, passports, international law. I'd ruined my digestion on the gastronomy of three continents. I'd tested the potency of a dozen national drinks at the price of innumerable hangovers – all for Uncle Sam. I'd choked over the ablatives, subjunctives and vocabularies of half a dozen different languages. I'd cemented international relations with as many foreign countries. I'd even learned how to train falcons, housebreak dogs, and teach seals to play "Silent Night" on a mouth organ for my country. Plumber, ironmonger, impresario; I'd even hauled the Embassy garbage. And where was it all leading?

I peered down the hole at the dim blue lights of the landing field.

The light beside me flashed green.

The dispatcher shouted, "Go."

I went.

Made in the USA
Coppell, TX
06 January 2022